PENG

I CAN ~~NOT~~ DRAW CATS

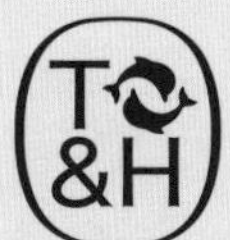

CONTENTS

CHAPTER 1
THE BASICS

CATS FROM HEAD TO TAIL

EARS AND NOSE * MUZZLE
EYES AND EYEBROWS * BODIES
STANDING, SITTING AND STRETCHING * YOGA
FUR MARKINGS * TAILS

CHAPTER 2
ANYTHING'S POSSIBLE

IT'S TIME TO GET CREATIVE

COMICAL CATS * GEOMETRIC
CATS * ARTY CATS
HIRAMEKI * GROUP PORTRAITS

HUMAN -LIKE CATS
HANGING AROUND AND HIDING AWAY
CAT COIFFURE * TATTOOS * CATS
AND OTHER CREATURES * FAMOUS
RELATIONS * PICTURE POSTCARDS
CAT MASK * TALKING CAT

CHAPTER 3
THE ART OF CATS

BECOMING A MASTER CAT PAINTER

SKETCHING * PAINTING ON CARDBOARD
FROM DARK TO LIGHT * PHOTO
STUDIES * CAT PORTRAIT
ON WOOD

CATS

ARE STUBBORN AND CHEEKY,
HILARIOUS AND UNPREDICTABLE,
LIKE WILD ANIMALS AND CUDDLY TOYS
AT THE SAME TIME.

YOU CAN LIVE WITH THEM,
FEED THEM, STROKE THEM AND SPOIL
THEM. AND YOU CAN ALSO <u>DRAW</u>
THEM! YES, YOU CAN.

DON'T BELIEVE ME?
THEN WAIT AND SEE!

PENG'S CATS, MOMO AND COSIMO

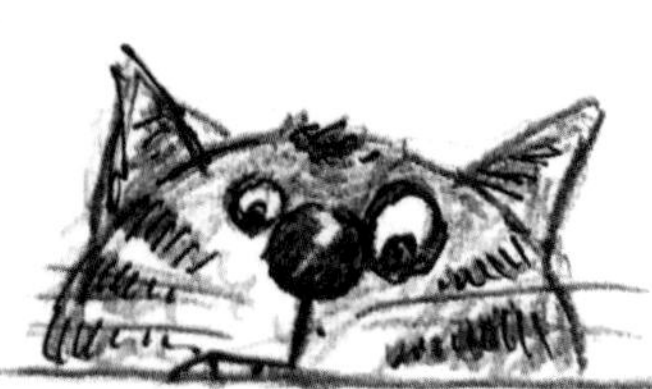
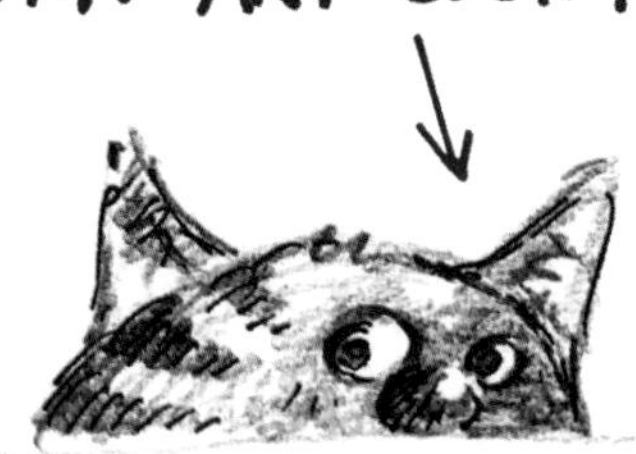

HOW TO USE
THIS BOOK

BASICALLY
EVERYTHING IS ALLOWED!

- DOODLE WHEREVER THERE'S SPACE
- DRAW OVER THE LINES OR COLOUR THEM IN
- COPY • SCRIBBLE • EXPERIMENT
- PASTE THINGS IN
- ADD YOUR OWN IDEAS

THIS BOOK IS FULL OF IDEAS, TIPS AND SUGGESTIONS, BUT WHAT YOU DO WITH THEM IS YOUR DECISION. YOUR DRAWINGS COULD BE SIMPLE, REALISTIC OR COMPLICATED.

IT'S ALL UP TO YOU!

MAKE THIS BOOK YOURS!

TOOL KIT

1
2
3
4
5
6
START WITH:
1. SOFT PENCILS (4B OR 6B)
2. BALLPOINT PEN (BLACK)
3. COLOURED PENCILS
4. ERASABLE PENCIL (YELLOW)
5. ERASER
6. PENCIL SHARPENER

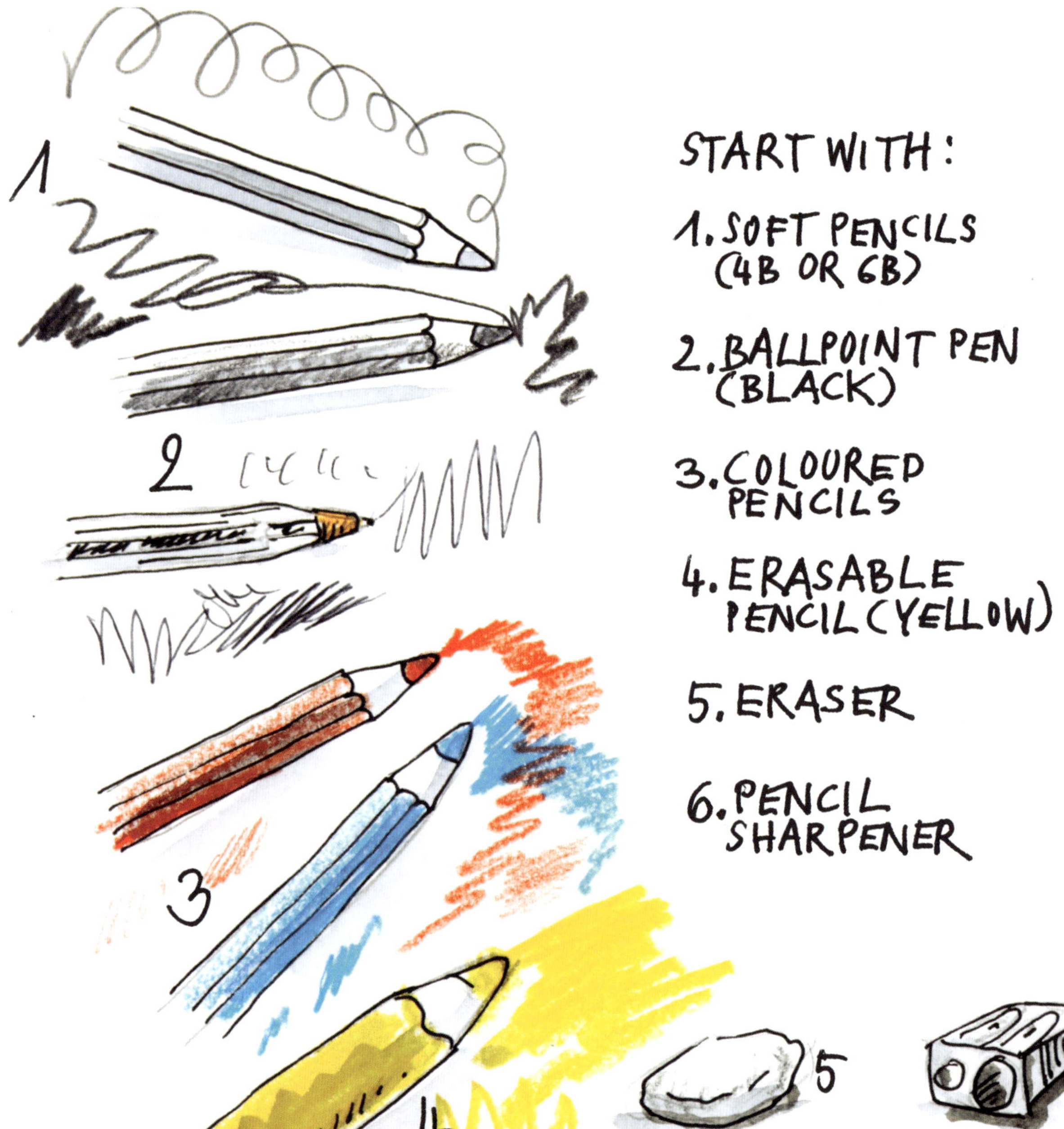

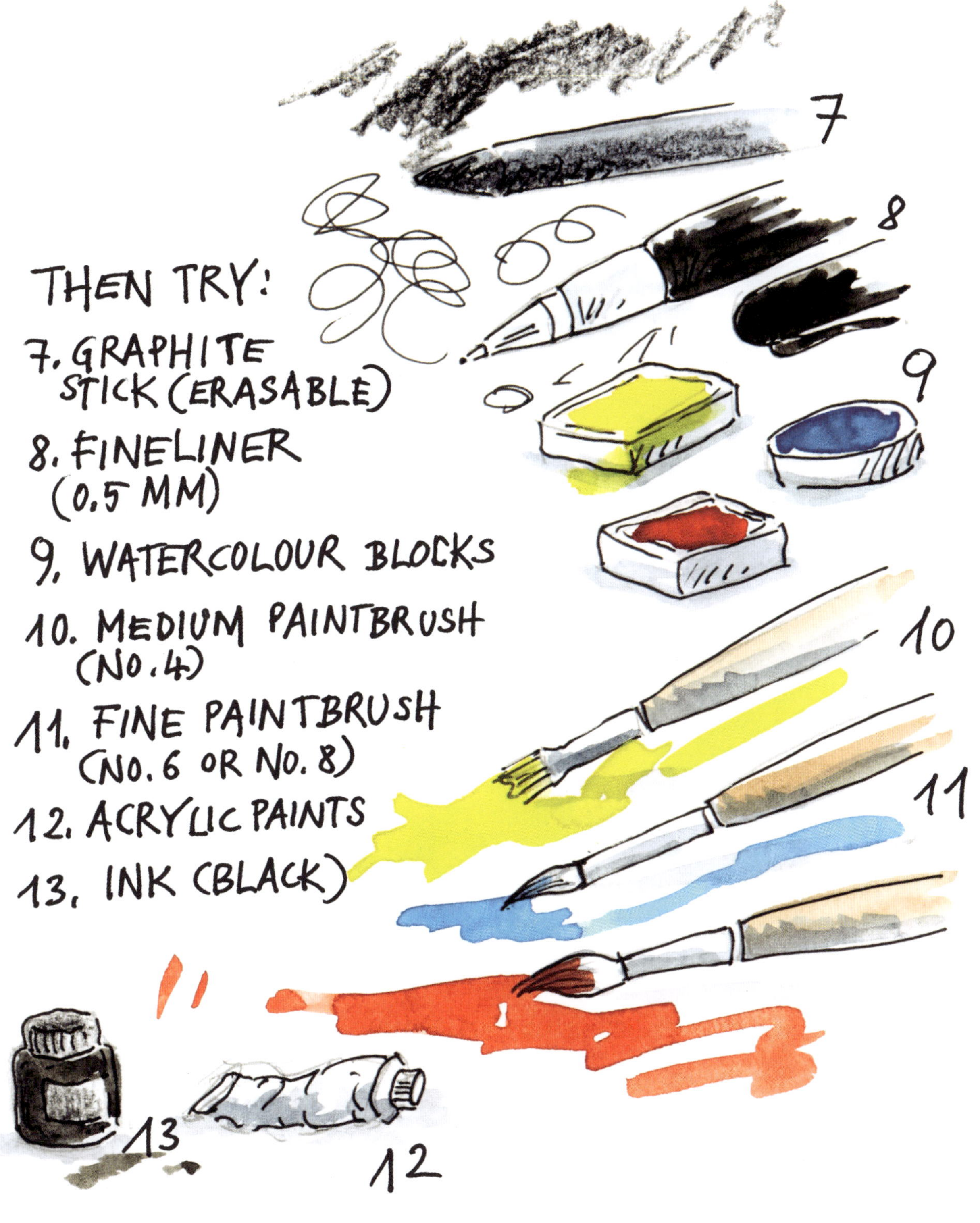

THEN TRY:
7. GRAPHITE STICK (ERASABLE)
8. FINELINER (0.5 MM)
9. WATERCOLOUR BLOCKS
10. MEDIUM PAINTBRUSH (NO. 4)
11. FINE PAINTBRUSH (NO. 6 OR NO. 8)
12. ACRYLIC PAINTS
13. INK (BLACK)
7
8
9
10
11
12
13

CHAPTER 1

THE BASICS

CATS FROM HEAD TO TAIL

EARS NOSE FUR

WHISKERS

EYES

BODIES ...

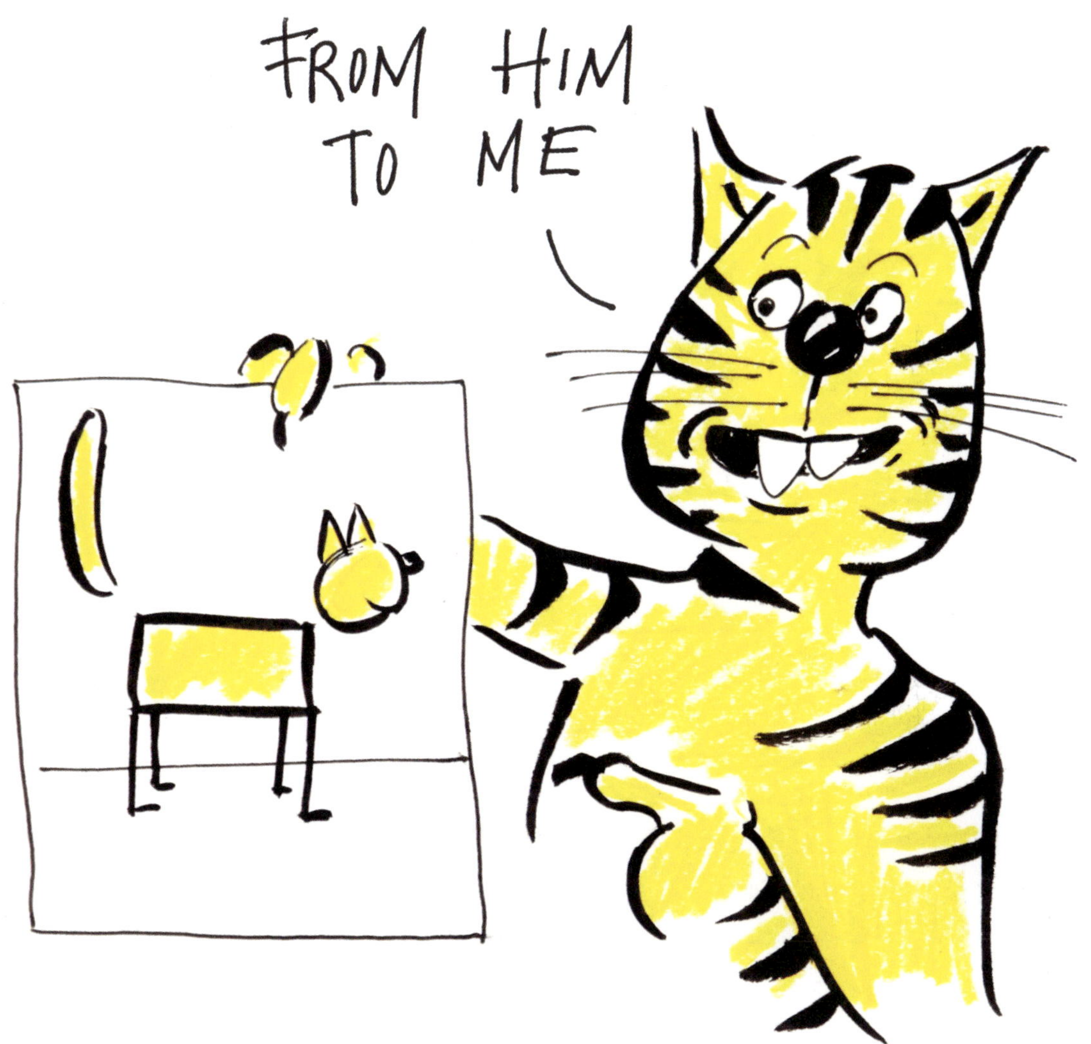

FROM HIM
TO ME

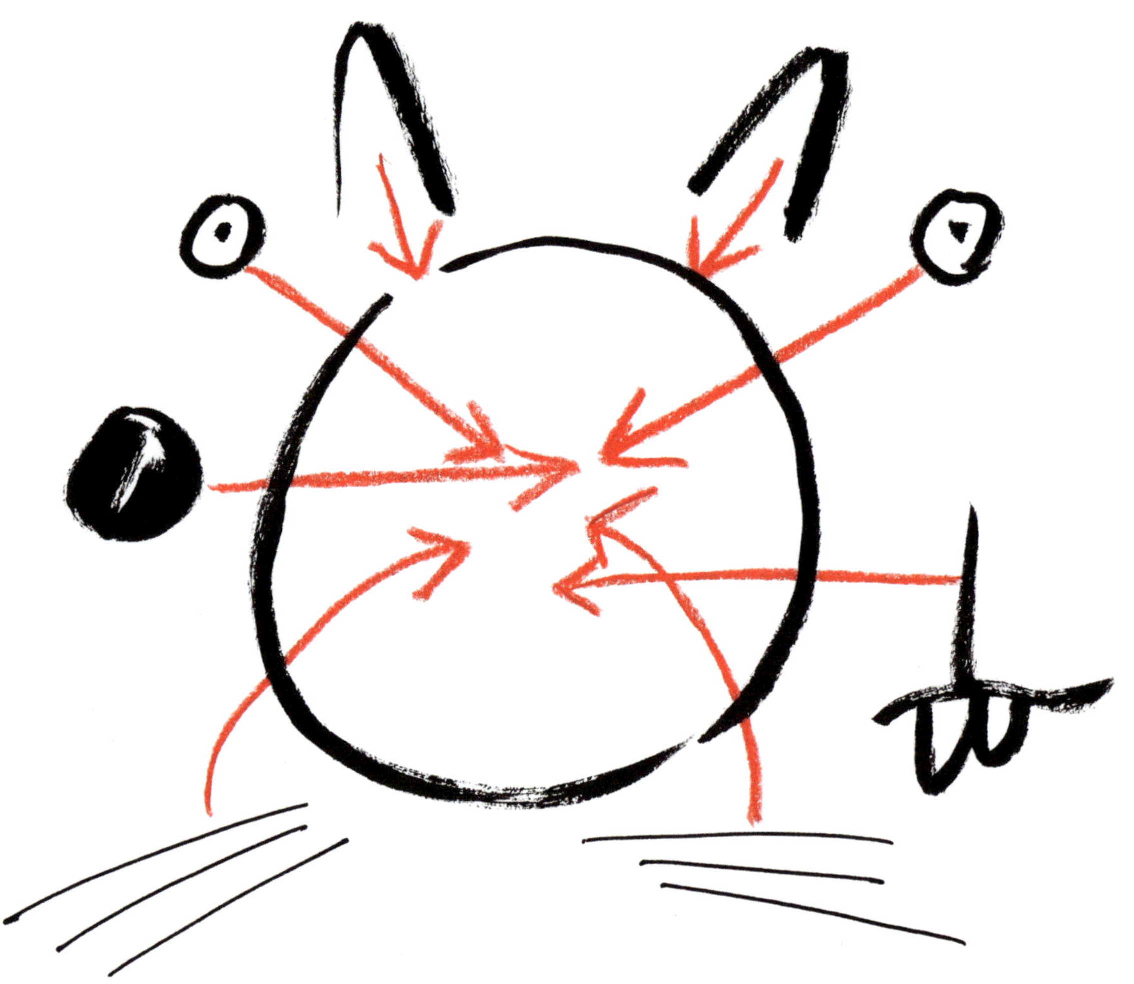
LET'S START WITH
HOW TO BUILD A CAT'S FACE
CONFUSED?
DON'T WORRY.

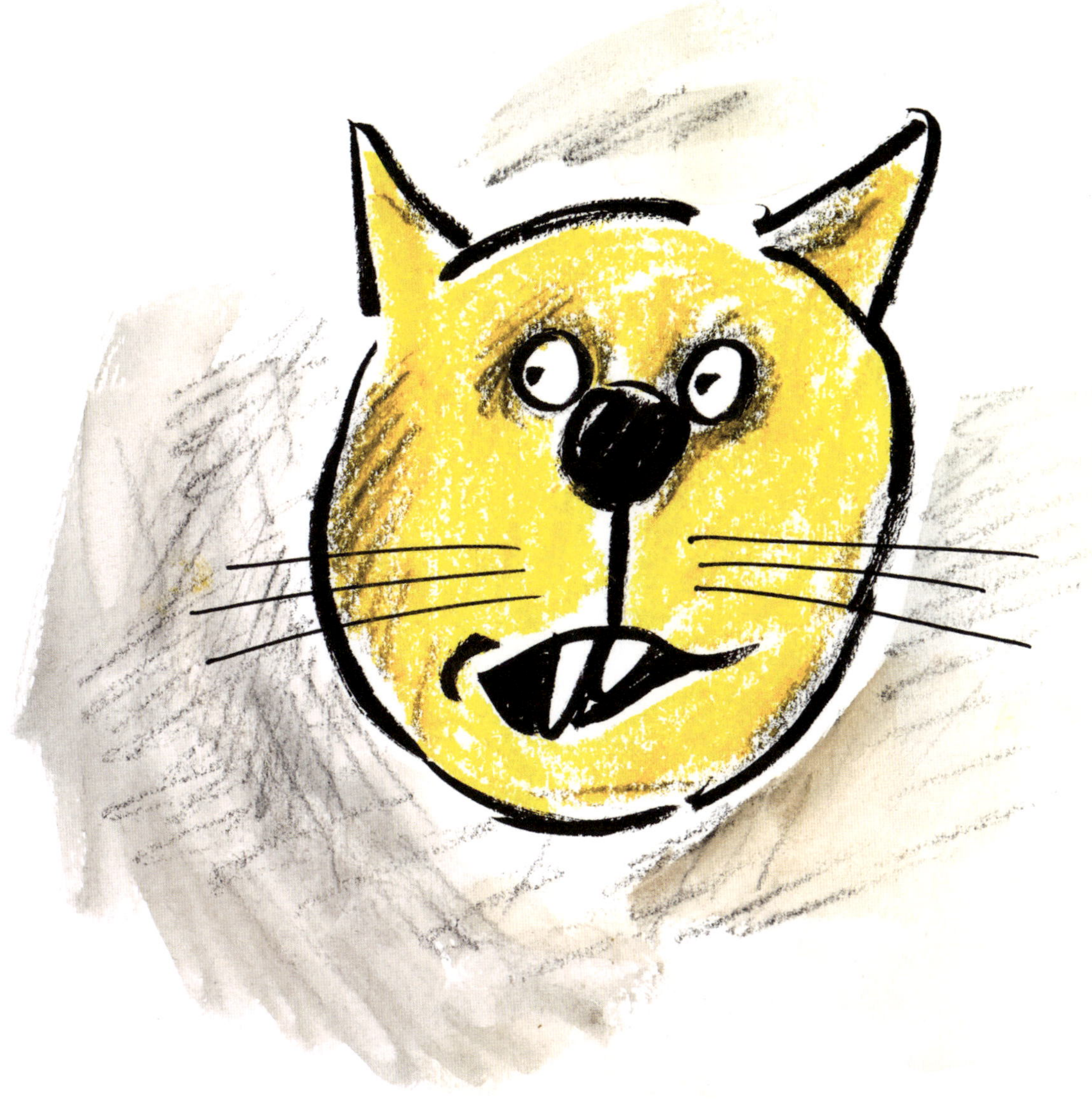

LET'S BREAK IT DOWN AND LOOK
AT THE MOST IMPORTANT DETAILS
YOU NEED TO BUILD A SIMPLE CAT.

WHEN **EARS** AND **NOSES** WORK TOGETHER...

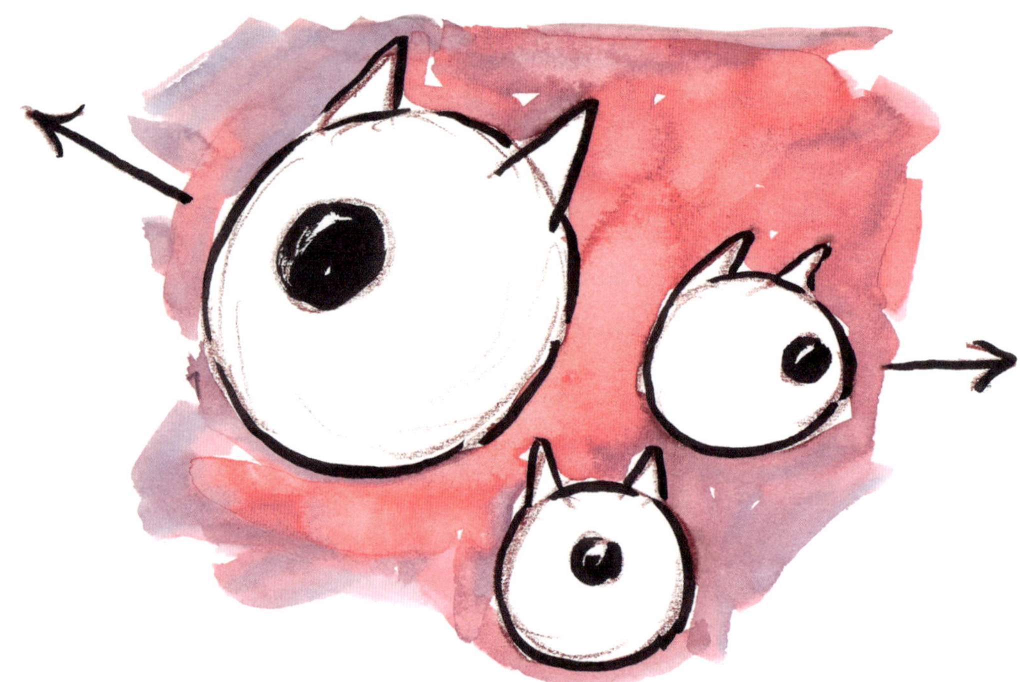

THEY SHOW WHICH DIRECTION THE HEAD IS POINTING

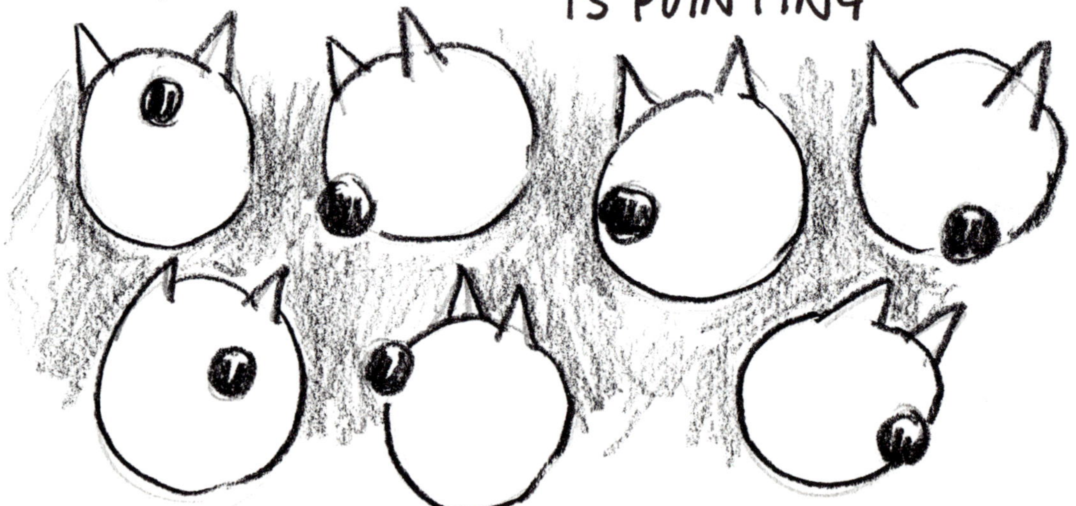

ADD THE EARS TO THESE HEADS

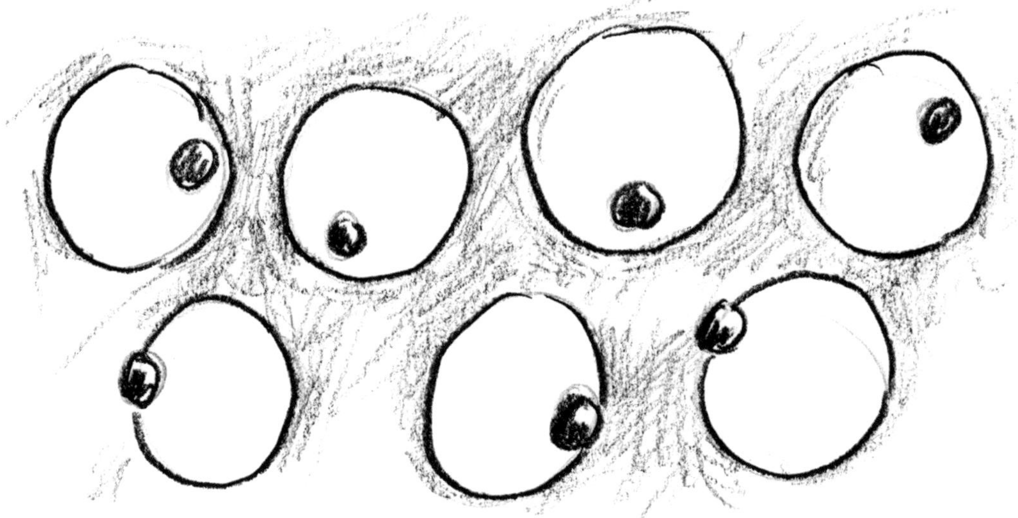

NOW ADD SOME NOSES HERE

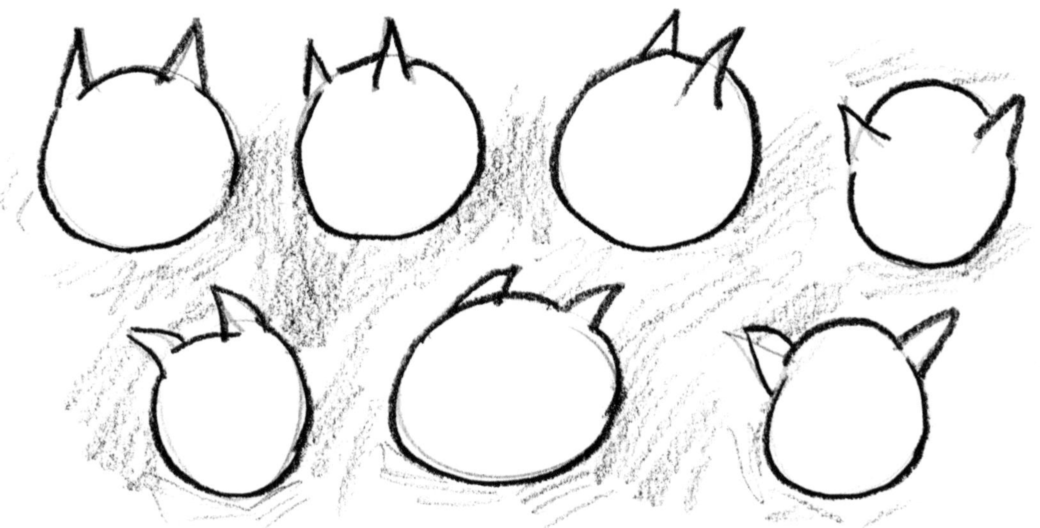

NOT TOO HARD, RIGHT?

YOU'VE DRAWN A HEAD, NOW ADD A **CURVE**

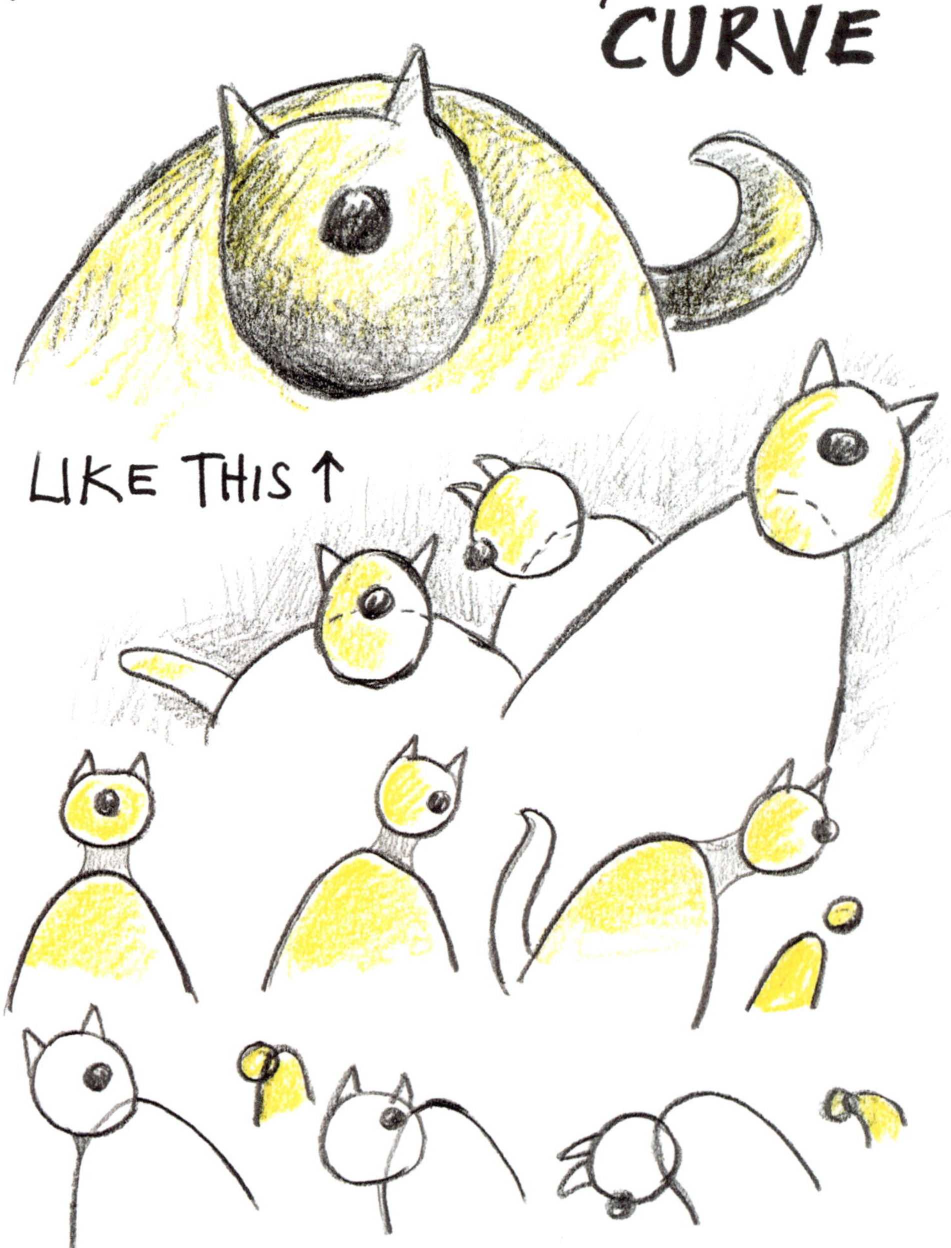

SUDDENLY YOUR CATS CAN MOVE AROUND.

TRY IT OUT HERE ↓

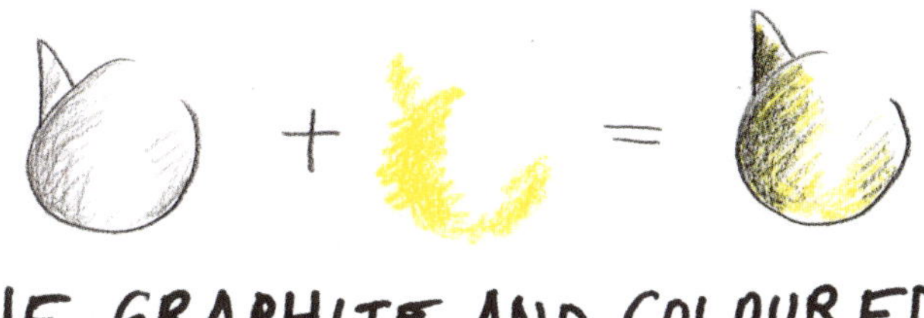

COMBINE GRAPHITE AND COLOURED
PENCIL

THE **MUZZLE** IS A GOOD WAY TO ADD EMOTIONS.

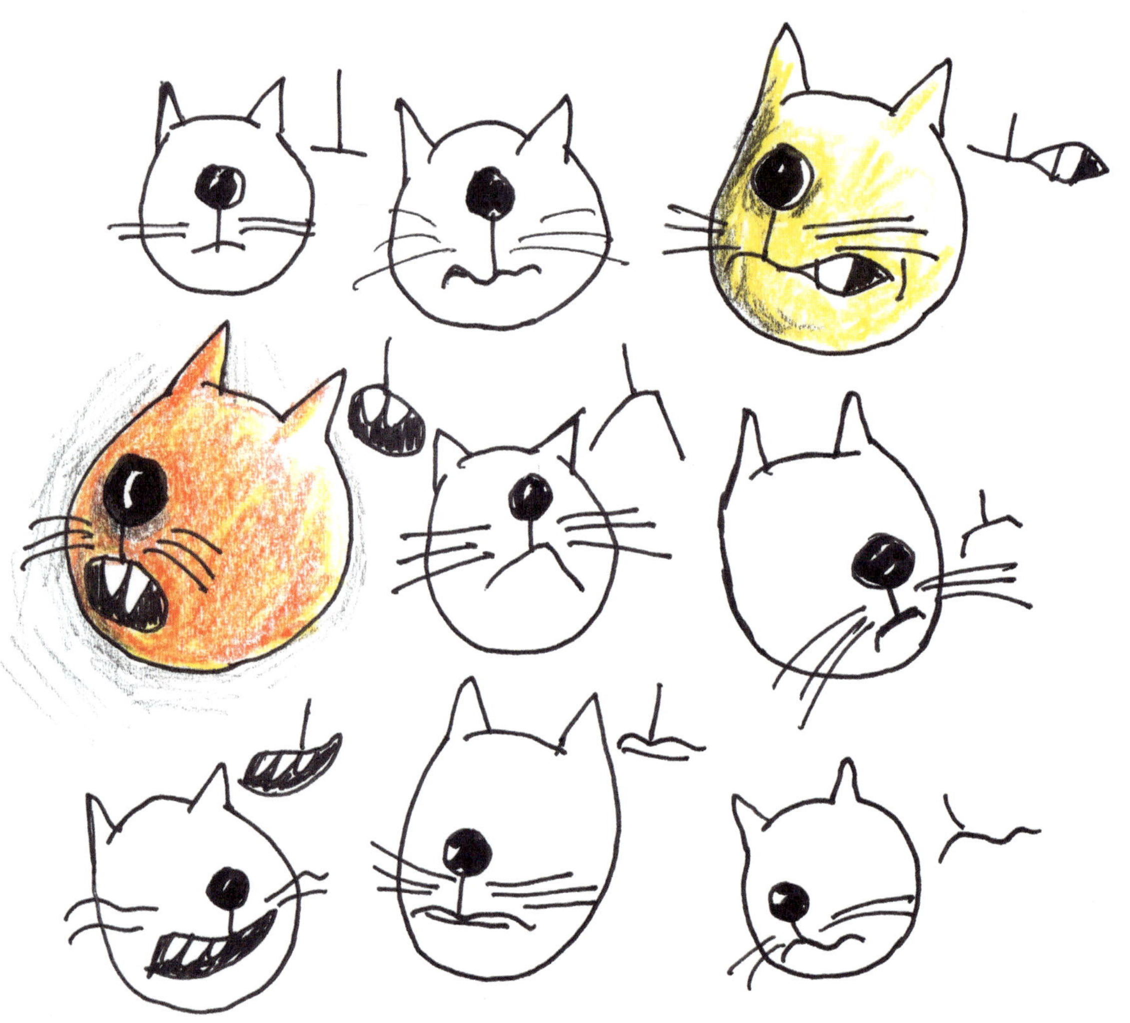

NOW IT'S YOUR TURN

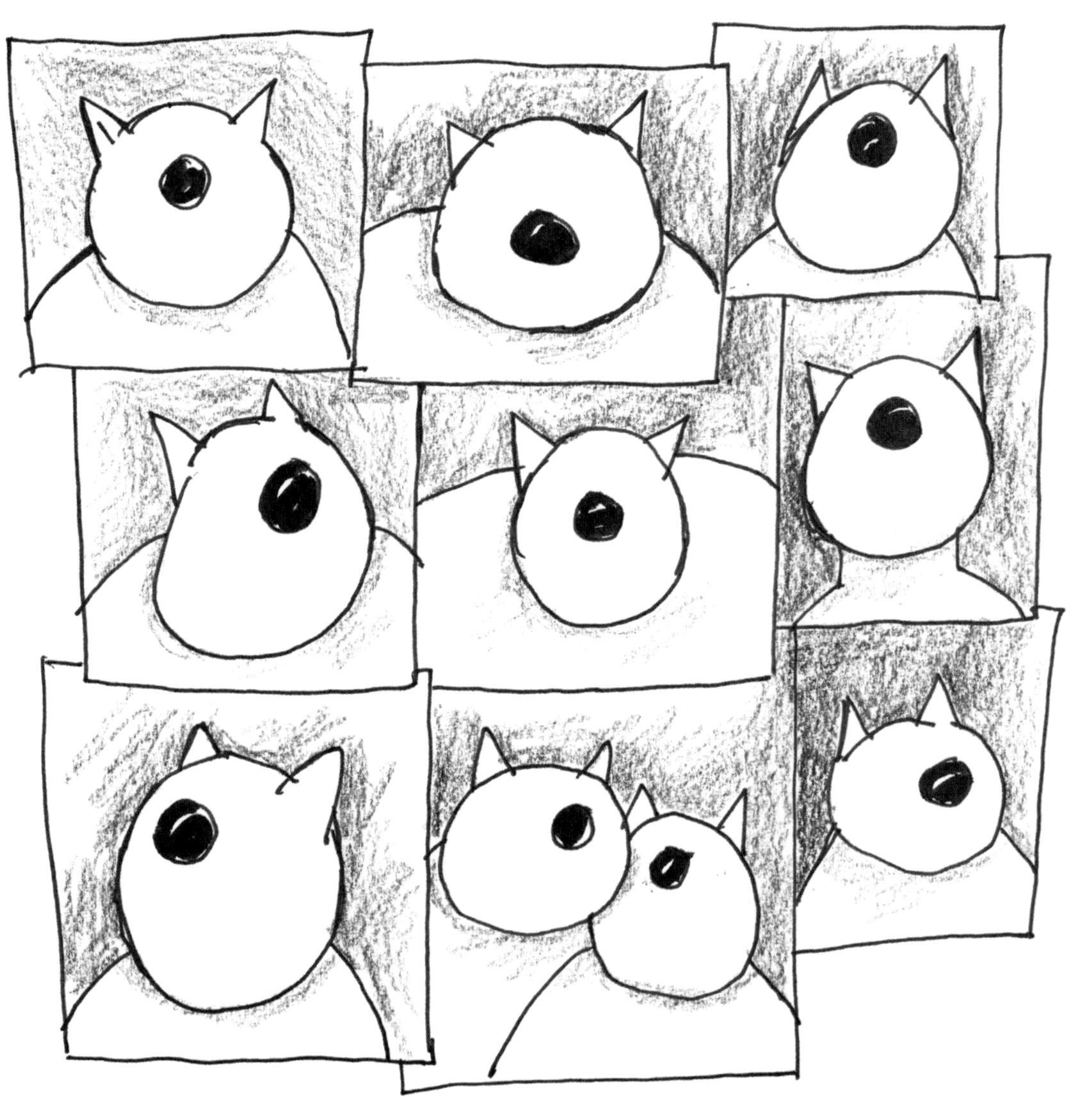

↑ FINELINER AND 4B PENCIL

EYES AND EYEBROWS
ARE GREAT FOR ADDING EXPRESSION.

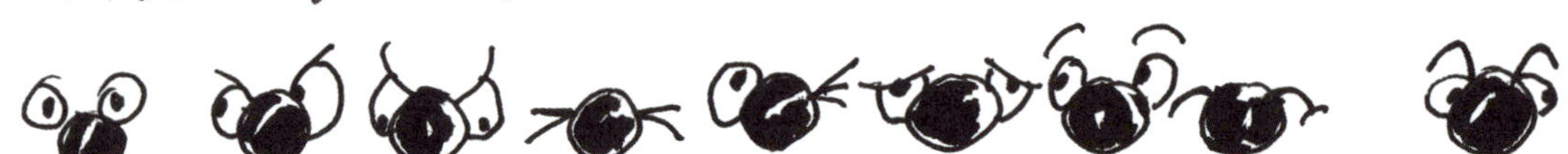

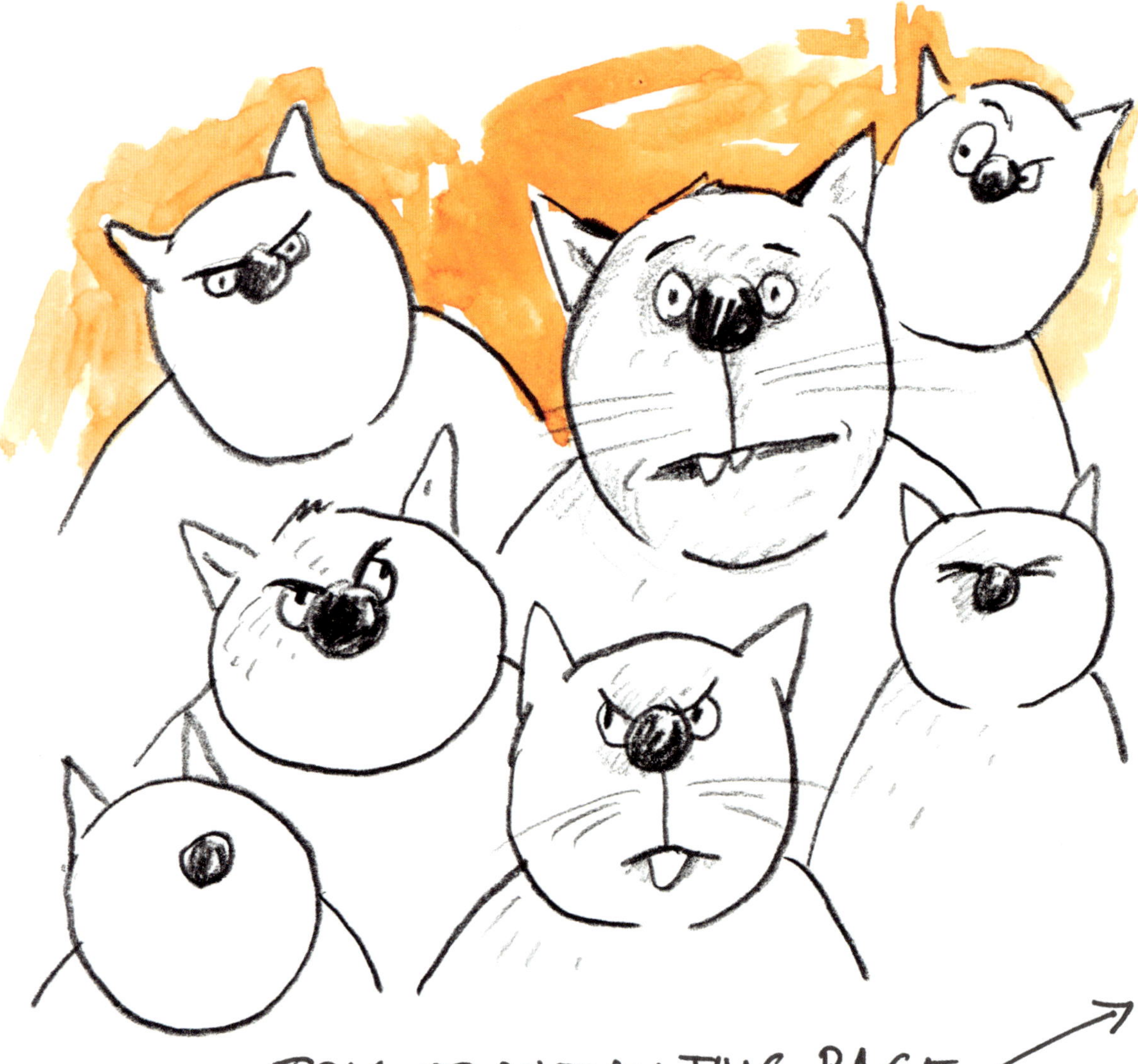

TRY IT OUT ON THIS PAGE

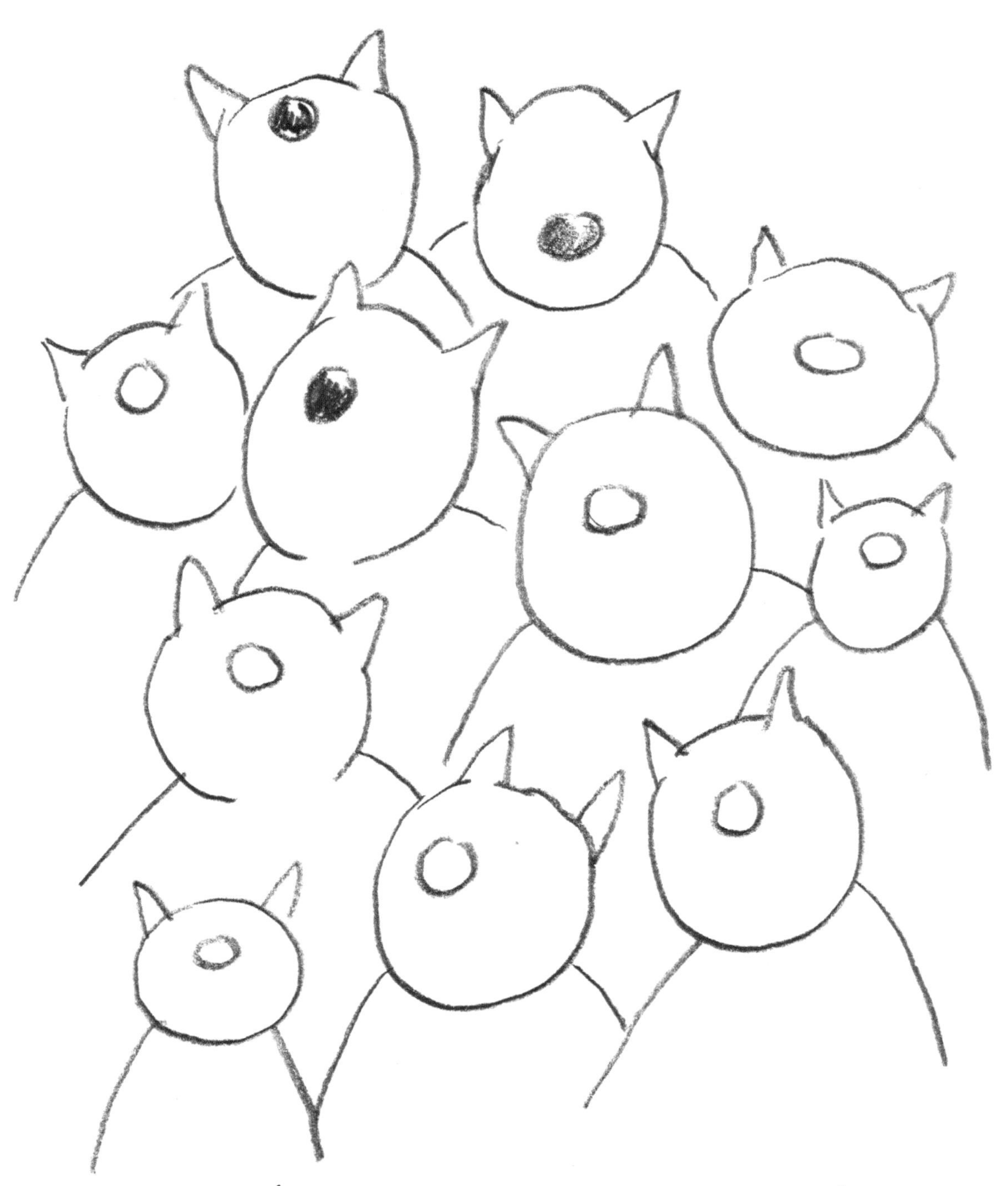

DON'T FORGET THE MUZZLE!

IDEAS FOR DRAWING
EXPRESSIONS

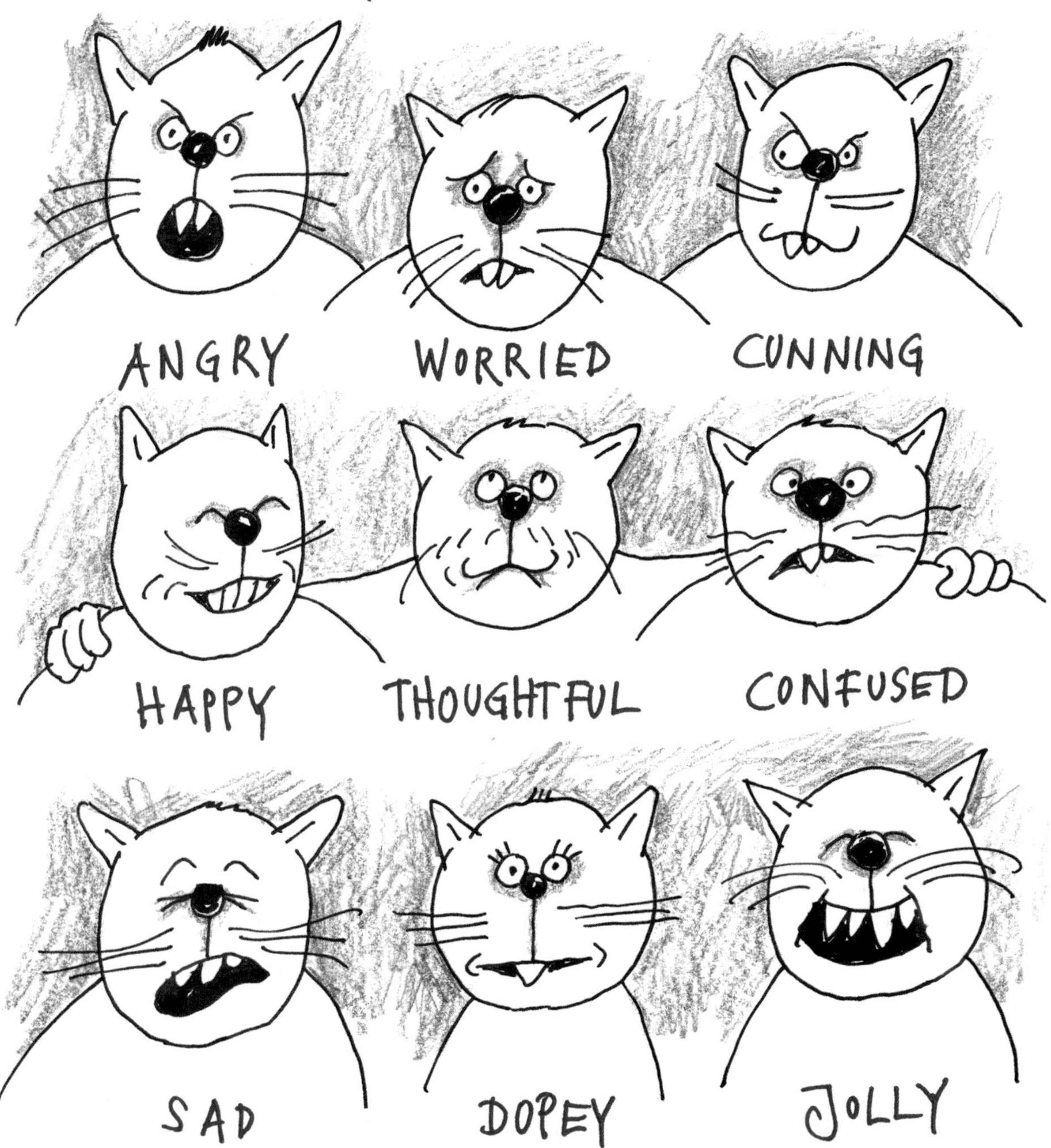

TRY IT YOURSELF
↓

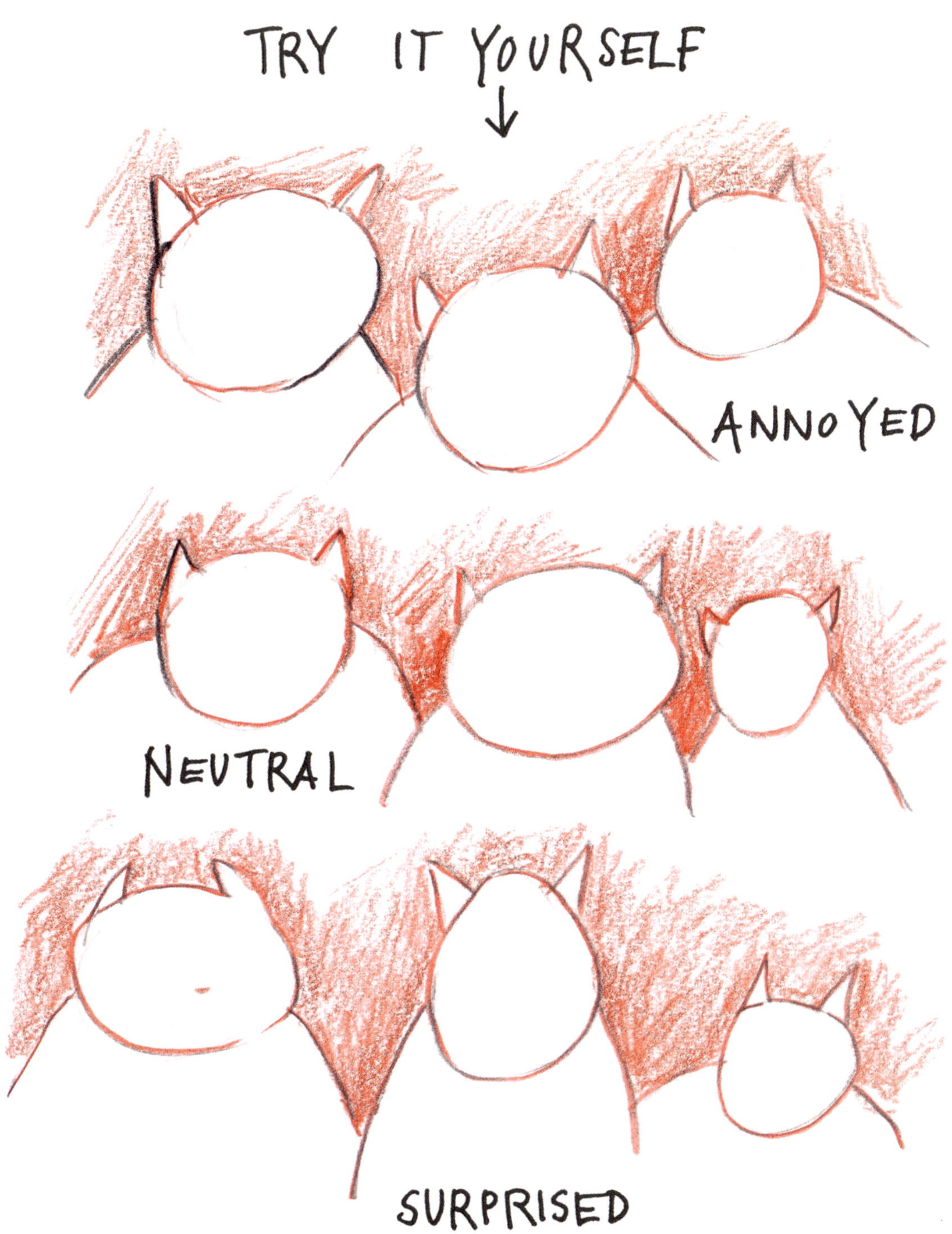

ANNOYED
NEUTRAL
SURPRISED

TIME FOR THE
WHOLE CAT

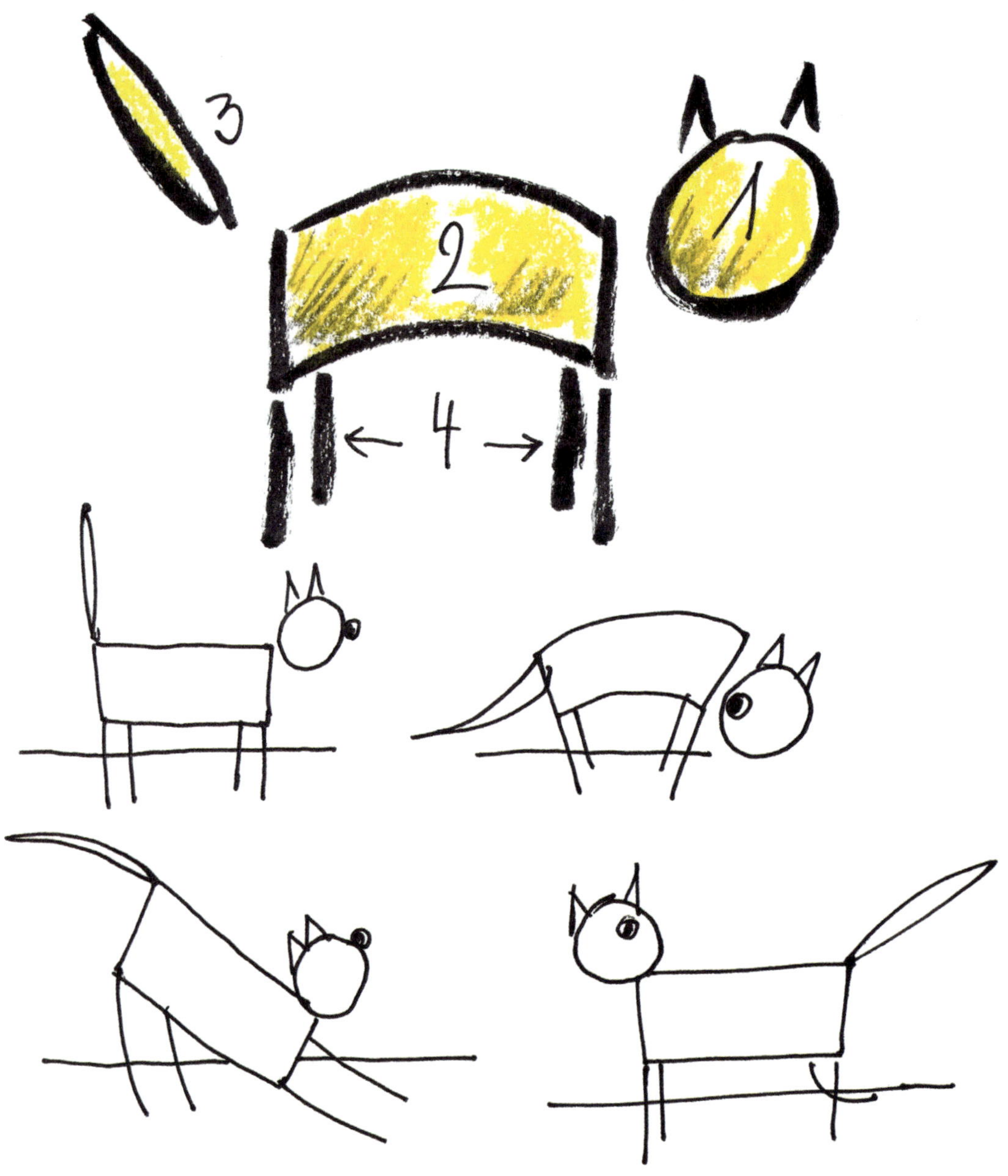

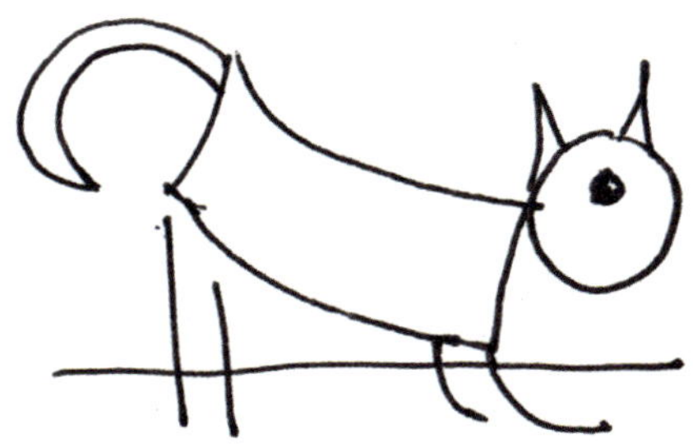

THEY CAN STAND, STRETCH AND LOOK IN ANY DIRECTION.

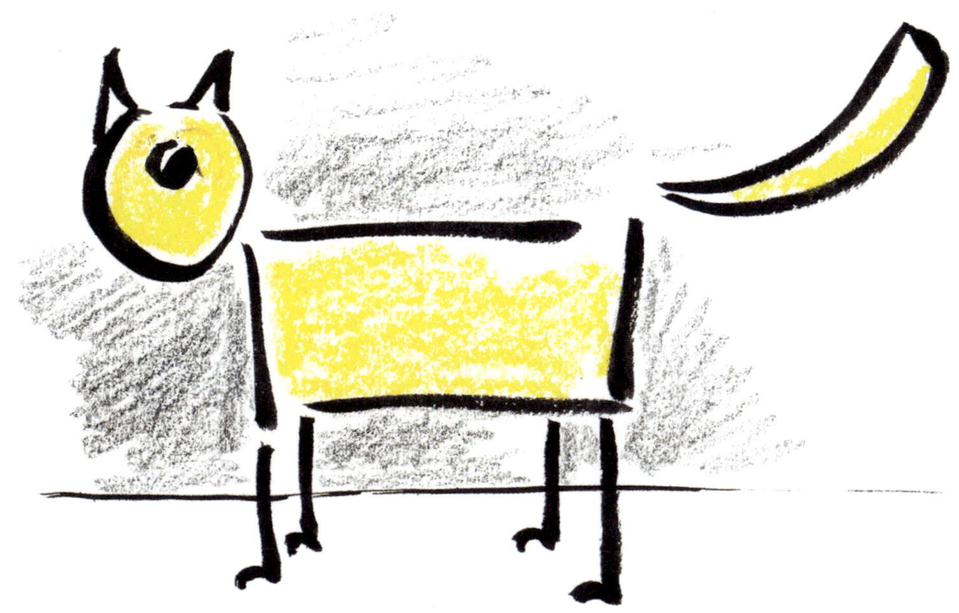

HOW GREAT IS THAT?

TIME TO PRACTISE
DRAW FIRST, THEN COLOUR

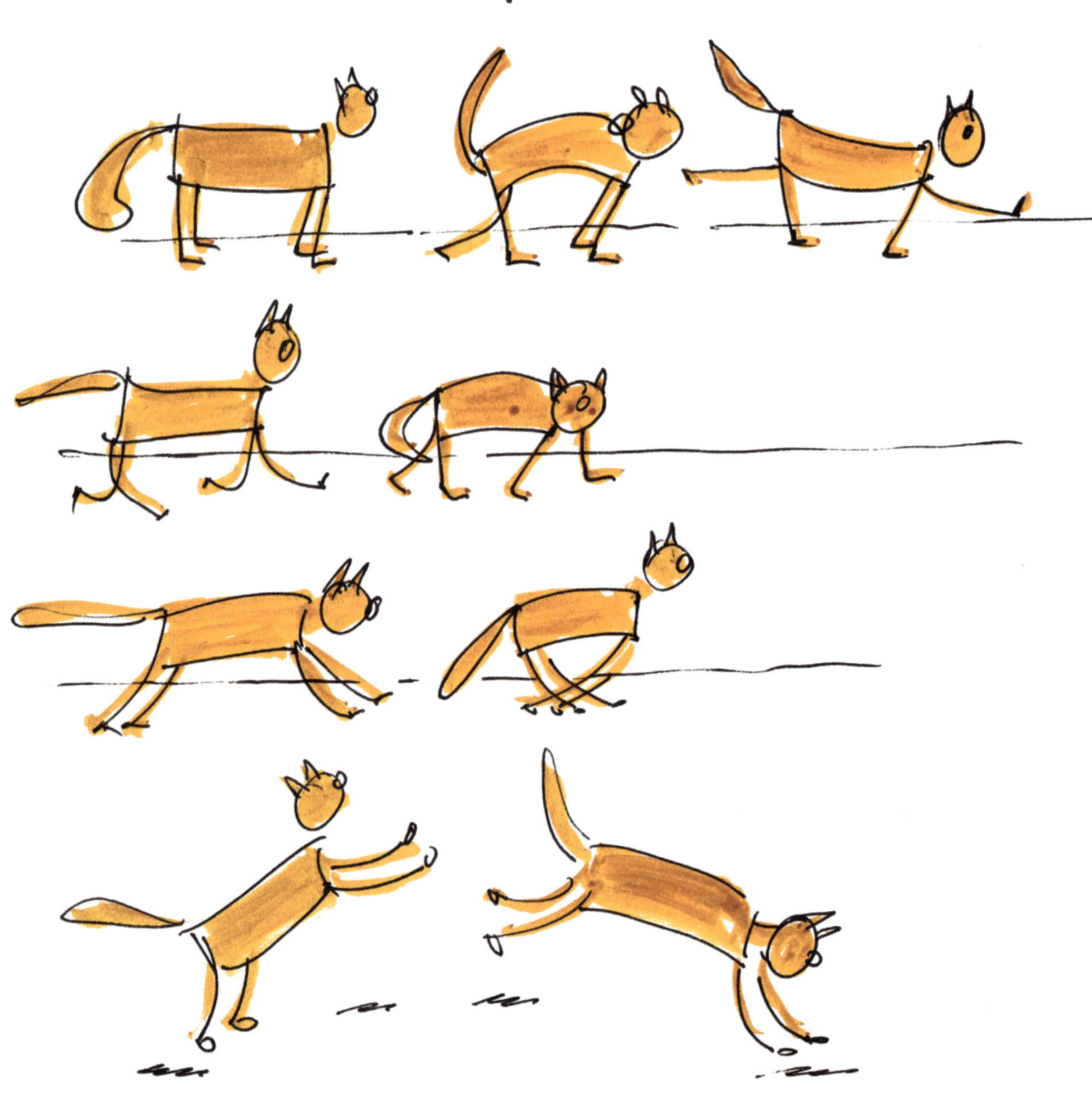

GO FOR IT!

SITTING CATS
FROM THE BACK OR FRONT

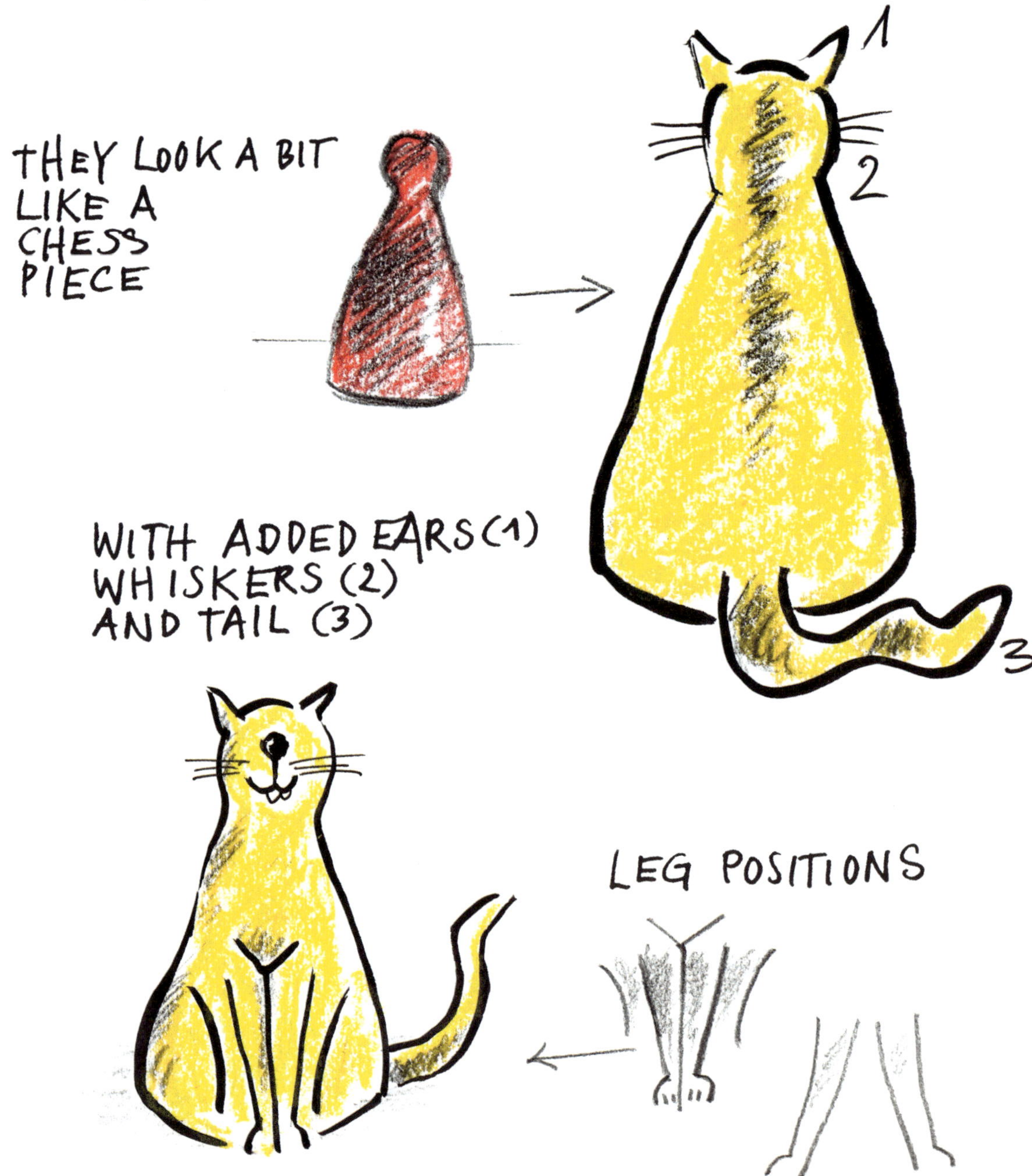

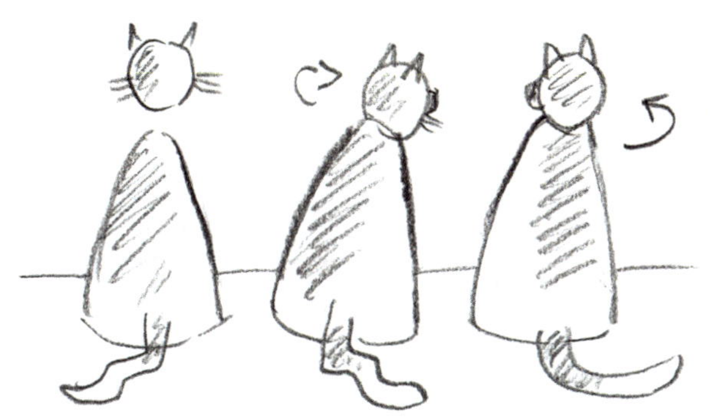

THEY CAN LOOK IN
DIFFERENT DIRECTIONS TOO,
TRY IT OUT!

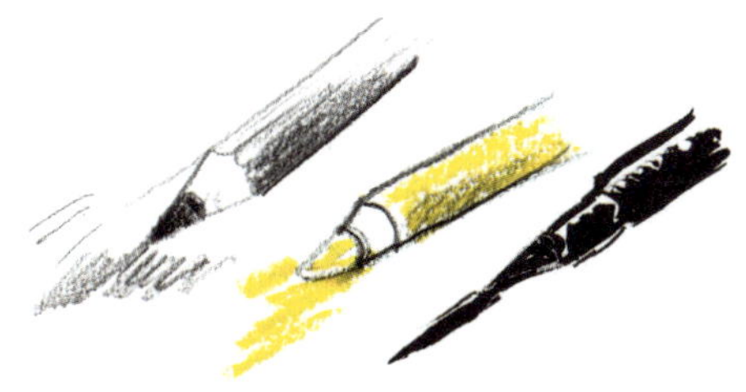

SITTING CATS
FROM THE SIDE

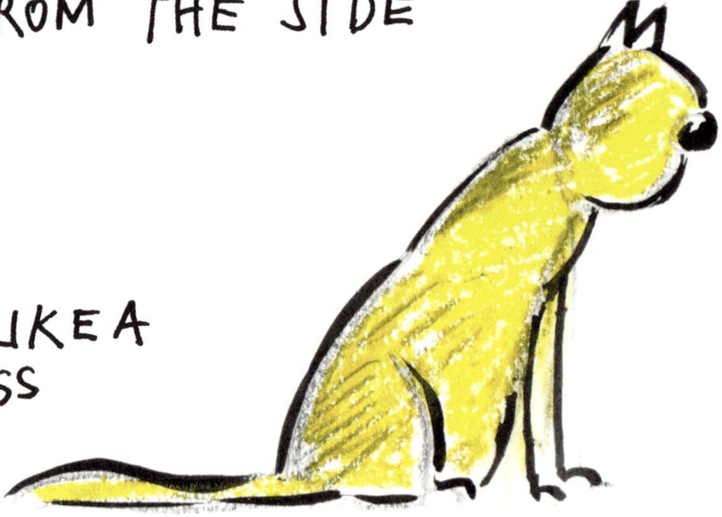

THEY LOOK LIKE A
FLOPPY CHESS
PIECE!

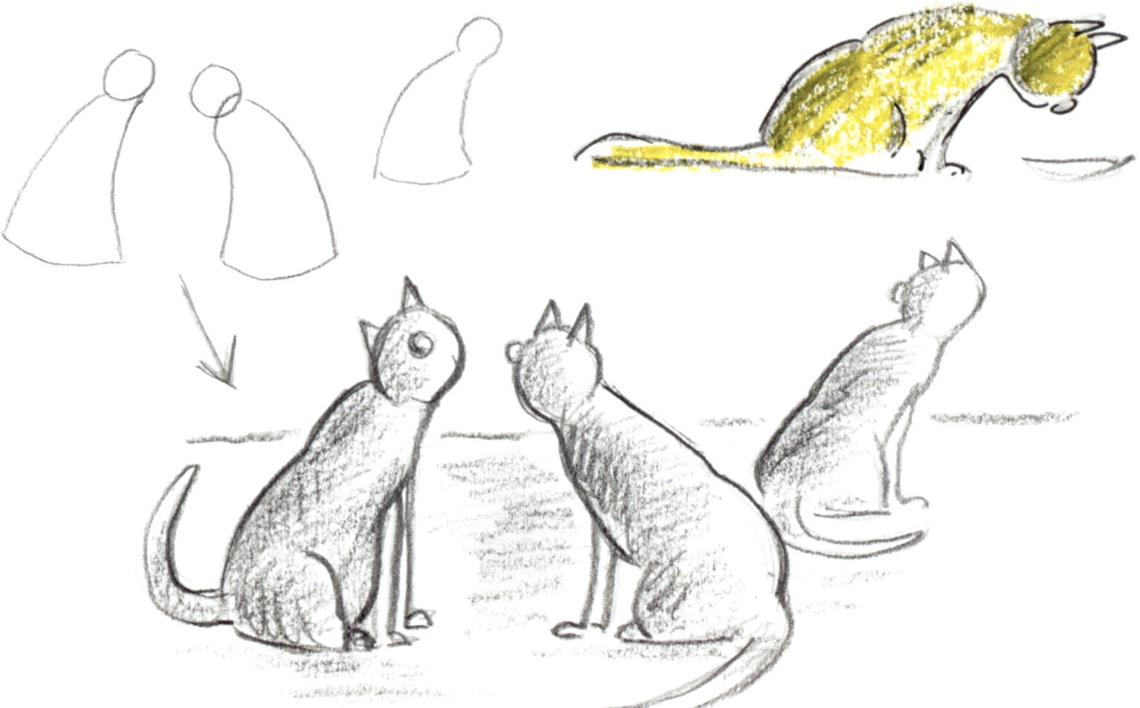

YOUR TURN!

DRAW MORE SITTING CATS

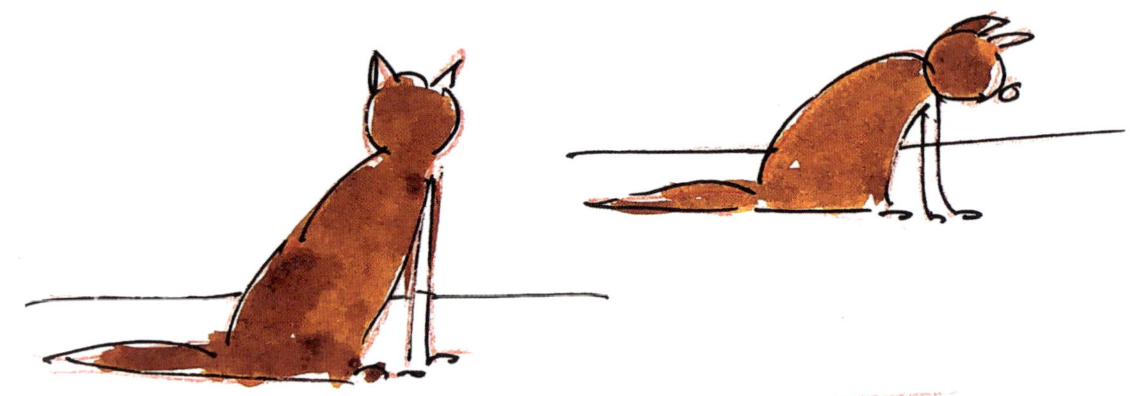

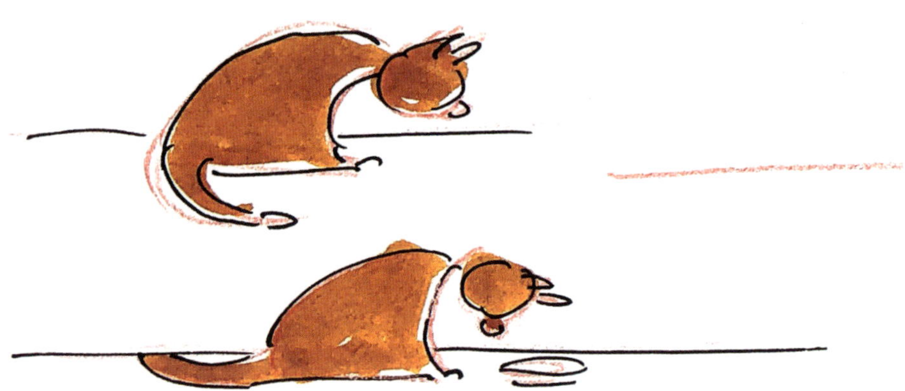

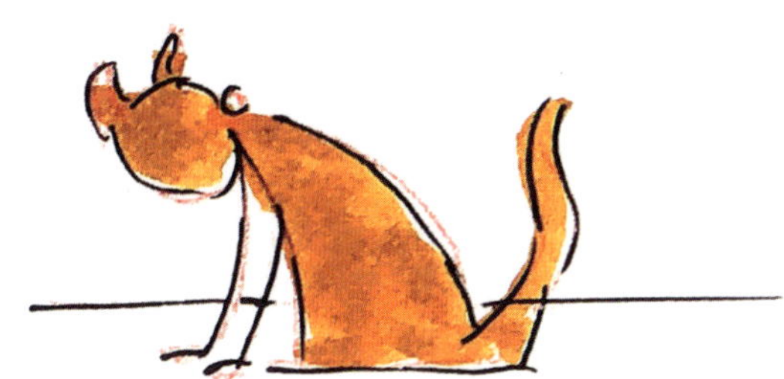

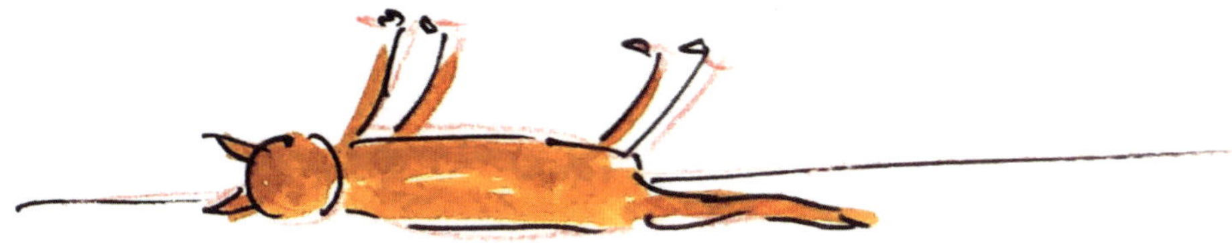

YOGA TIME!

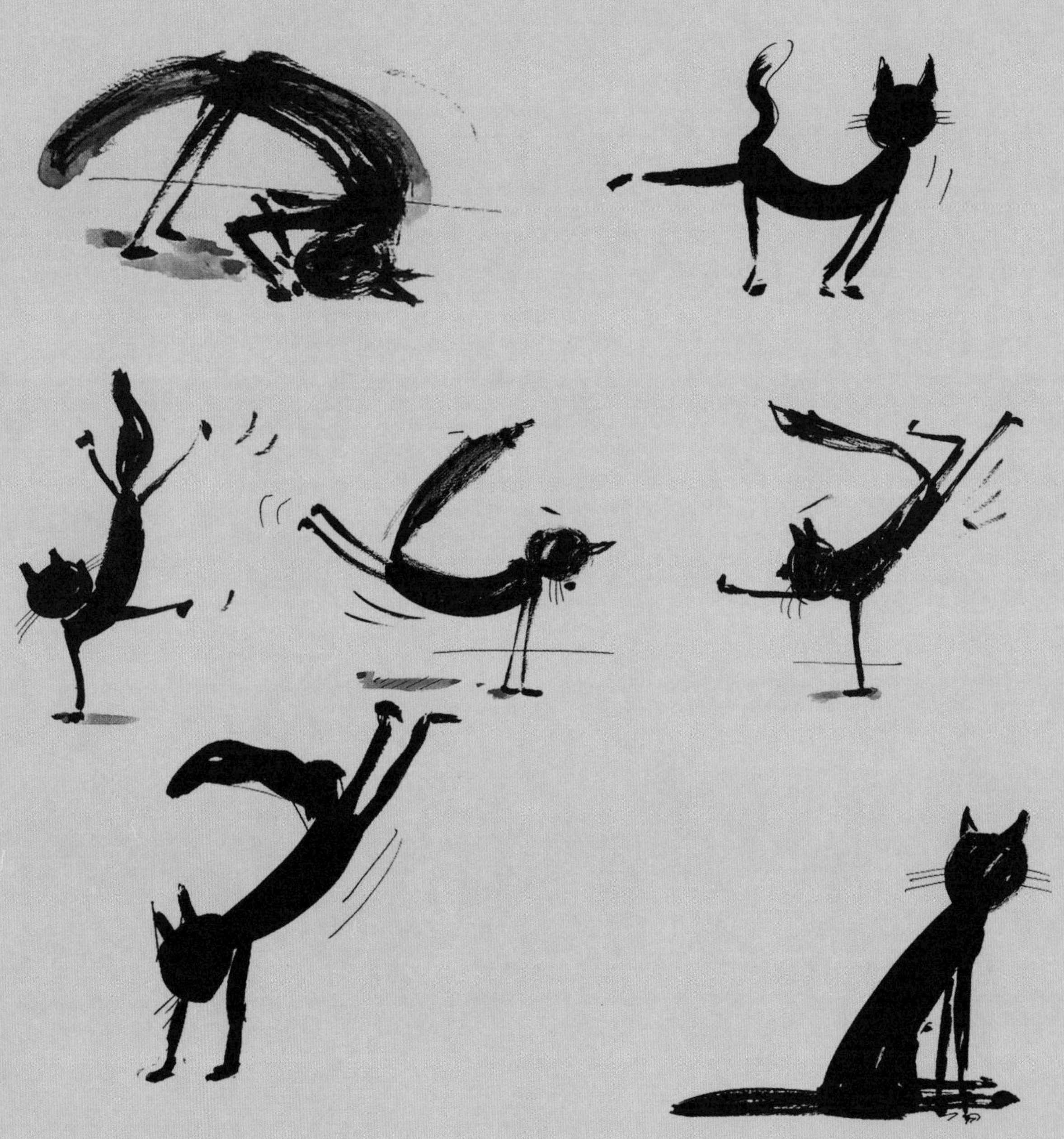

CAN YOU COME
UP WITH OTHER
POSES?
THEN GO FOR IT!

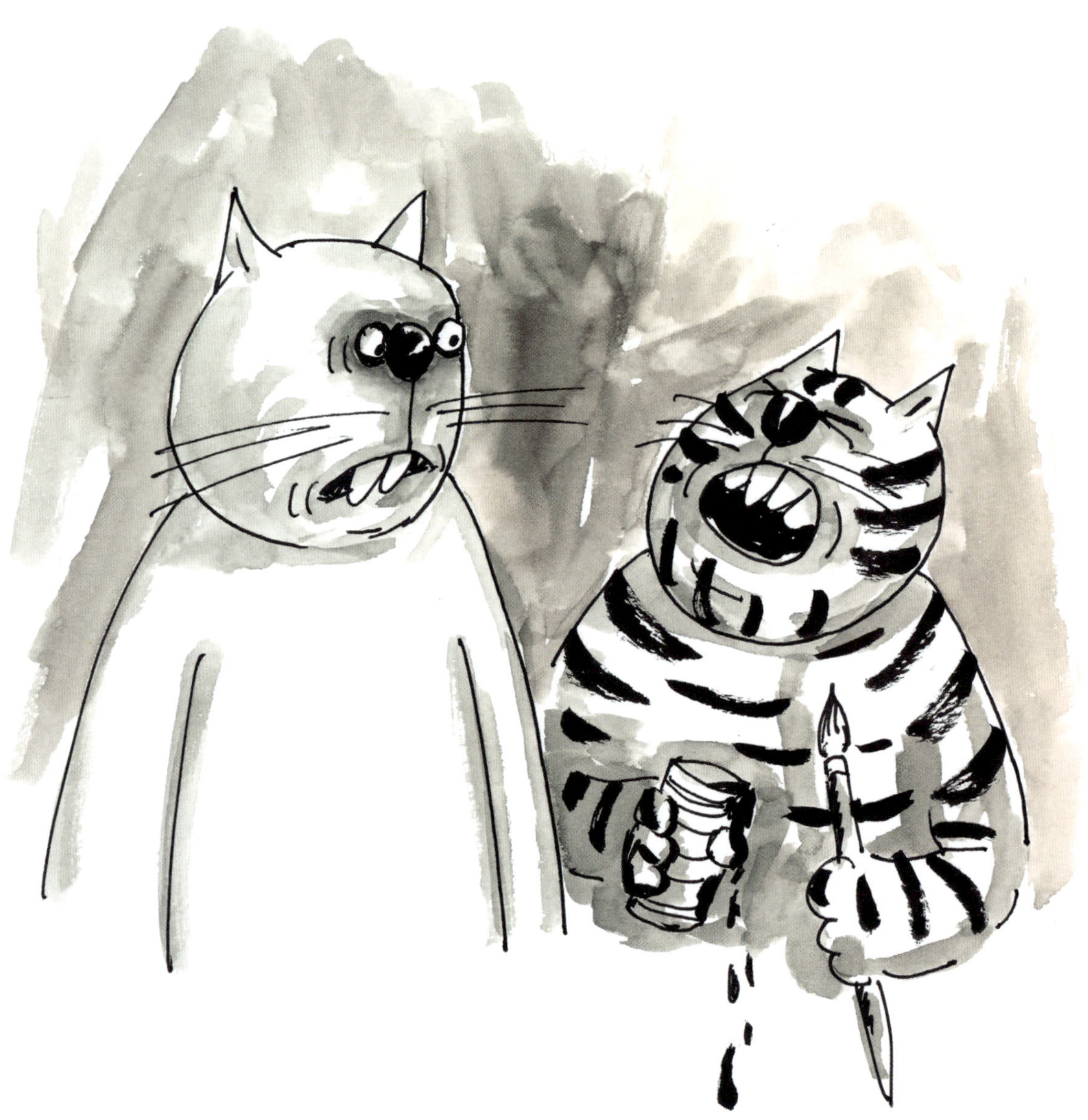

NO MARKINGS?
BOOORRRING!

MUCH BETTER!

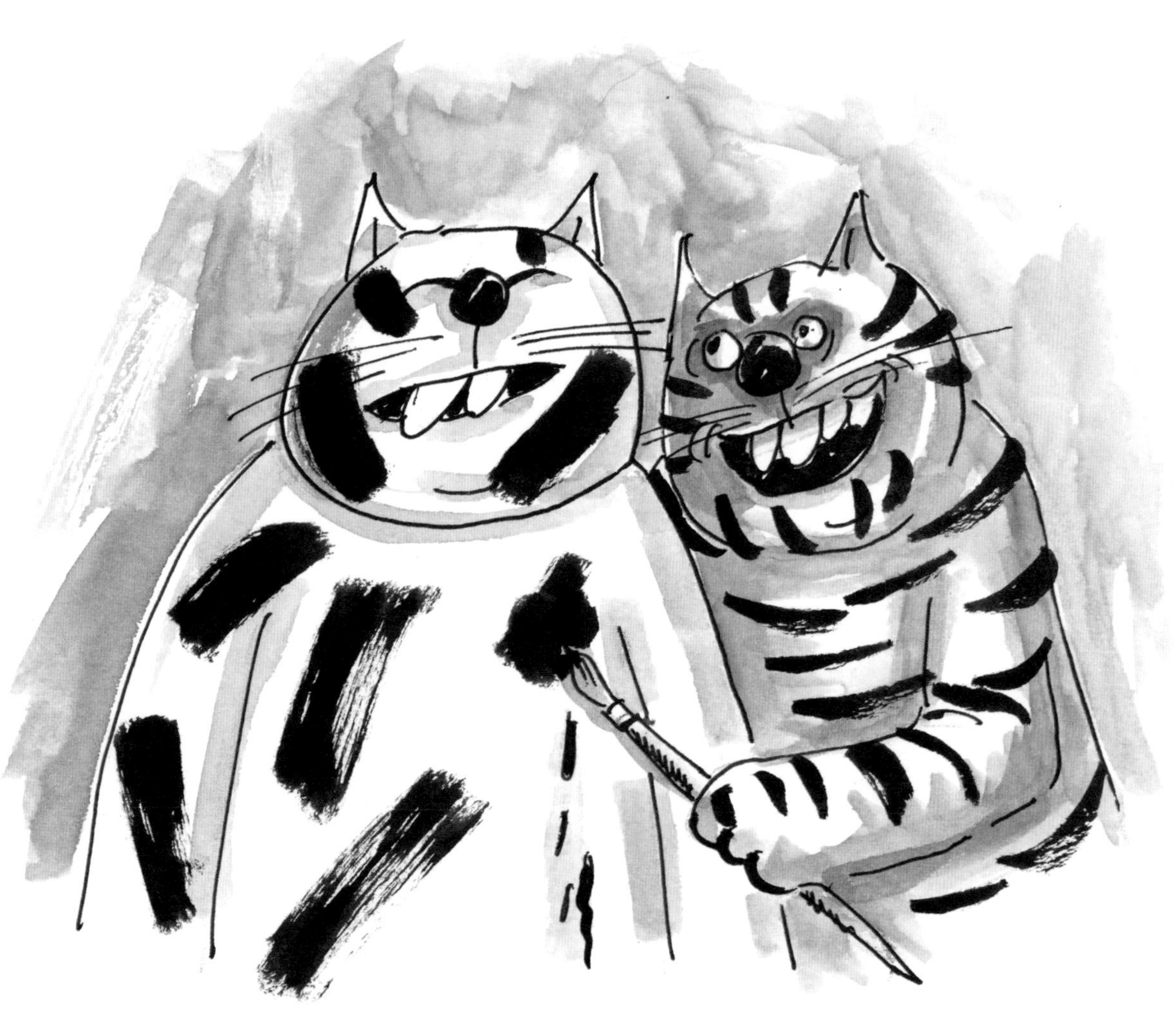

FUR MARKINGS
USING DIFFERENT TOOLS

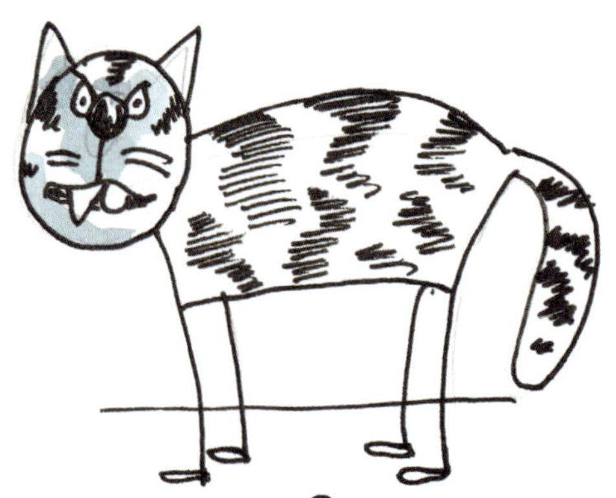

FINELINER

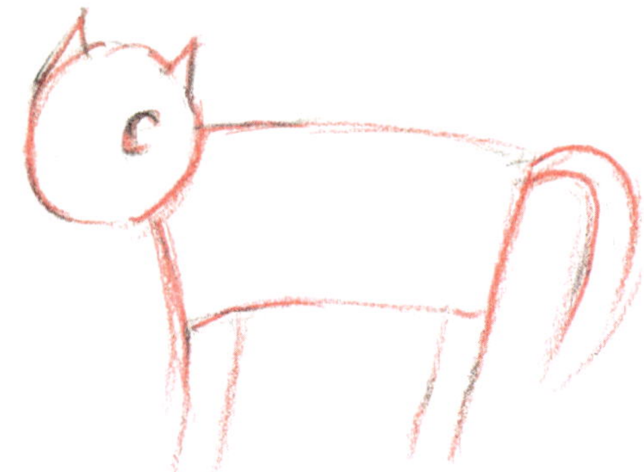

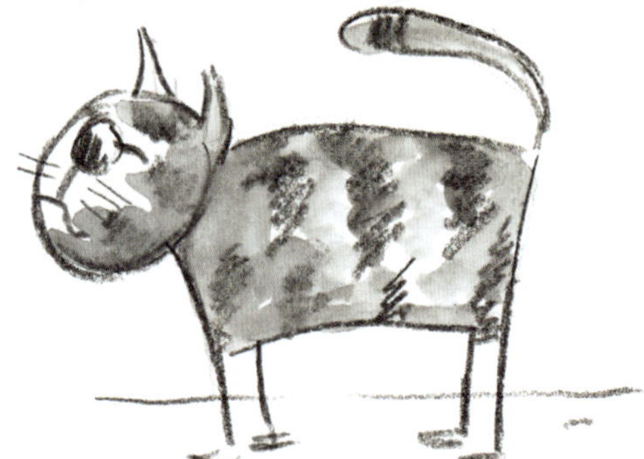

GRAPHITE PENCIL

INK AND BRUSH

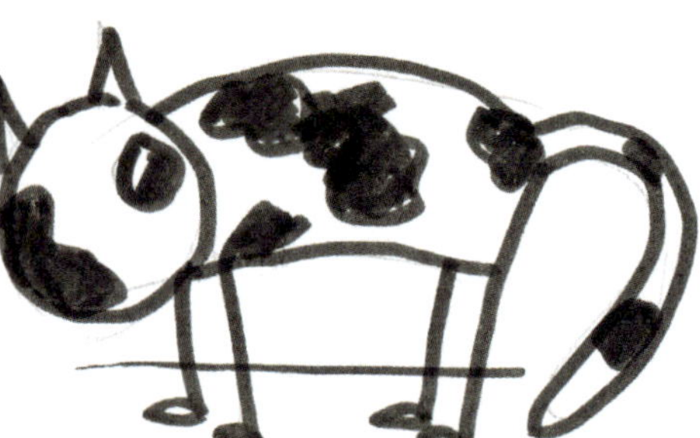

FELT-TIP PEN

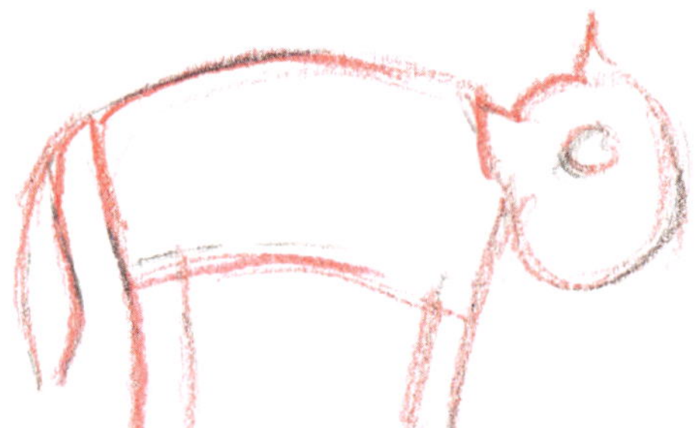

USE THE SPACE TO EXPERIMENT WITH OTHER PATTERNS AND TOOLS!

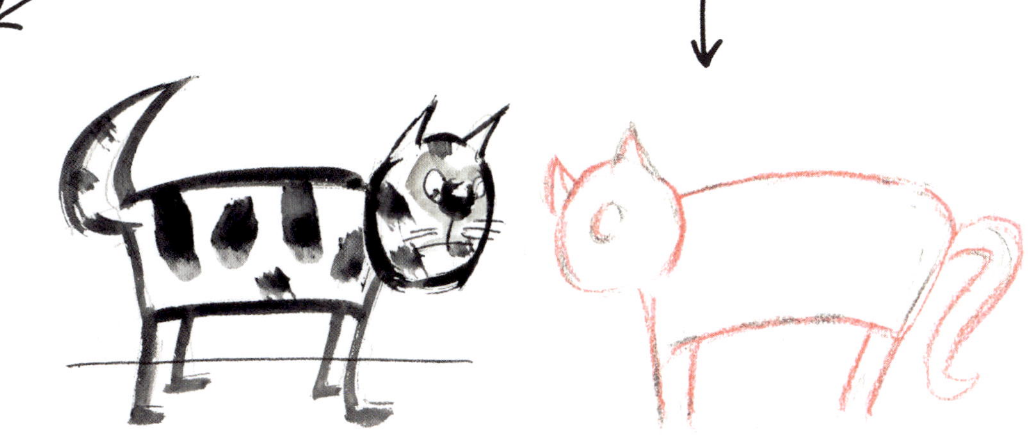

PAINTBRUSH

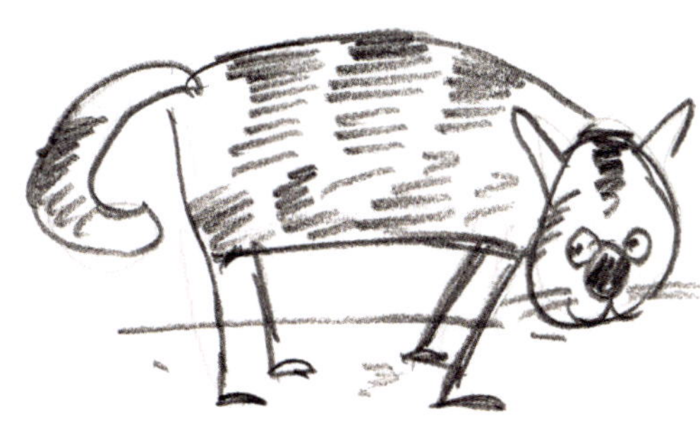

4B PENCIL

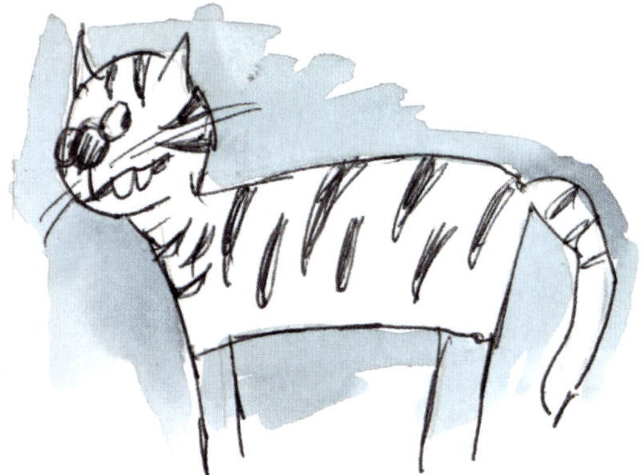

BALLPOINT PEN AND BRUSH

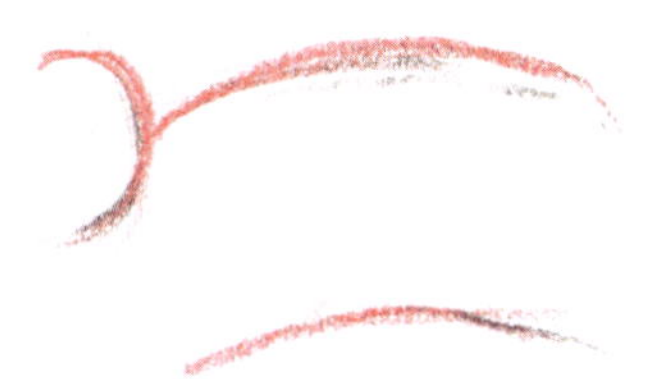

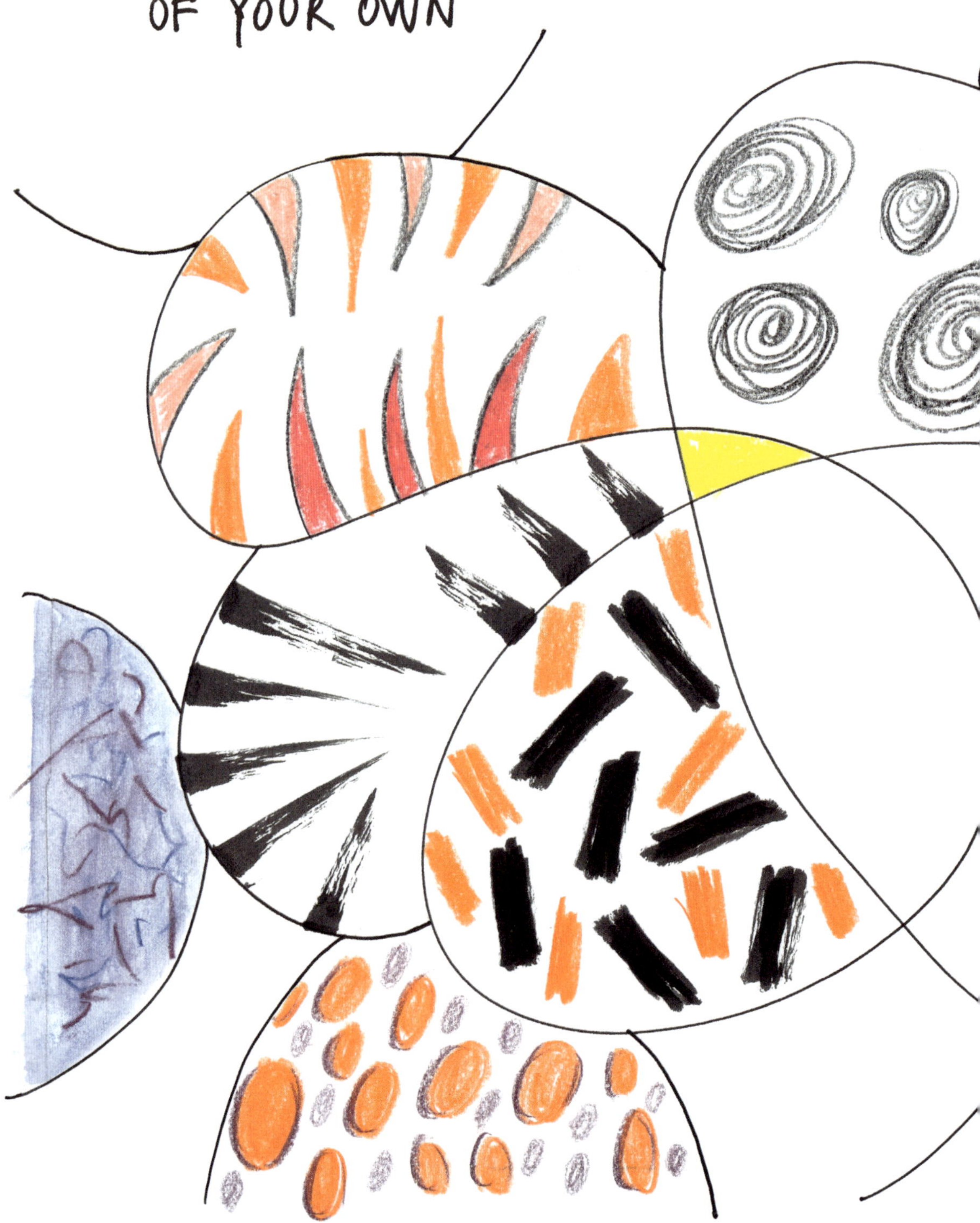

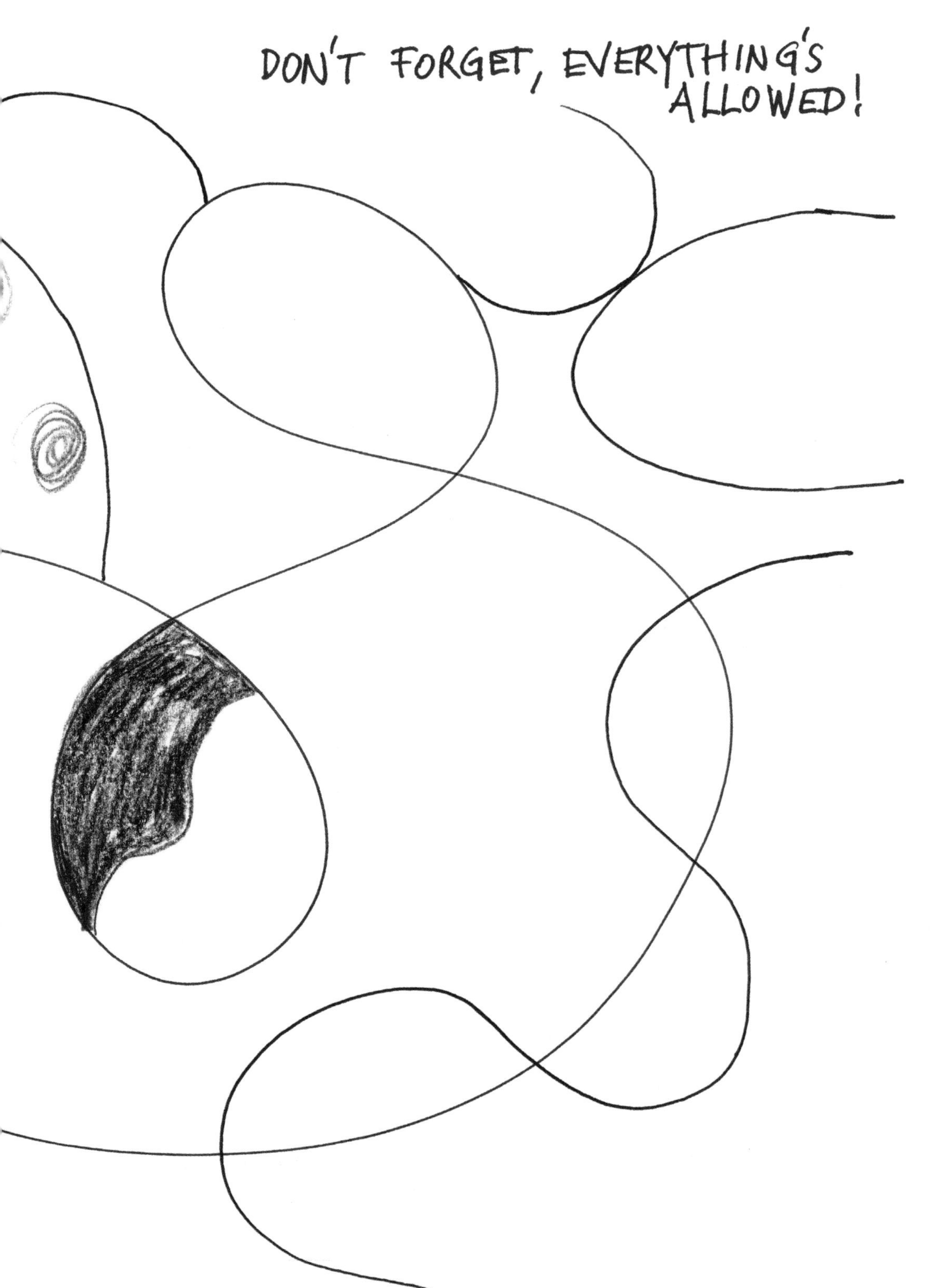

DON'T FORGET, EVERYTHING'S ALLOWED!
DON'T FORGET, EVERYTHING'S ALLOWED!

THESE CATS WOULD LIKE PATTERNS TOO

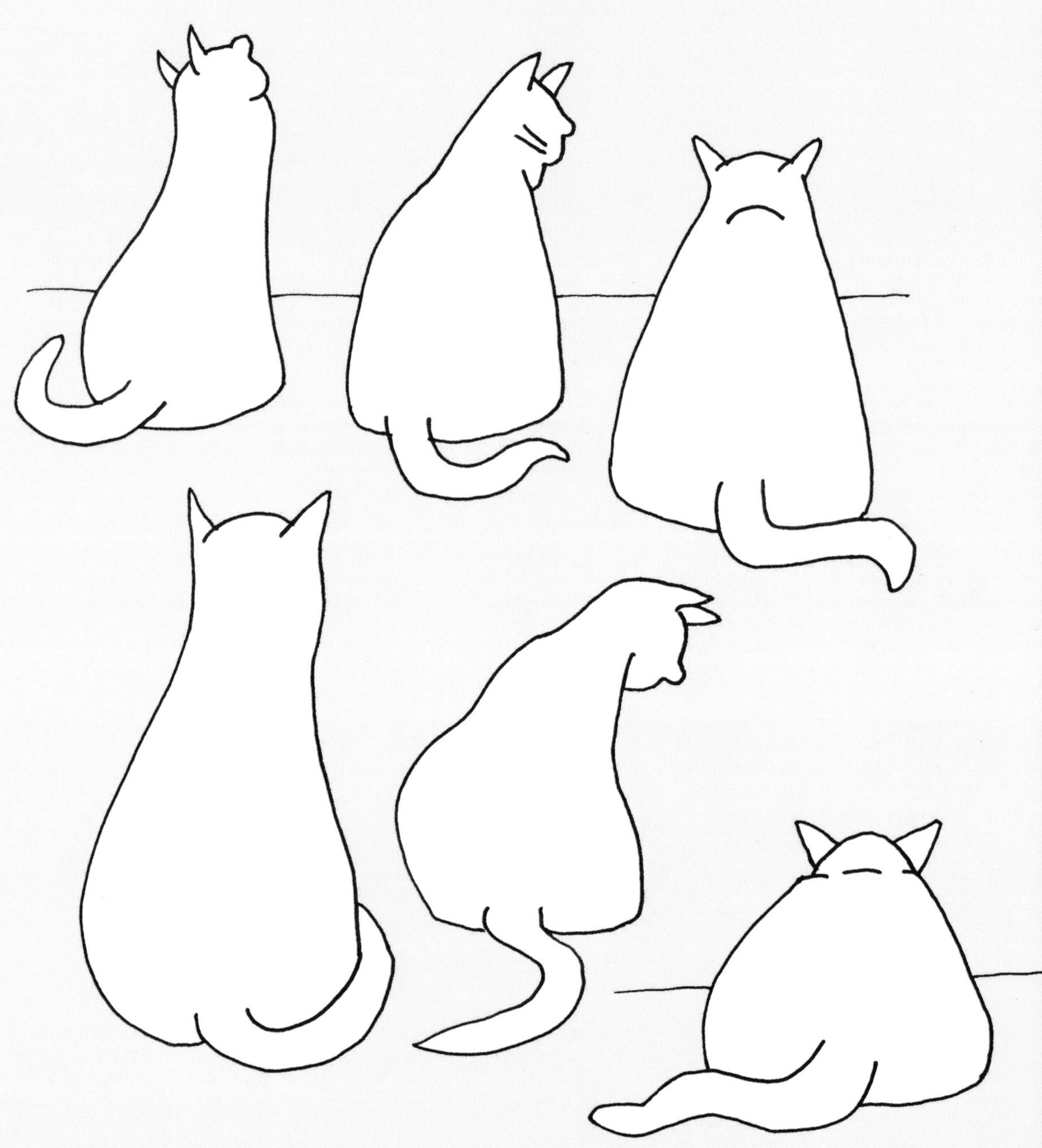

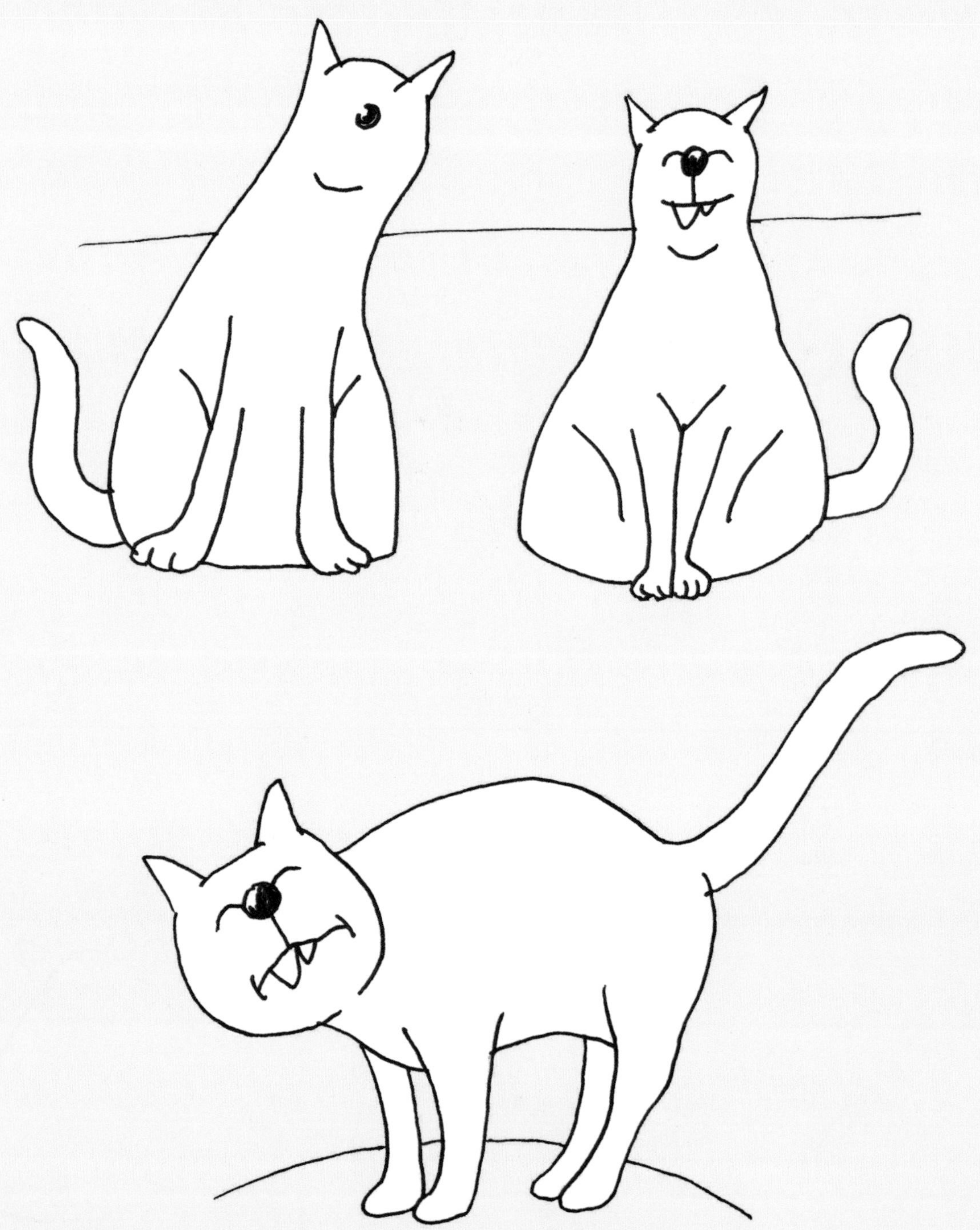

TAILS OF THE UNEXPECTED
SOME ARE PRETTIER THAN OTHERS!

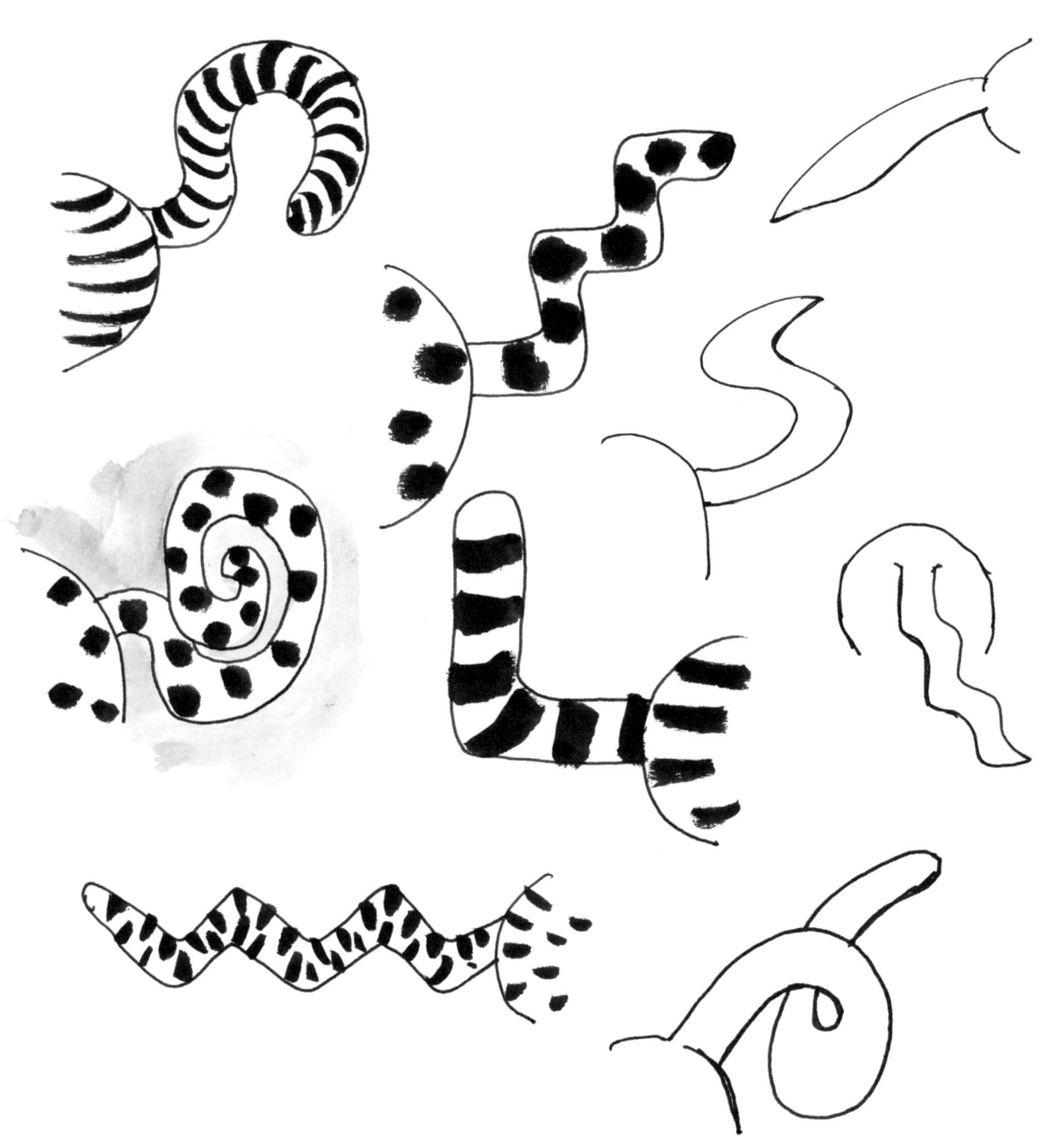

SOME ARE BLANK FOR YOU TO FILL IN!

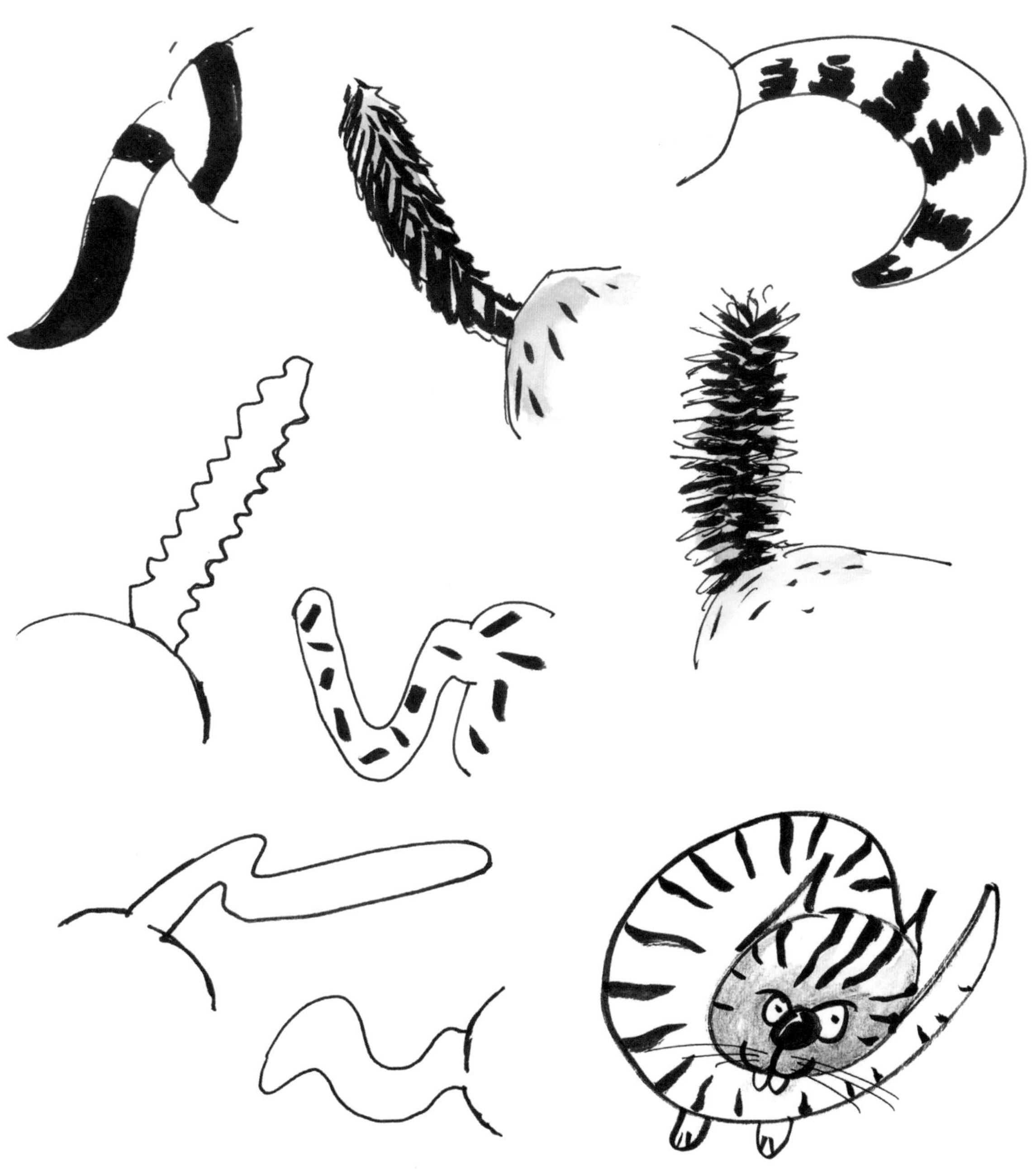

HERE ARE QUITE A FEW PLAYFUL KITTIES

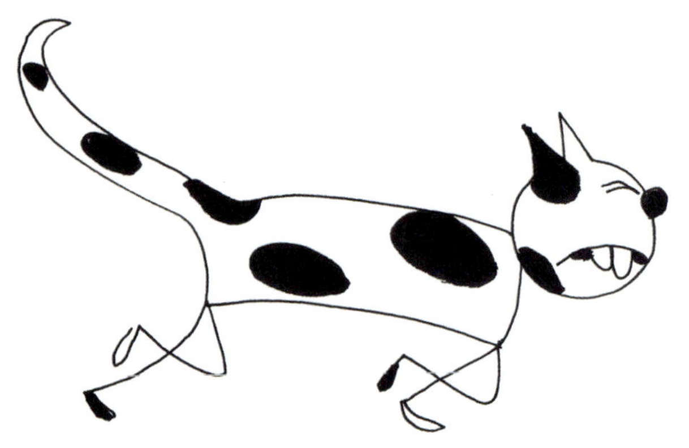

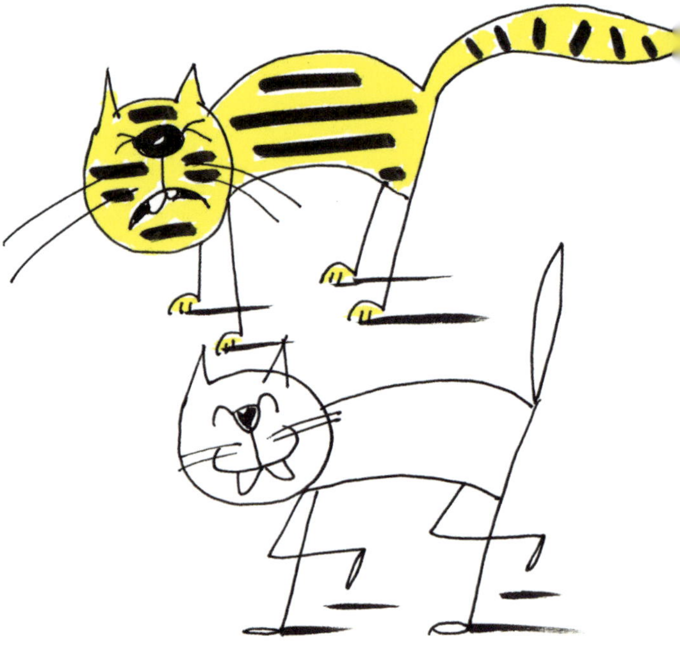

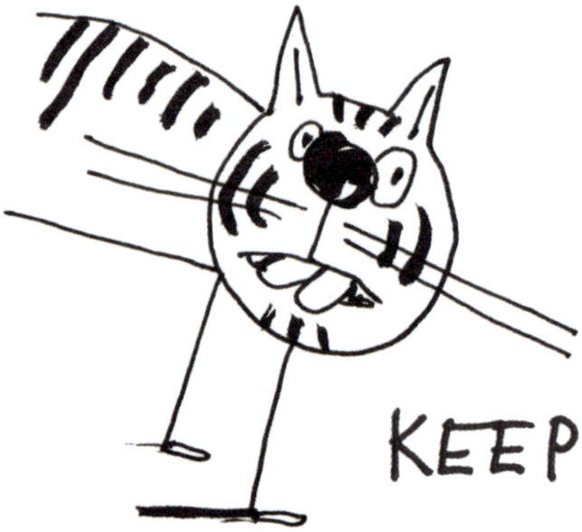

KEEP IT SIMPLE!

SQUEEZE IN AS MANY MORE AS YOU CAN

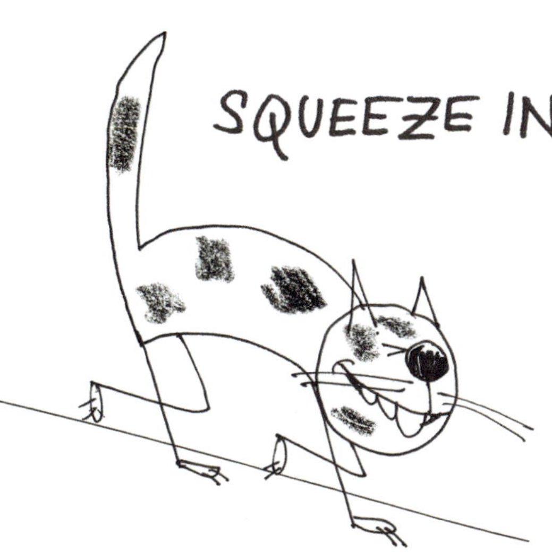

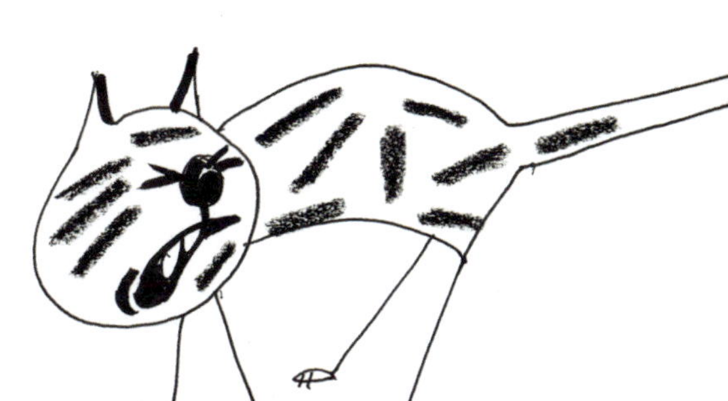

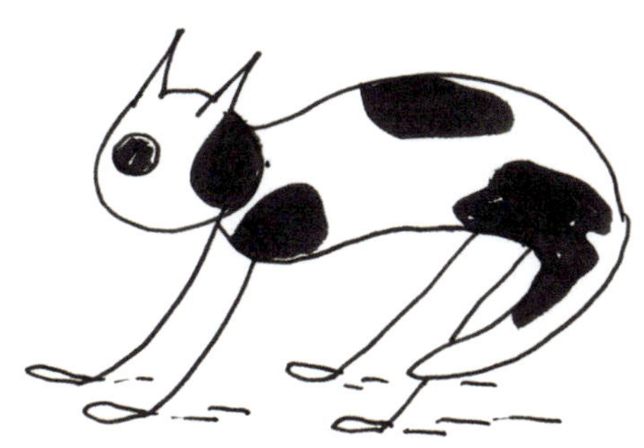

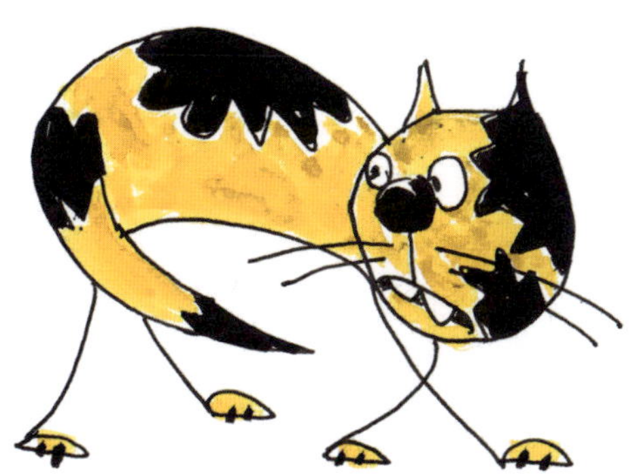

BACKGROUNDS AND SHADING
GIVE YOUR CATS A LITTLE MORE DEPTH

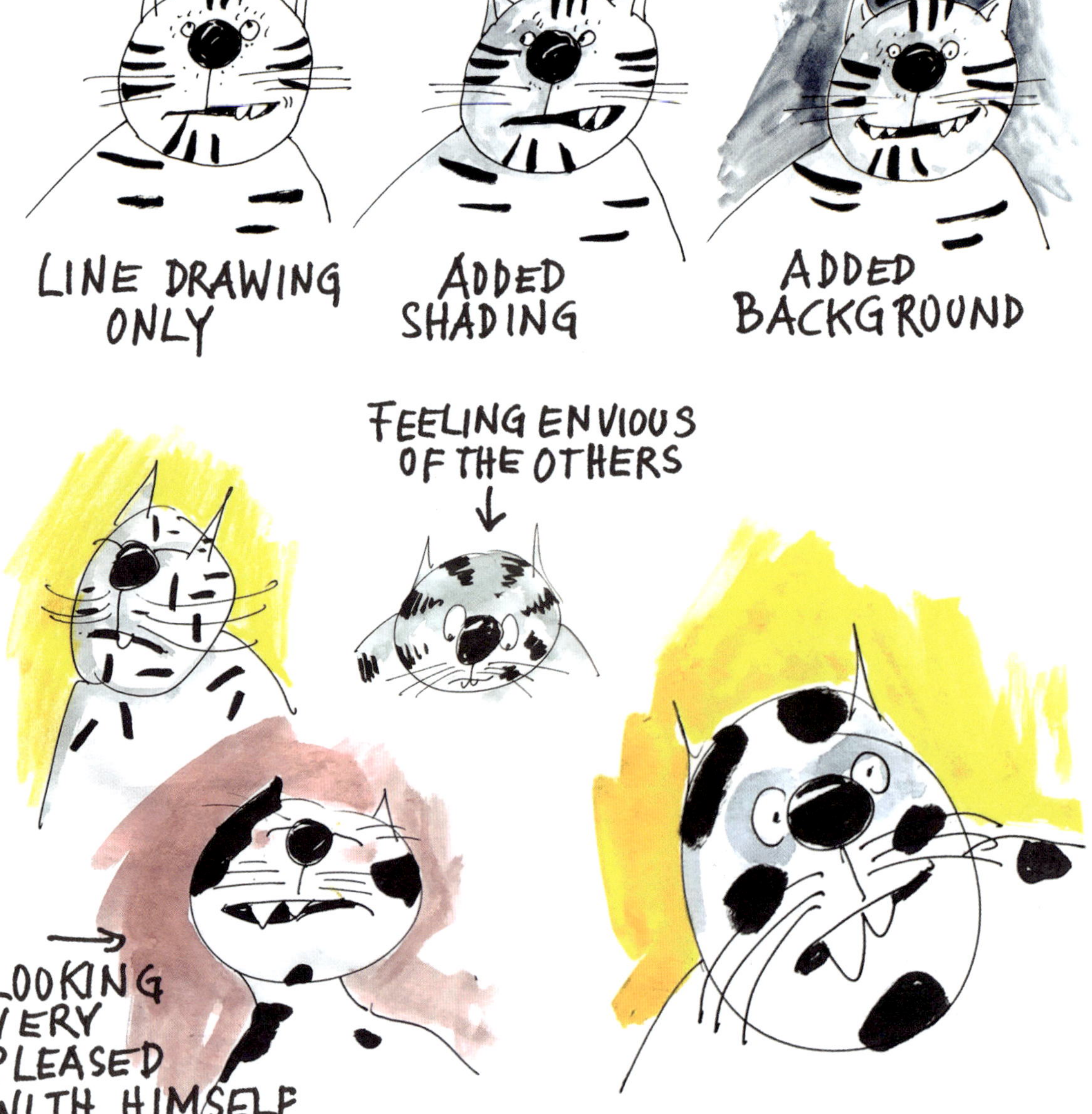

DRAW SOME CAT HEADS AND TRY
ADDING SHADING AND
BACKGROUNDS

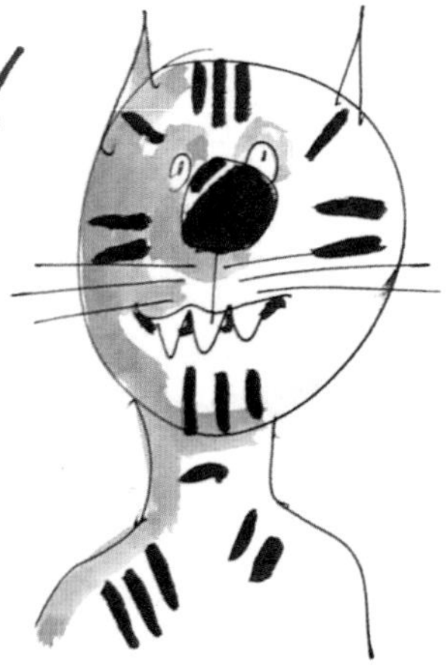

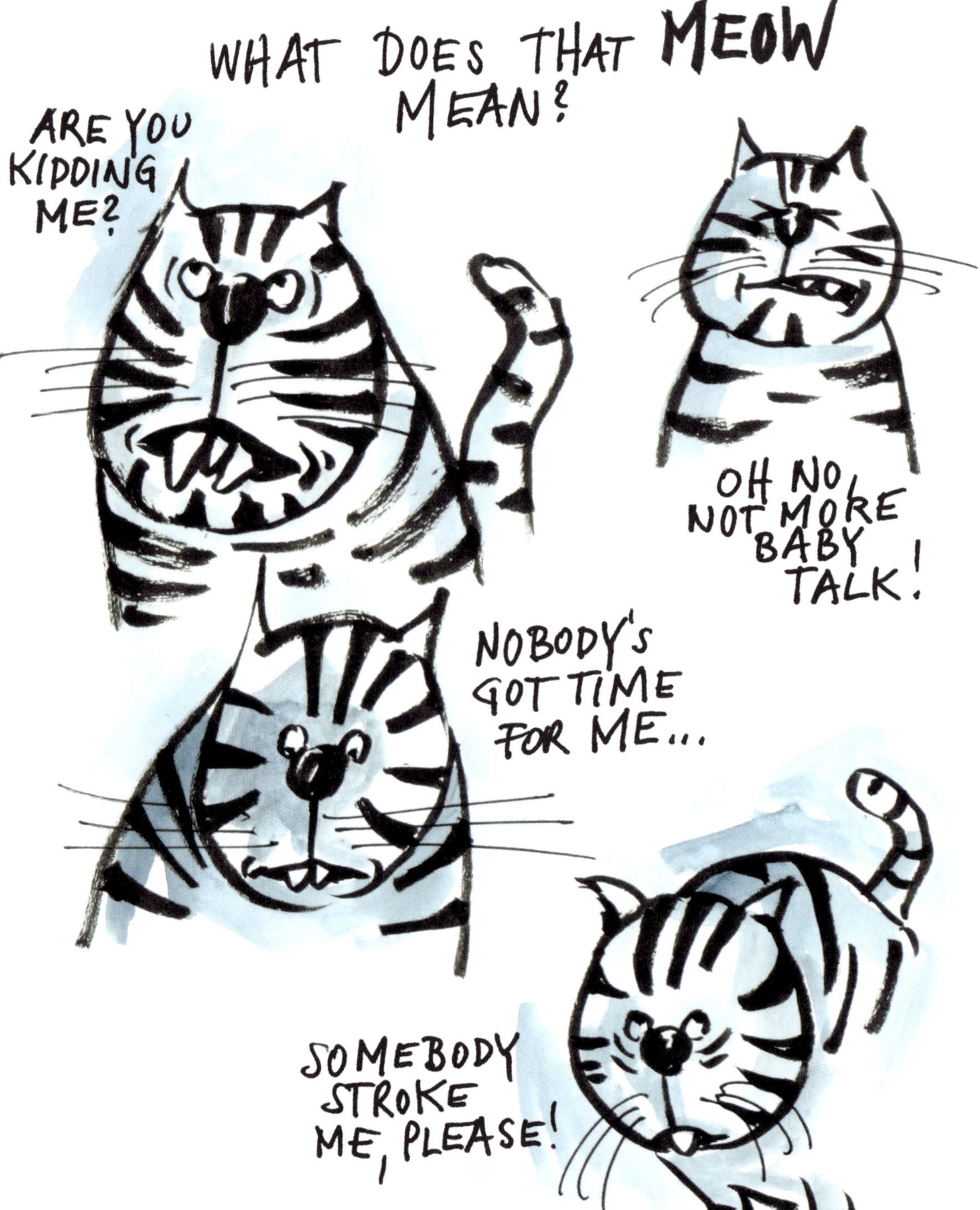

WHAT DOES THAT MEOW MEAN?
ARE YOU KIDDING ME?
OH NO NOT MORE BABY TALK!
NOBODY'S GOT TIME FOR ME...
SOMEBODY STROKE ME, PLEASE!

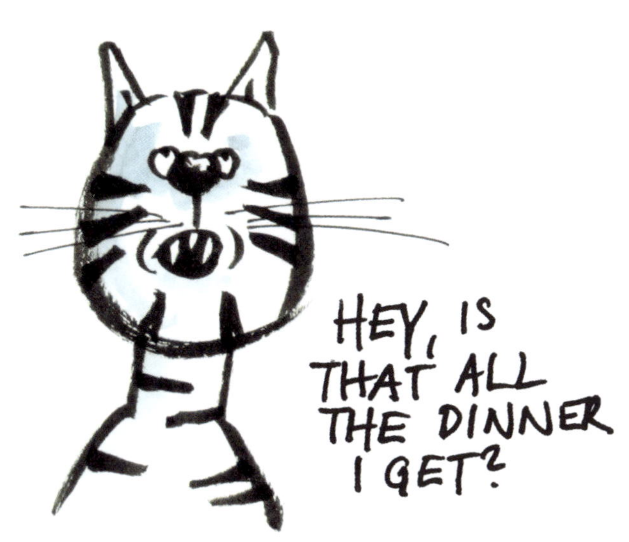

HEY, IS
THAT ALL
THE DINNER
I GET?

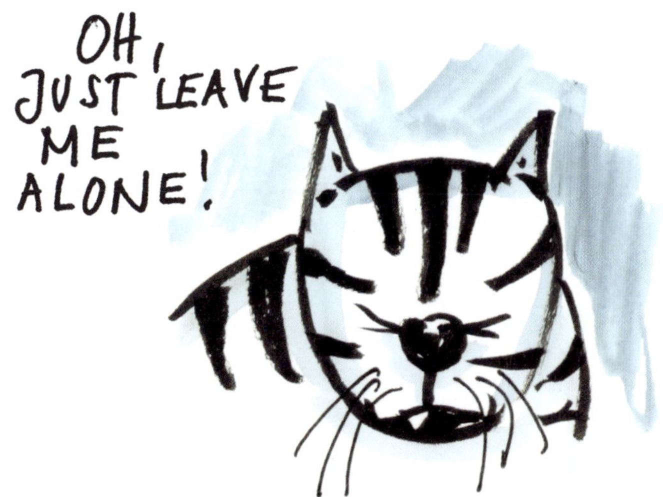

OH,
JUST LEAVE
ME
ALONE!

KITTY FARTS – EVERY CAT DOES THEM!

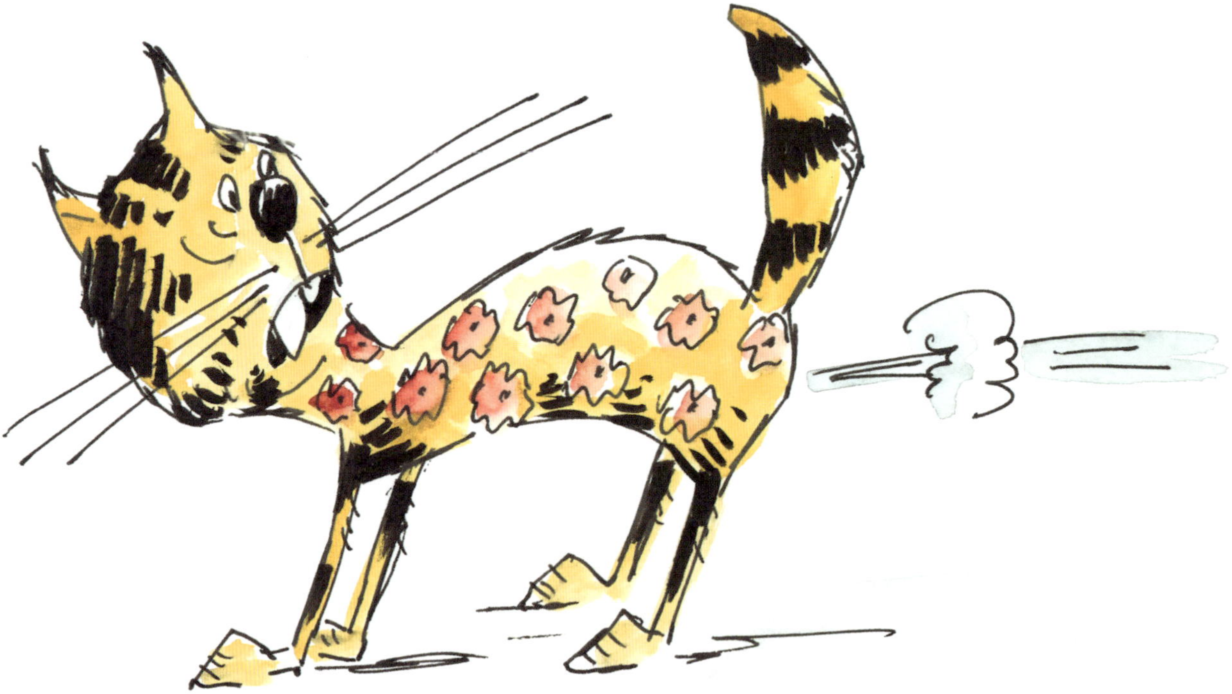

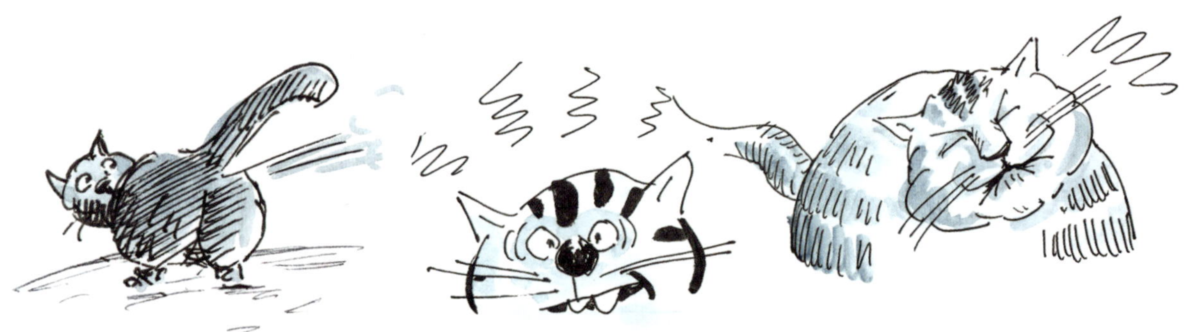

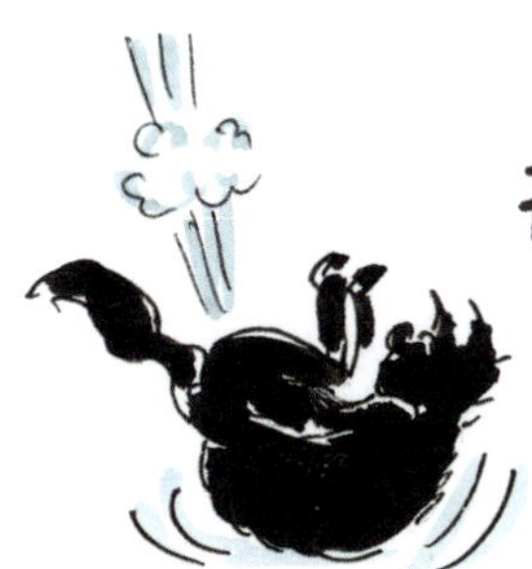

FARTING CATS ARE GUARANTEED
TO RAISE A LAUGH — TRY
DRAWING A FEW!

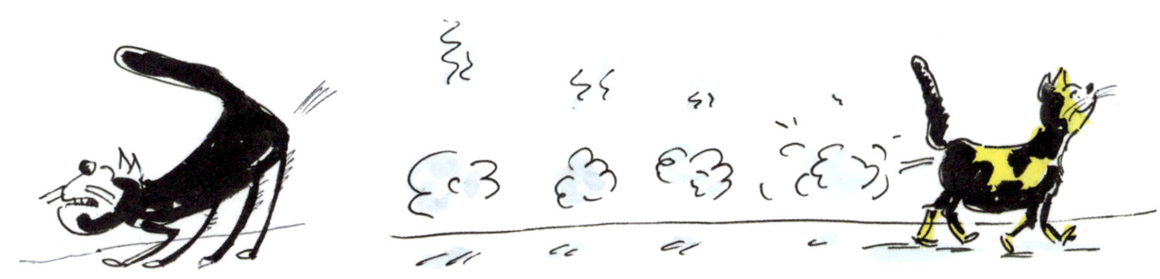

READY TO TRY SOMETHING NEW?
A DIFFERENT NOSE

LIKE THIS

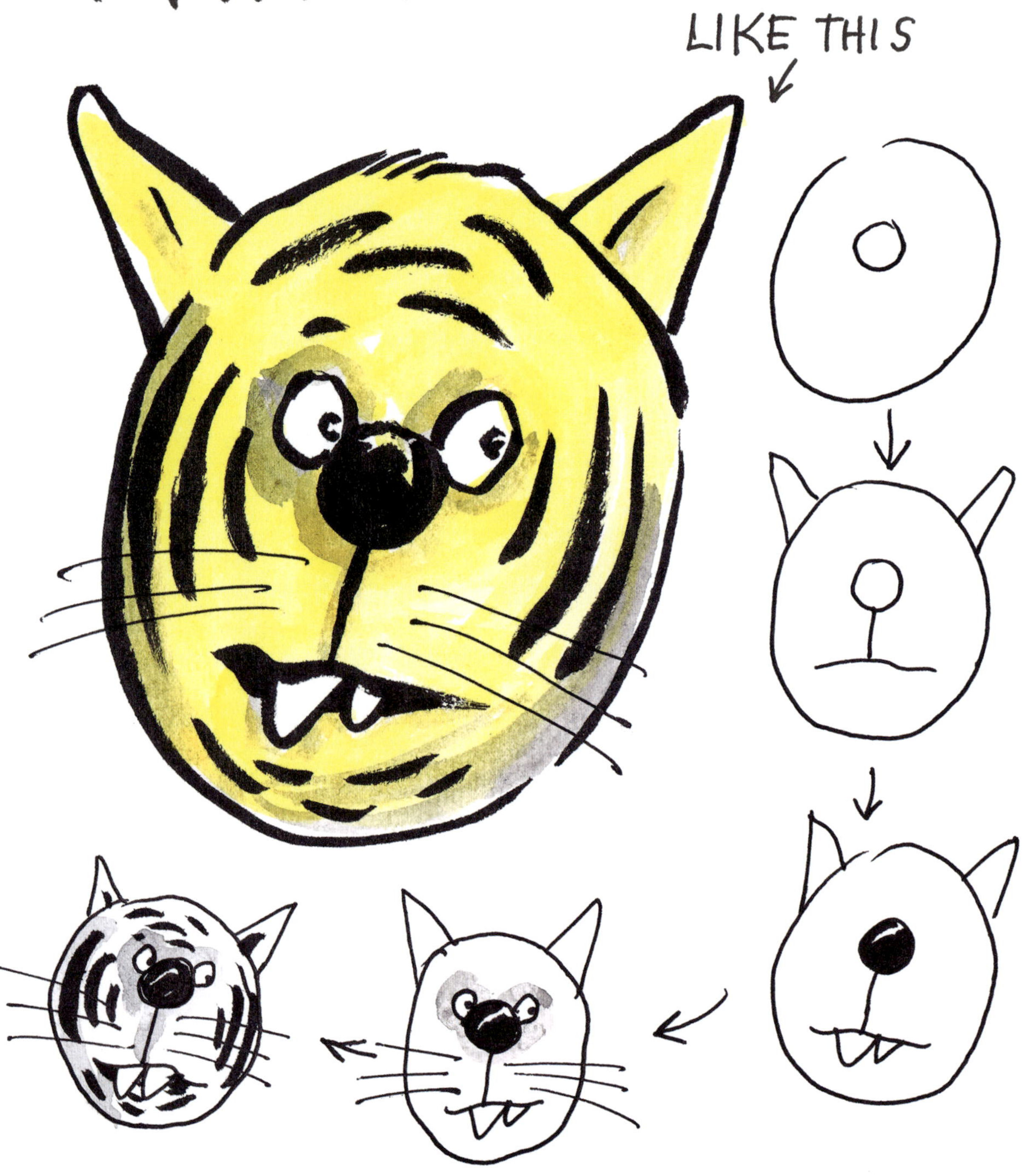

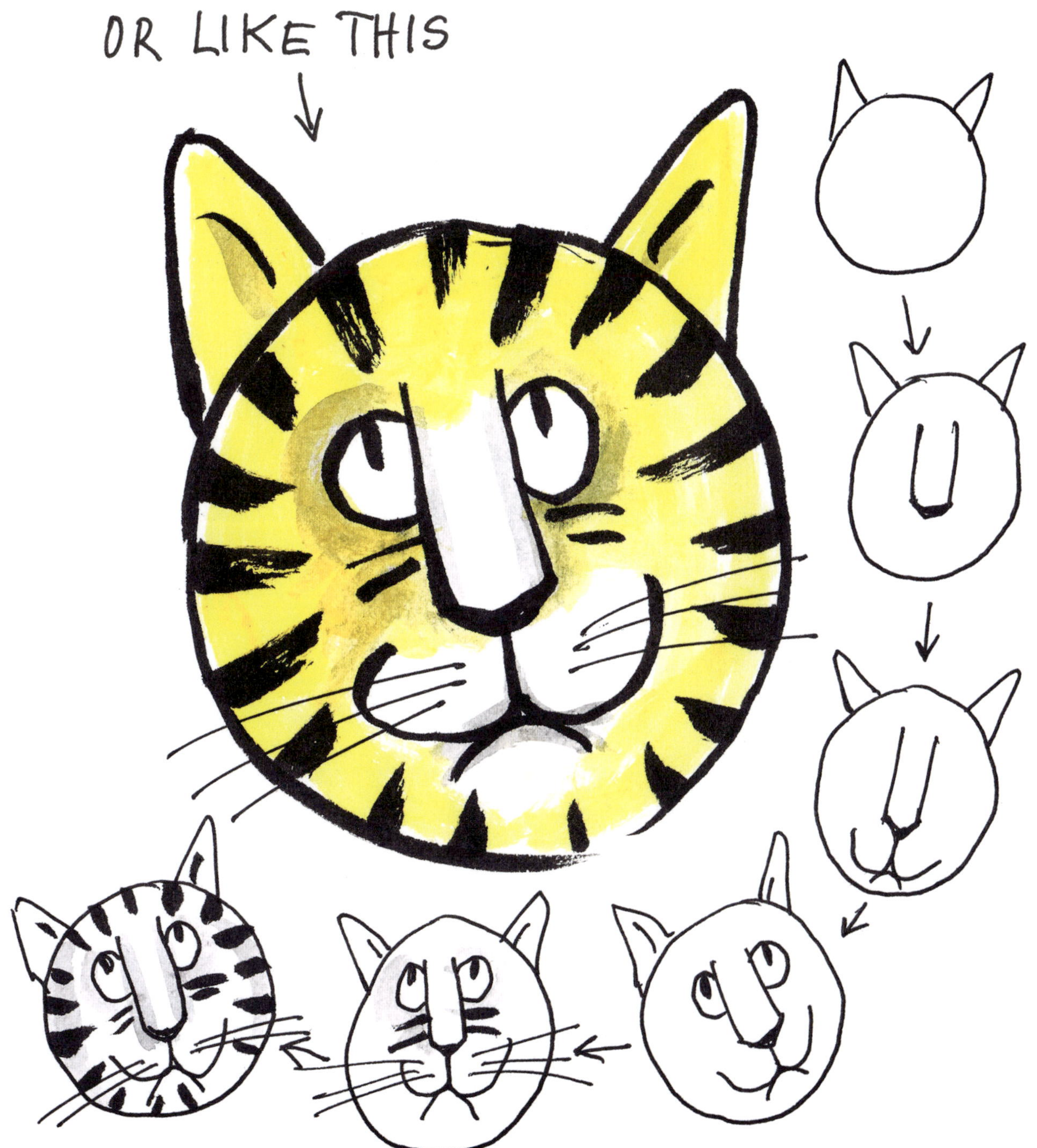

OR LIKE THIS

LET'S COMPARE NOSES

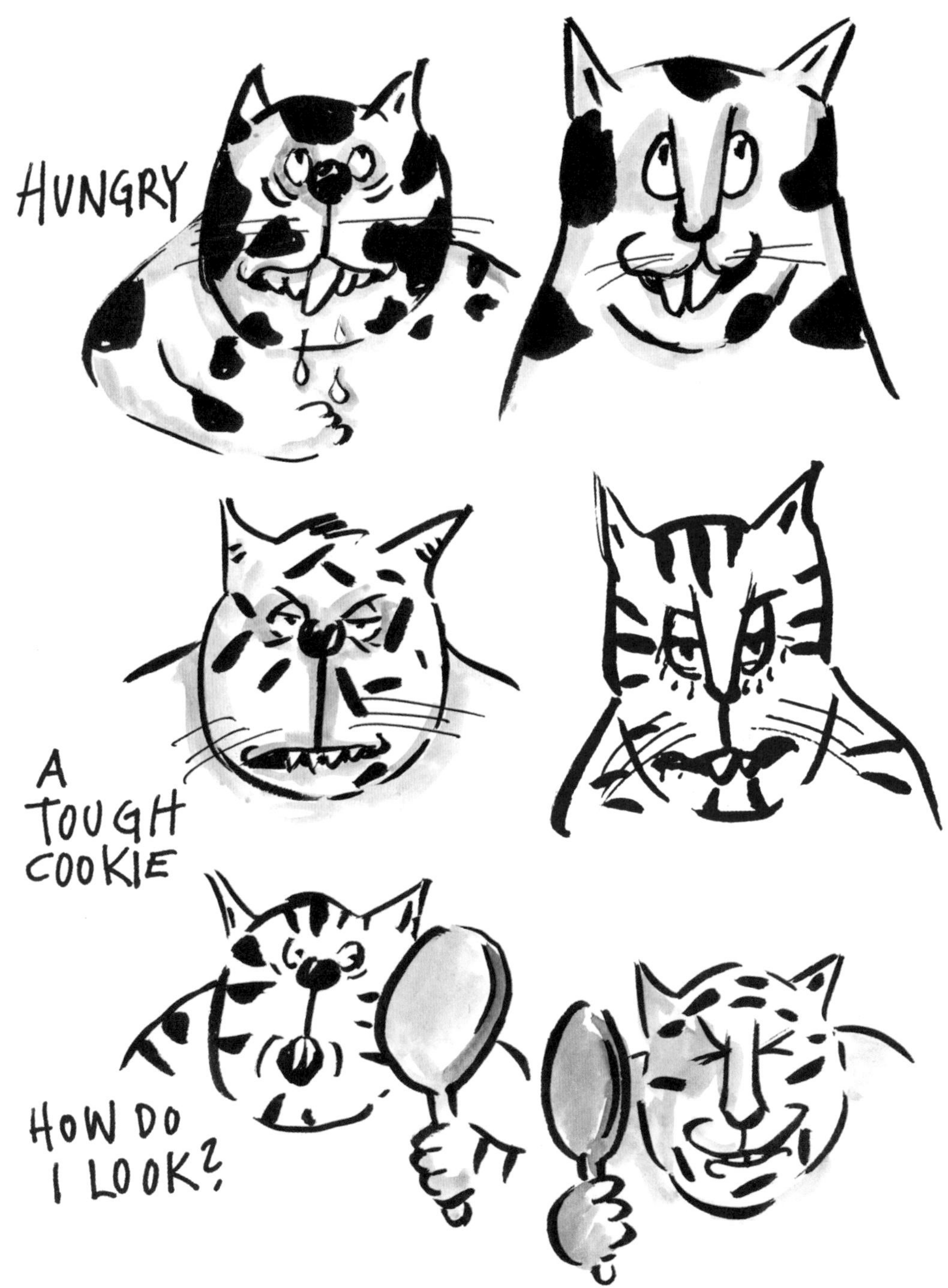

DRAW A PARTNER WITH THE OTHER KIND OF NOSE

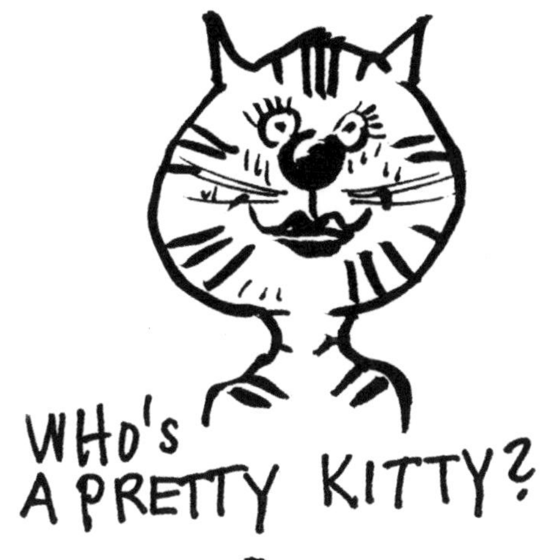

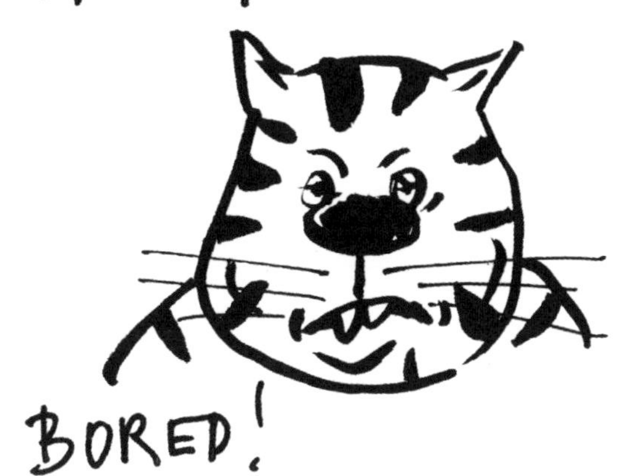

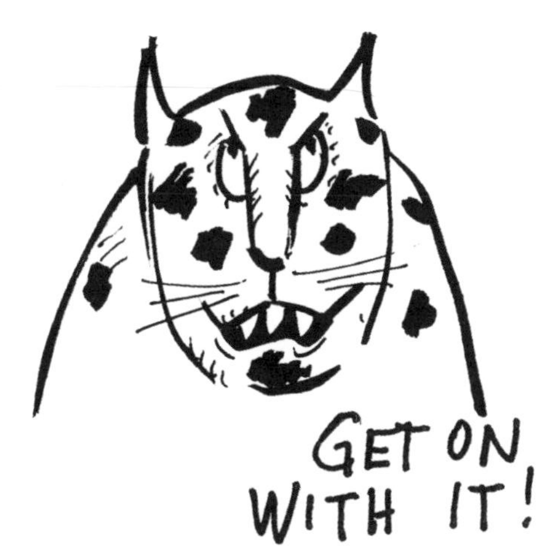

OUTDOOR EXERCISE

TRY DRAWING ON PEBBLES WITH A FELT-TIP
PEN OR INK AND BRUSH

LIKE THIS

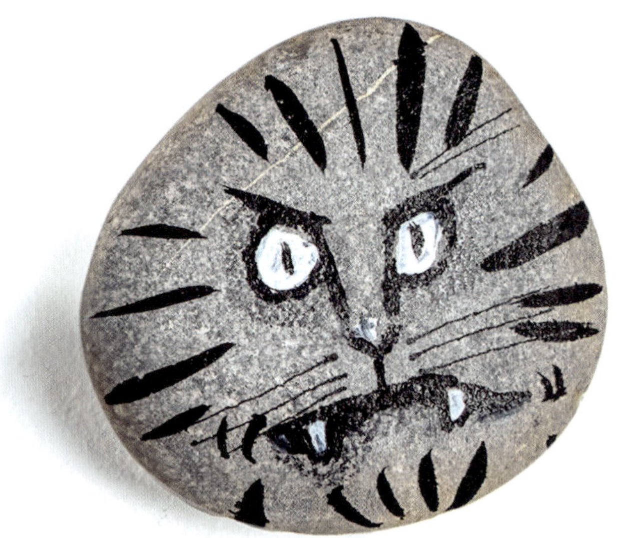

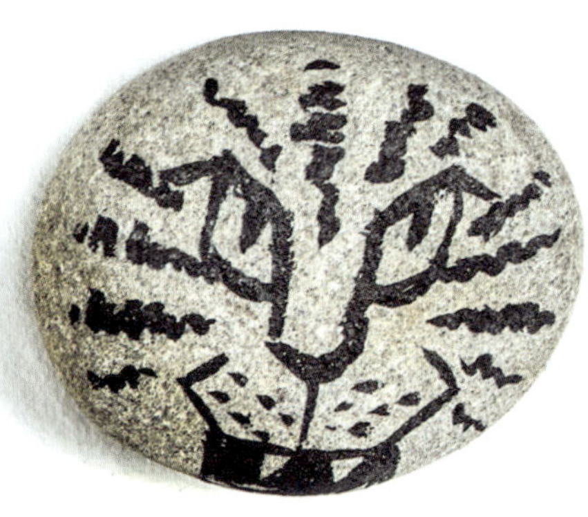

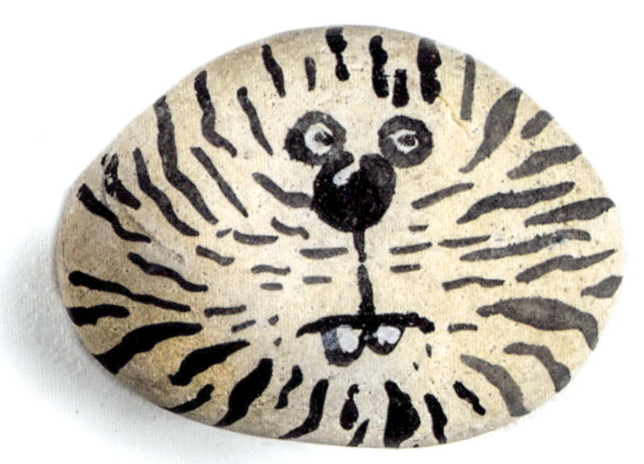

TRY . . .

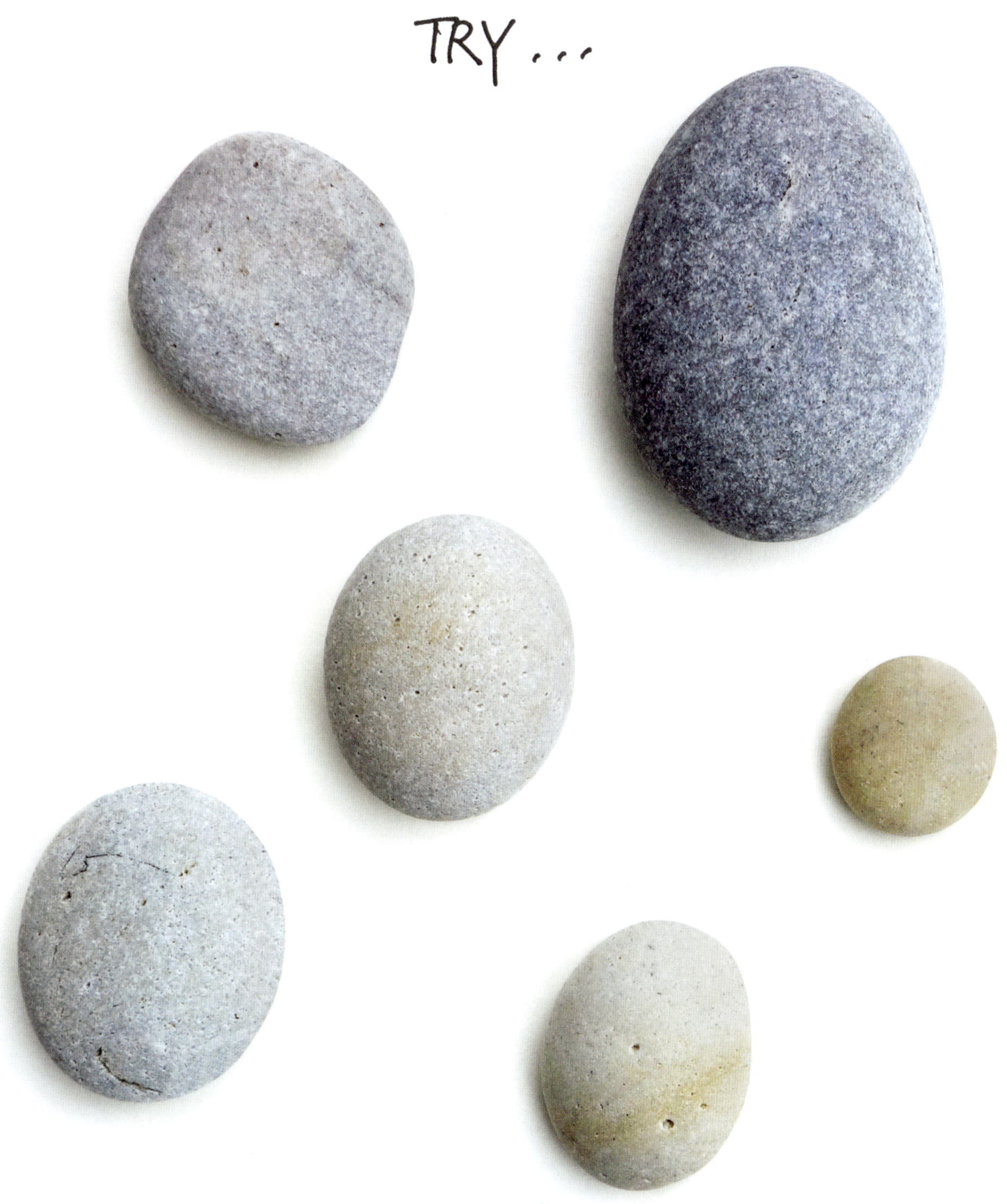

PENCIL PRACTICE
COPY THESE CATS...

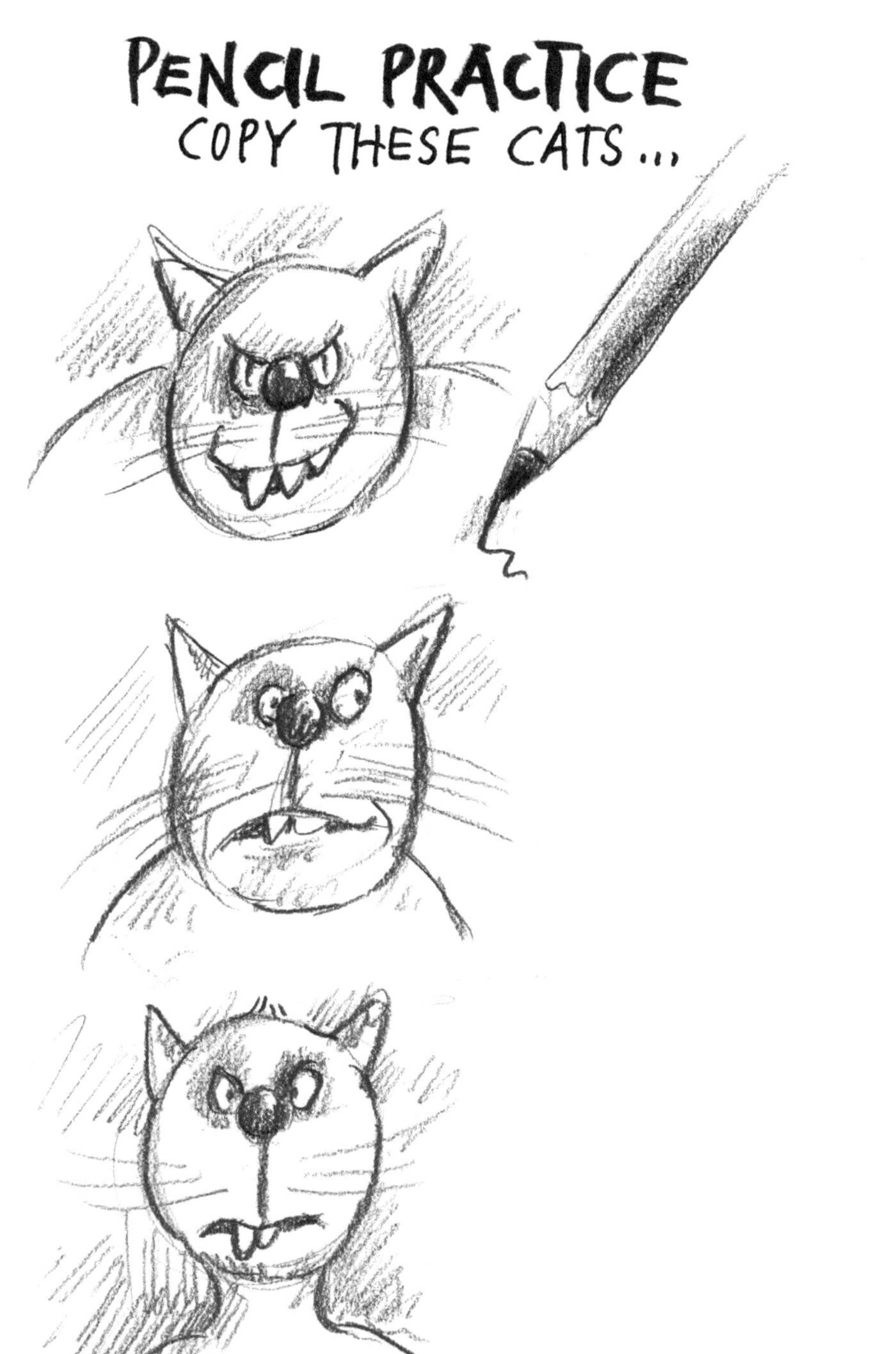

YOUR PENCIL CAN CREATE ⟶
A RANGE OF SHADES FROM LIGHT TO DARK

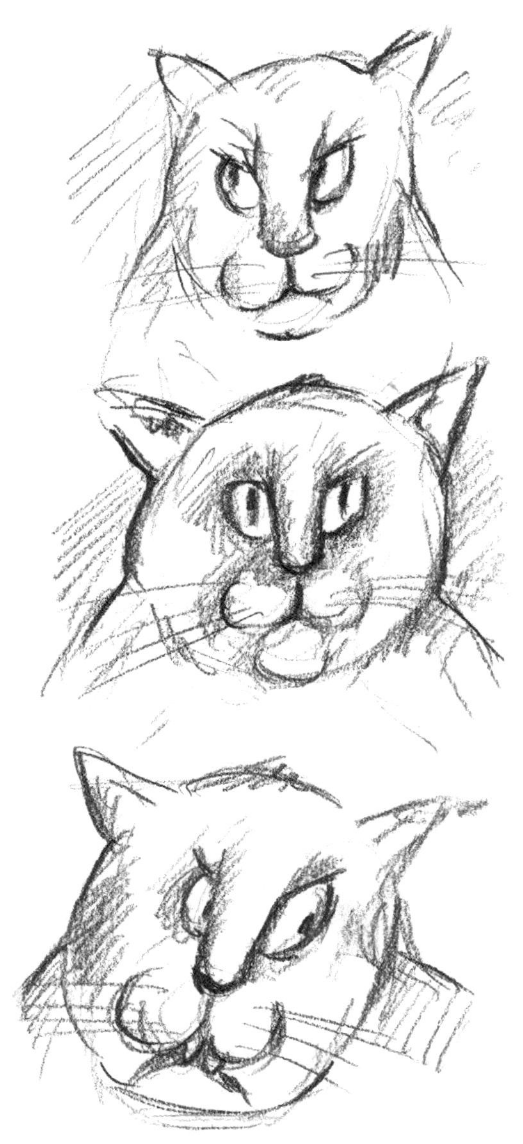

COLOURS + PATTERN = A COAT WITH MARKINGS

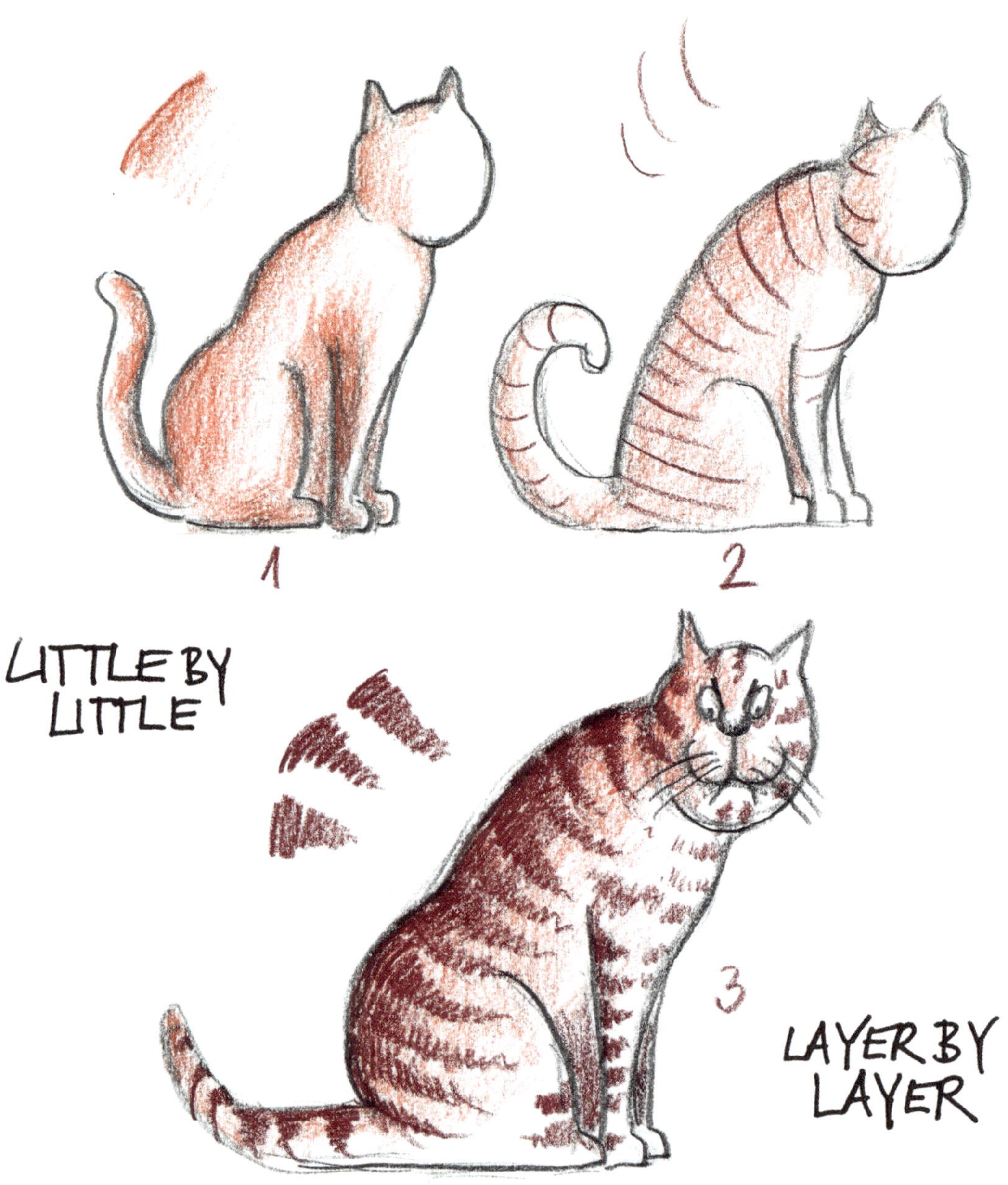

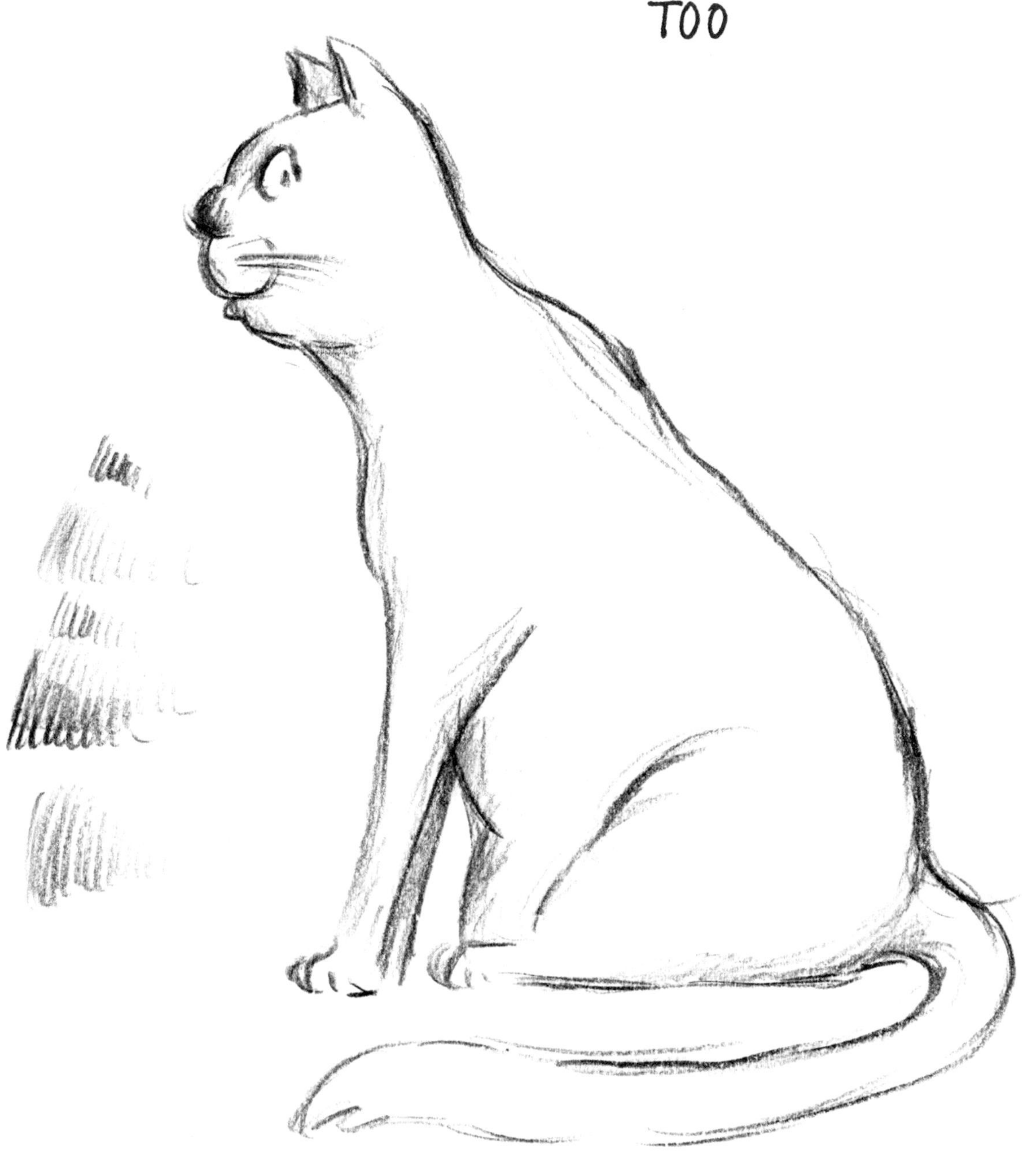

THIS CAT WOULD
LIKE A LOVELY
COAT WITH MARKINGS
TOO

MORE FURRY FRIENDS THAT NEED COLOURFUL COATS

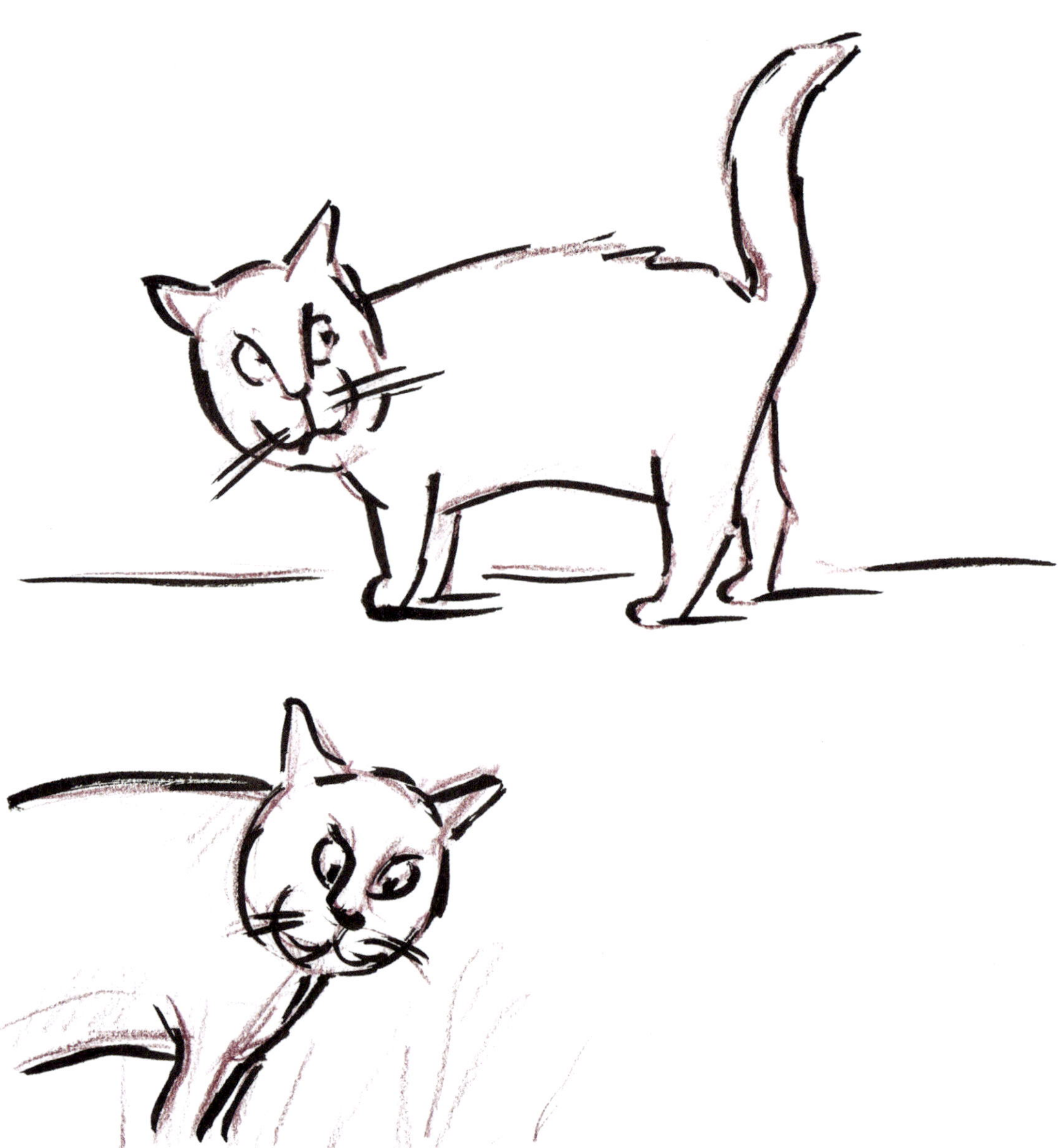

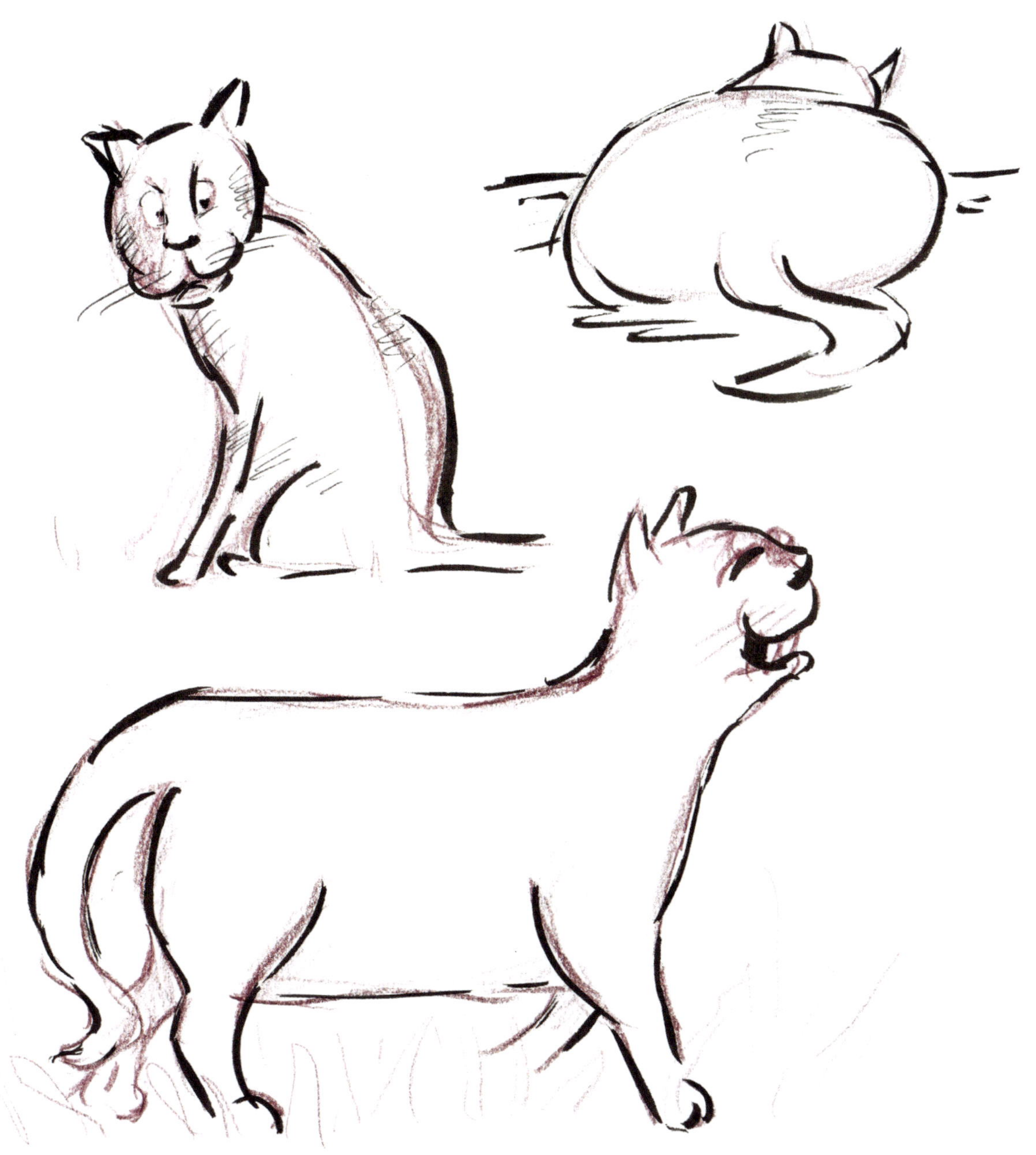

NOW TRY USING SEVERAL COLOURS, ONE LAYER AT A TIME

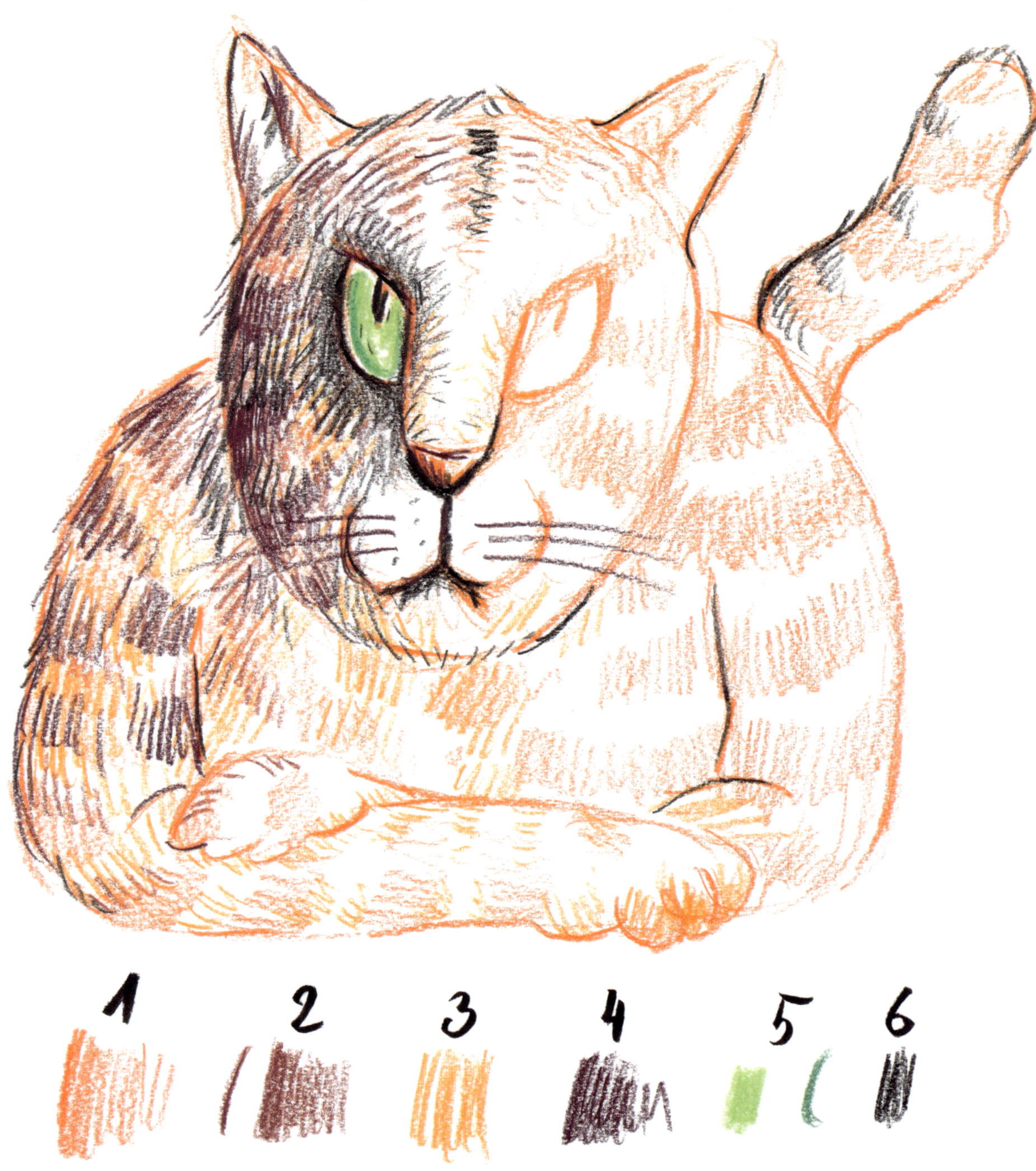

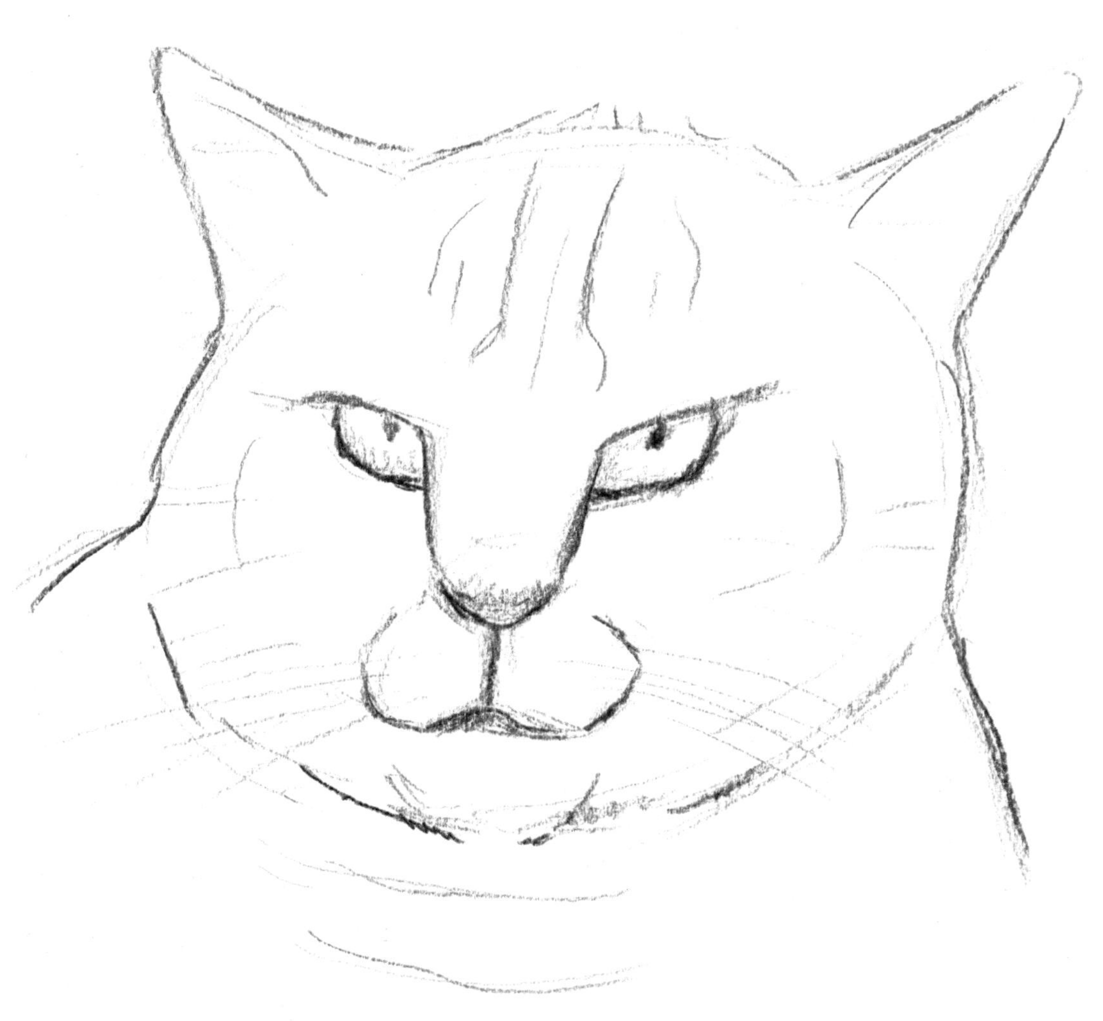

THE MORE LAYERS OF COLOUR YOU ADD,
THE MORE REALISTIC THE COAT WILL LOOK.
START WITH THE PALEST SHADES.

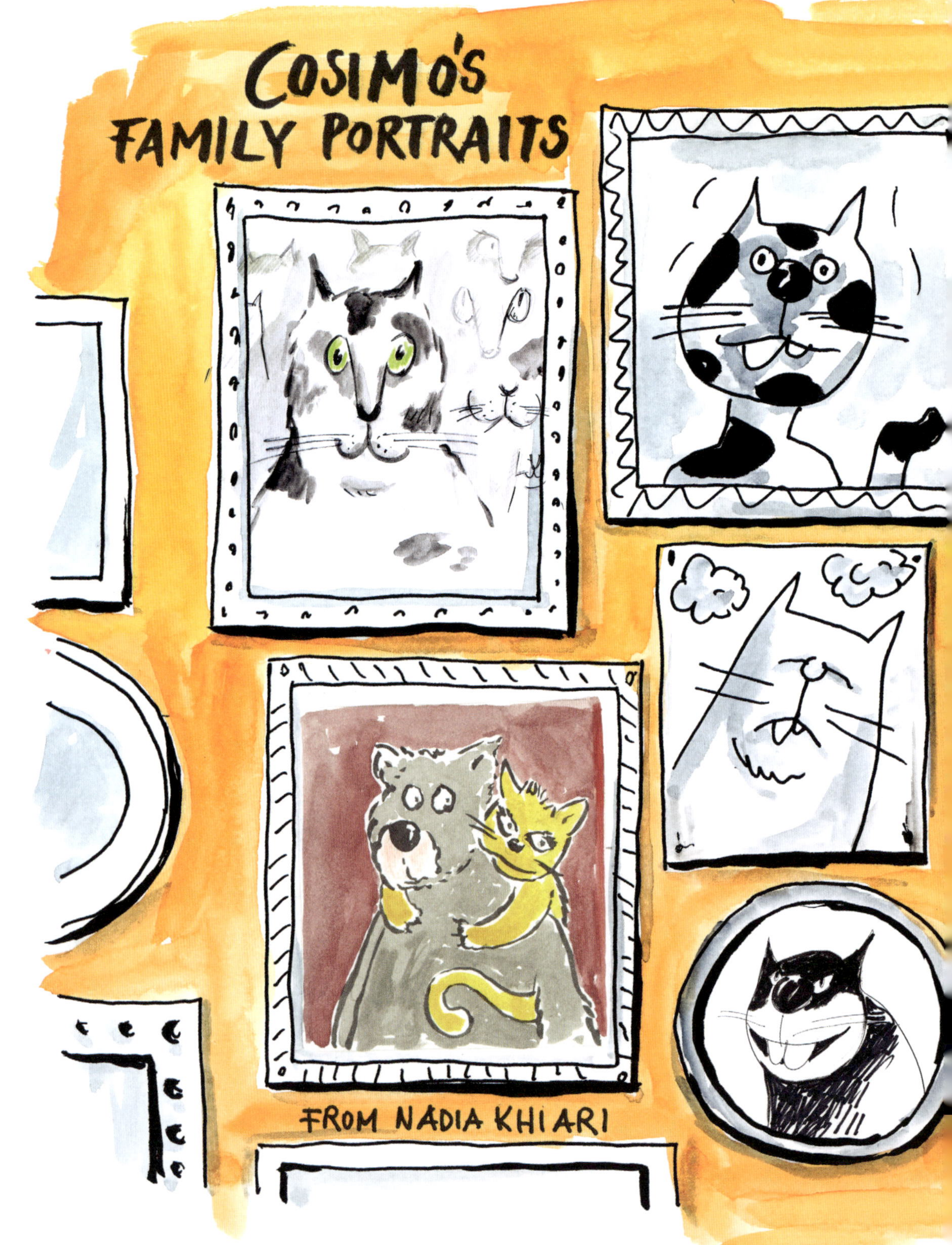

COSIMO'S FAMILY PORTRAITS
FROM NADIA KHIARI

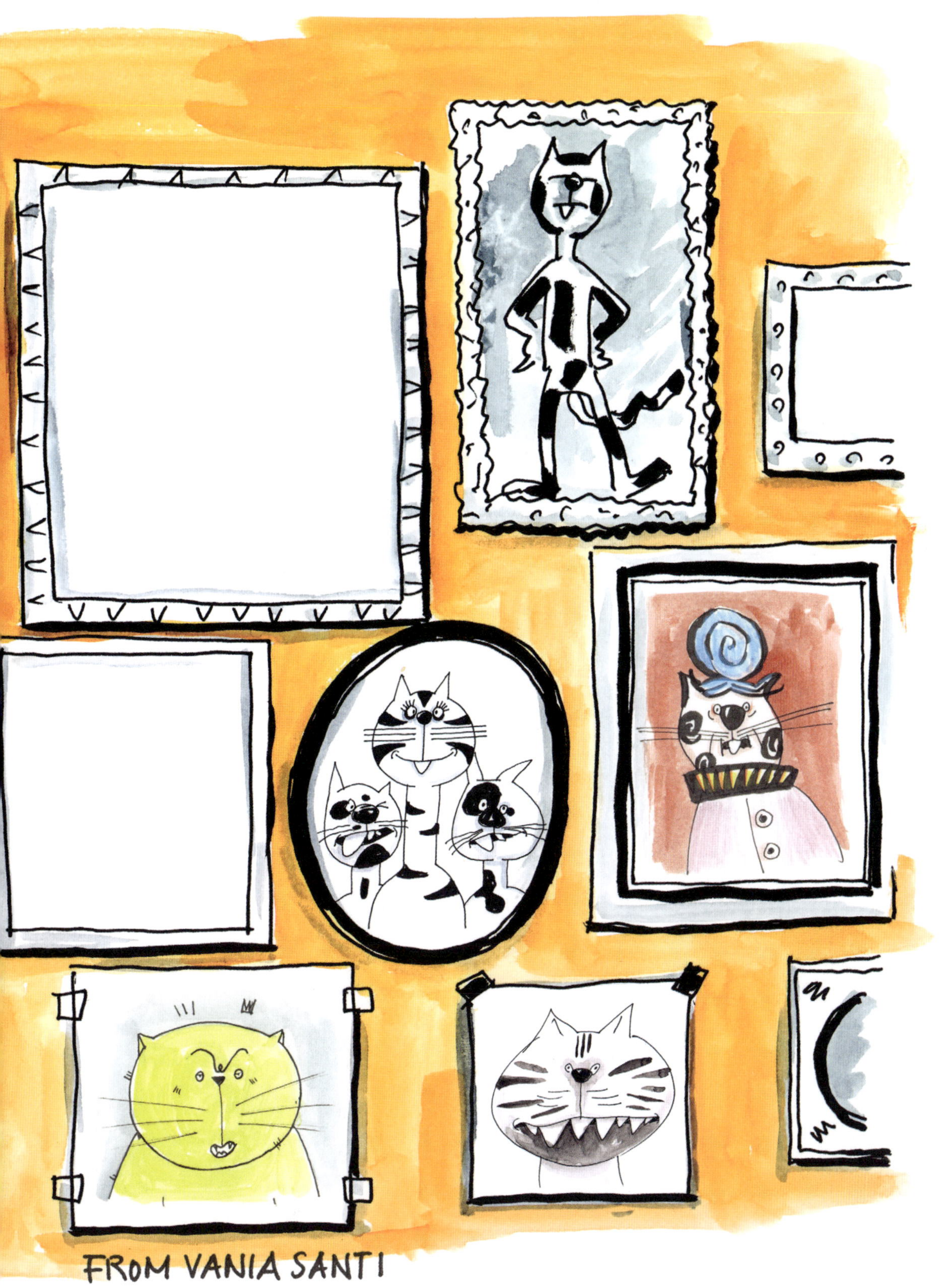

FROM VANIA SANTI

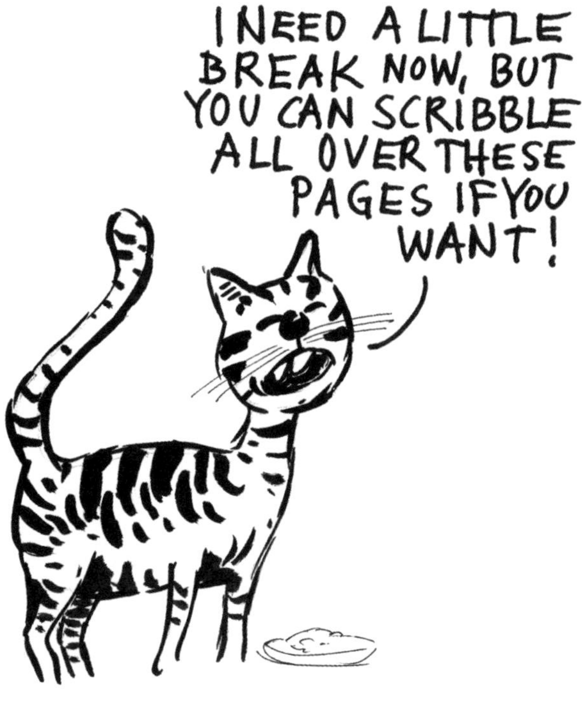

I NEED A LITTLE BREAK NOW, BUT YOU CAN SCRIBBLE ALL OVER THESE PAGES IF YOU WANT!

CHAPTER 2

ANYTHING'S POSSIBLE

IT'S TIME TO GET CREATIVE

GET INSPIRED BY THE SENSATIONALLY SILLY IDEAS IN THIS SECTION AND

DARE TO DO YOUR OWN THING!

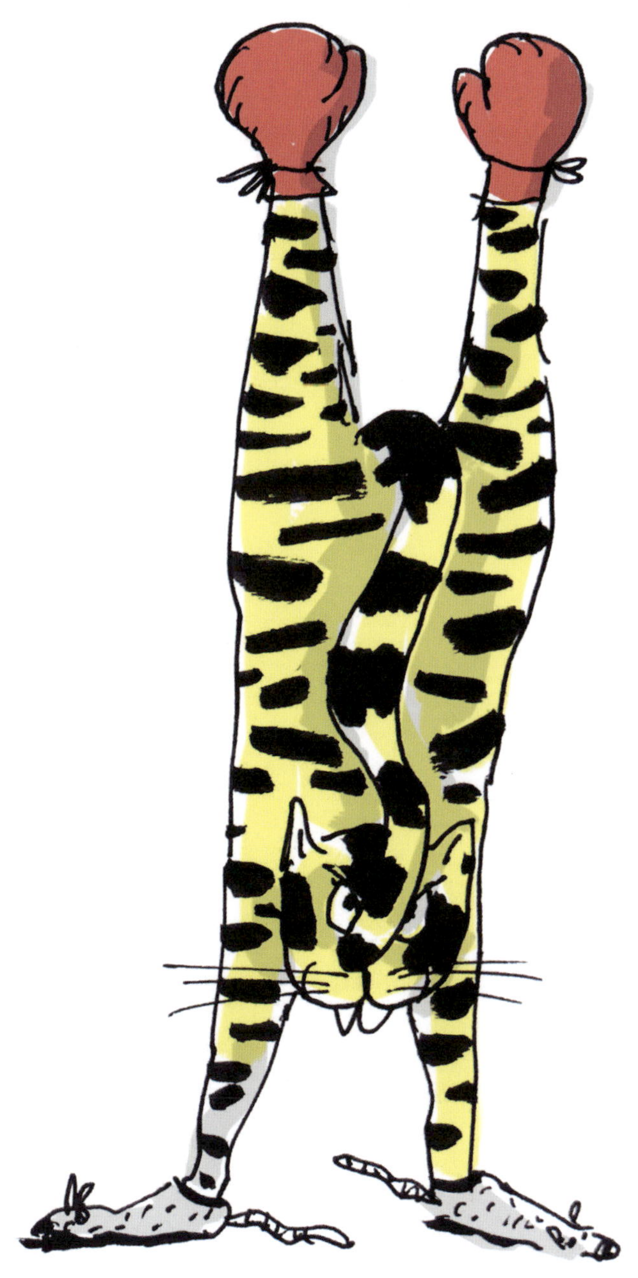

START WITH SOME
COMICAL CATS

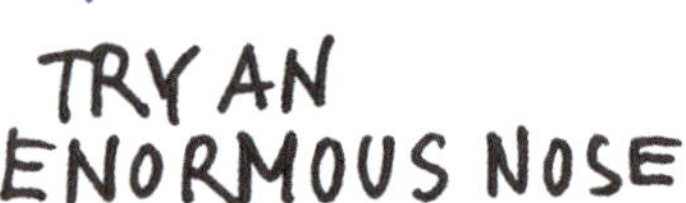

TRY AN ENORMOUS NOSE

OR NEAT LITTLE FANGS

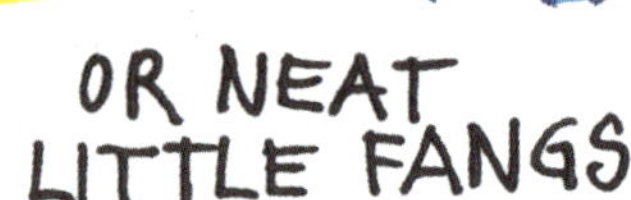

WITH SPOTS THAT FALL OFF

BEGIN WITH A BASIC CAT SHAPE AND INVENT SOME FANTASTIC FELINES OF YOUR OWN!

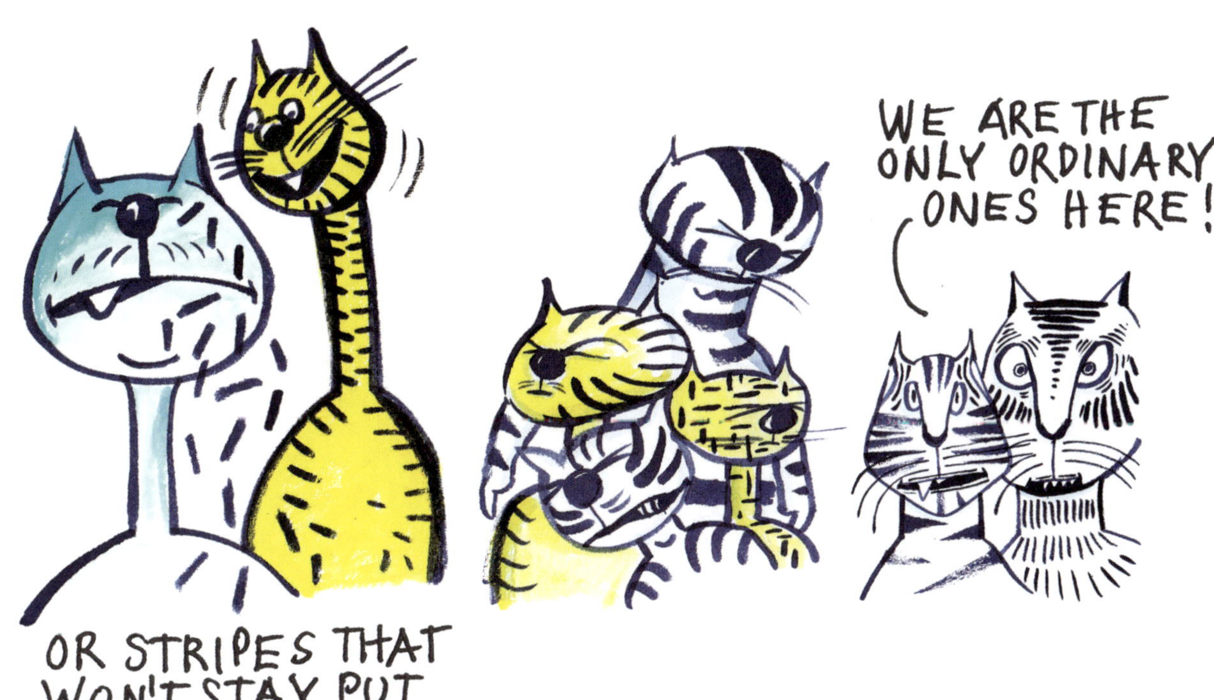

OR STRIPES THAT WON'T STAY PUT

... OR COPY!

GEOMETRIC CATS

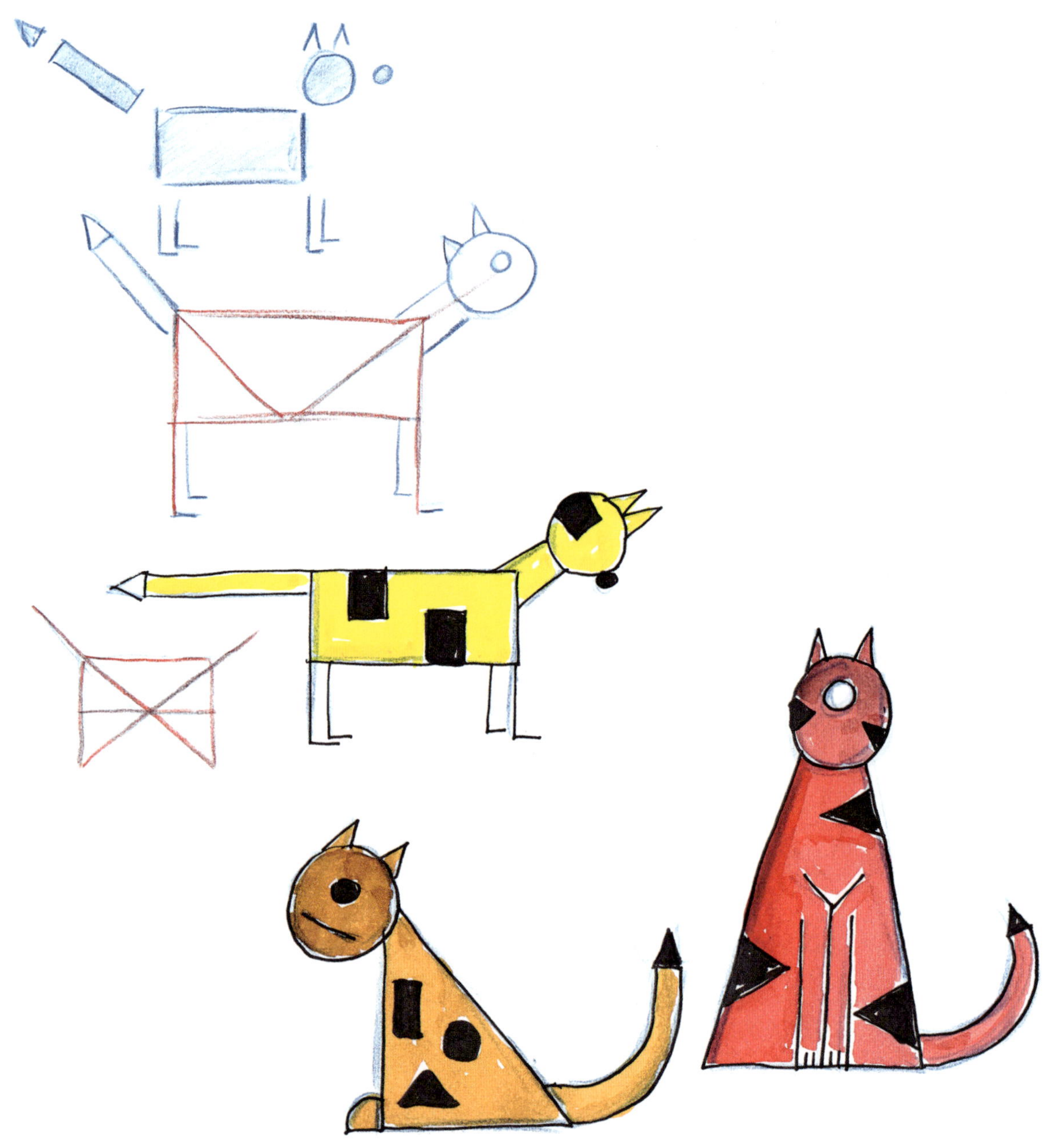

DRAW MORE CATS MADE FROM CIRCLES, SQUARES AND TRIANGLES.

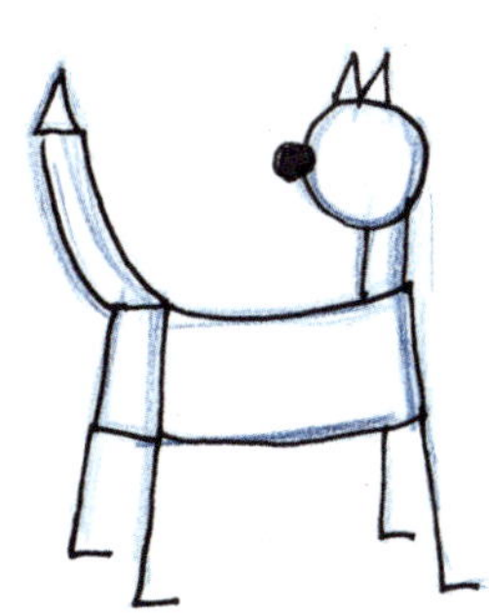

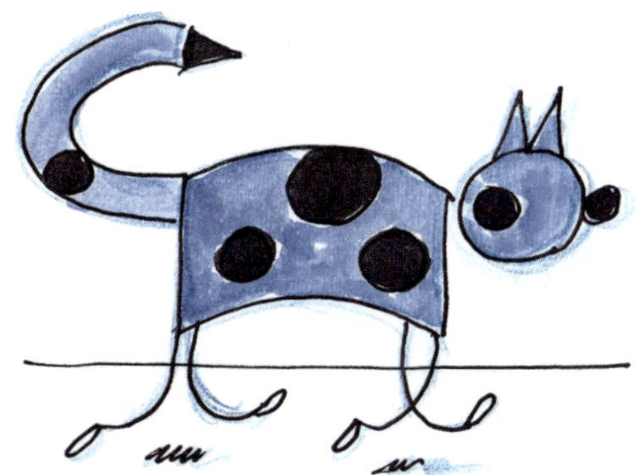

A CATALOGUE OF ARTY CATS

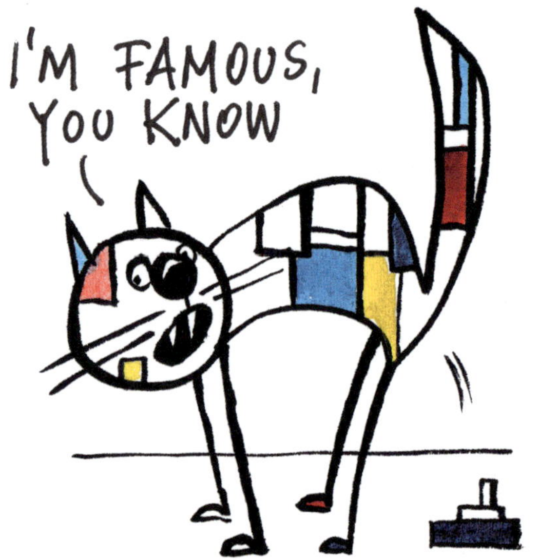

MONDRIAN CAT

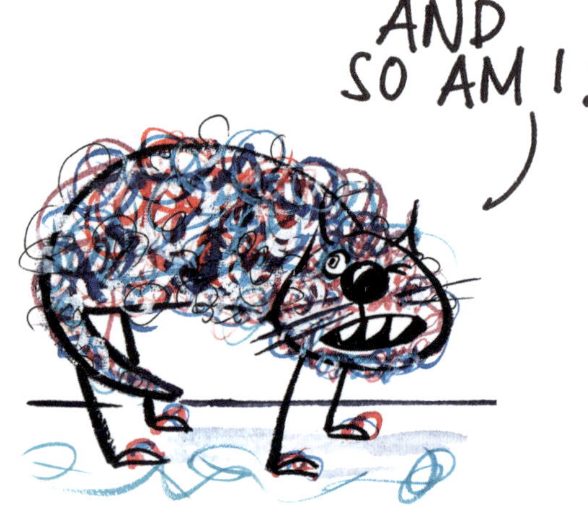

POLLOCK CAT

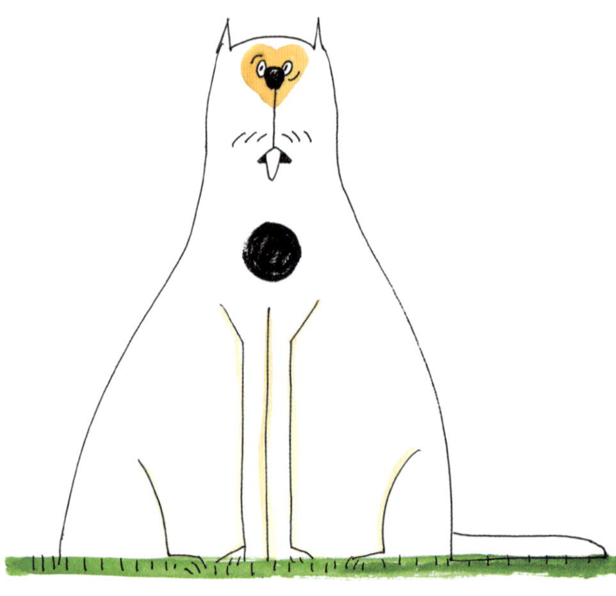

MINIMALIST CAT

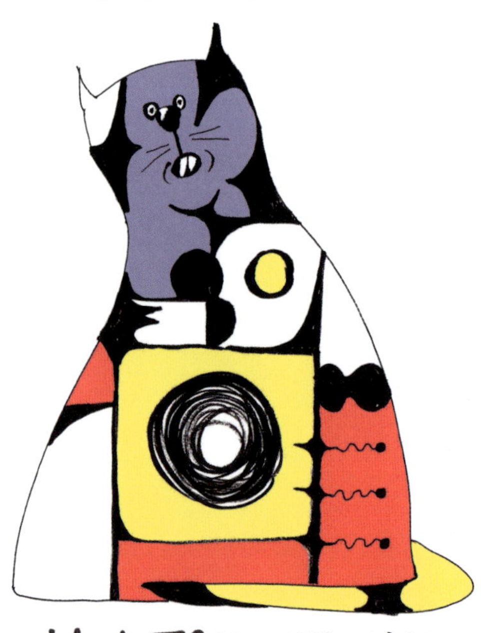

MODERNIST CAT

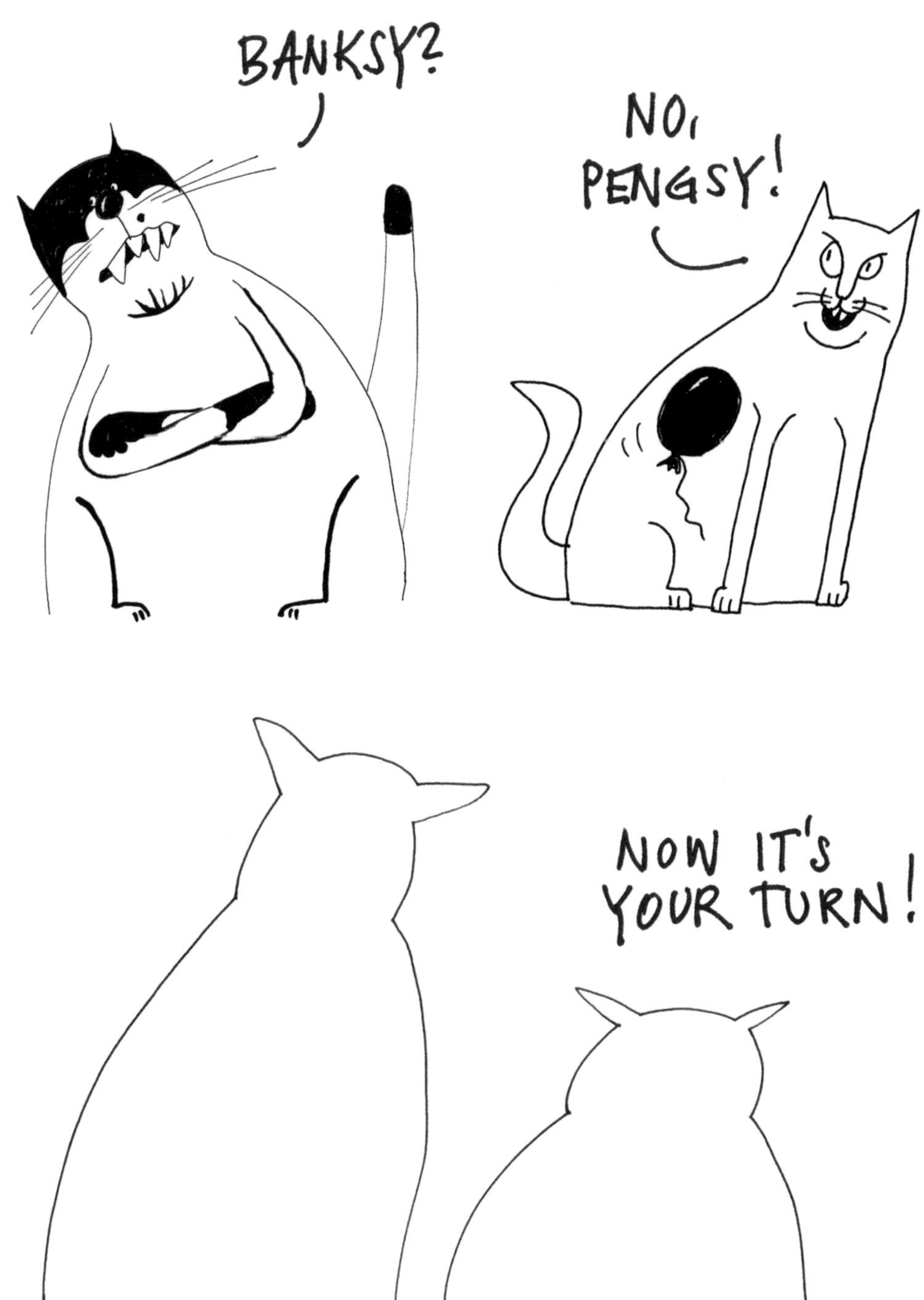

BANKSY?
NO, PENGSY!
NOW IT'S YOUR TURN!

THE WONDER OF WATERCOLOURS

WITH A LITTLE 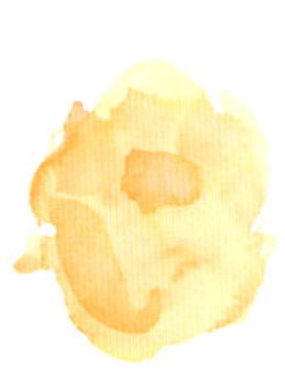 PRACTICE, YOU CAN GIVE COLOUR TO YOUR CATS AS WELL AS ADDING SHADING AND BACKGROUNDS.

DON'T MAKE THE PAINT TOO WET OR LET IT GET TOO DRY. IT SHOULD BE EASY TO FILL IN AREAS CLEANLY AND MAKE STROKES THAT HOLD THEIR SHAPE.

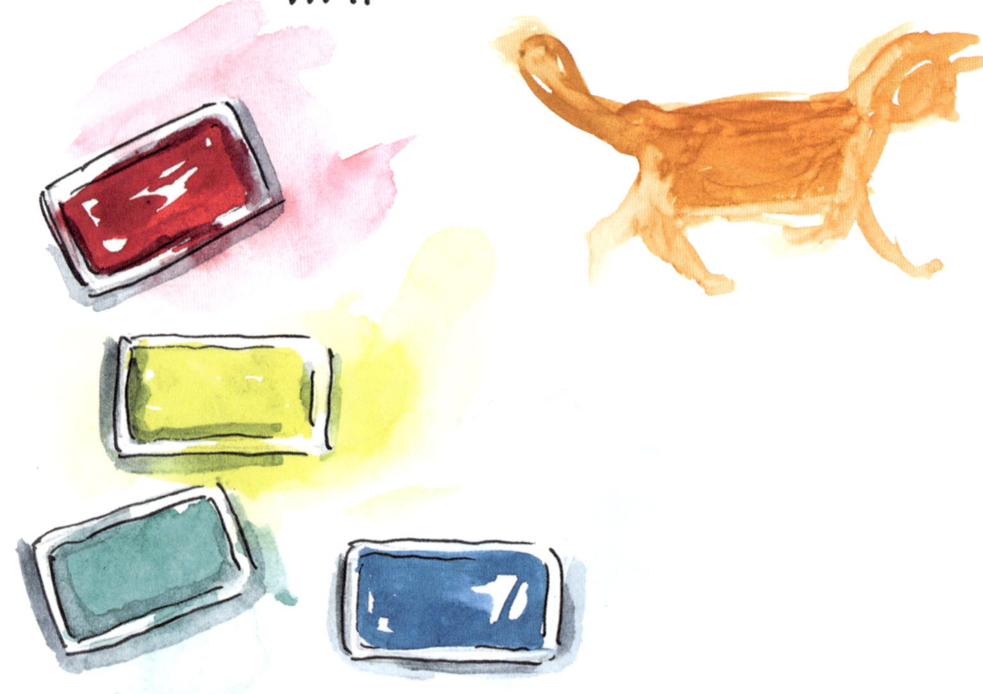

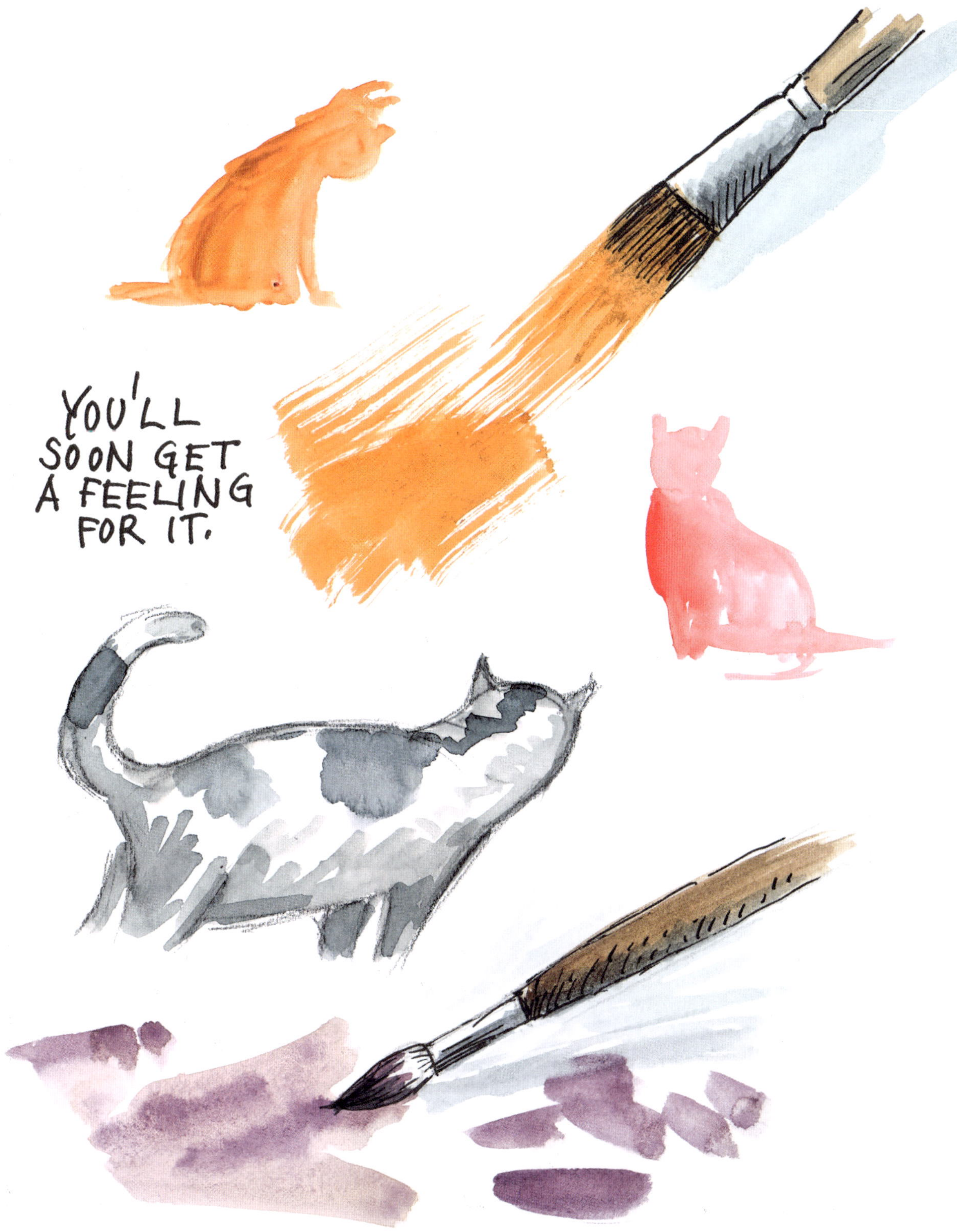

YOU'LL
SOON GET
A FEELING
FOR IT.

TRY OUT YOUR WATERCOLOURS

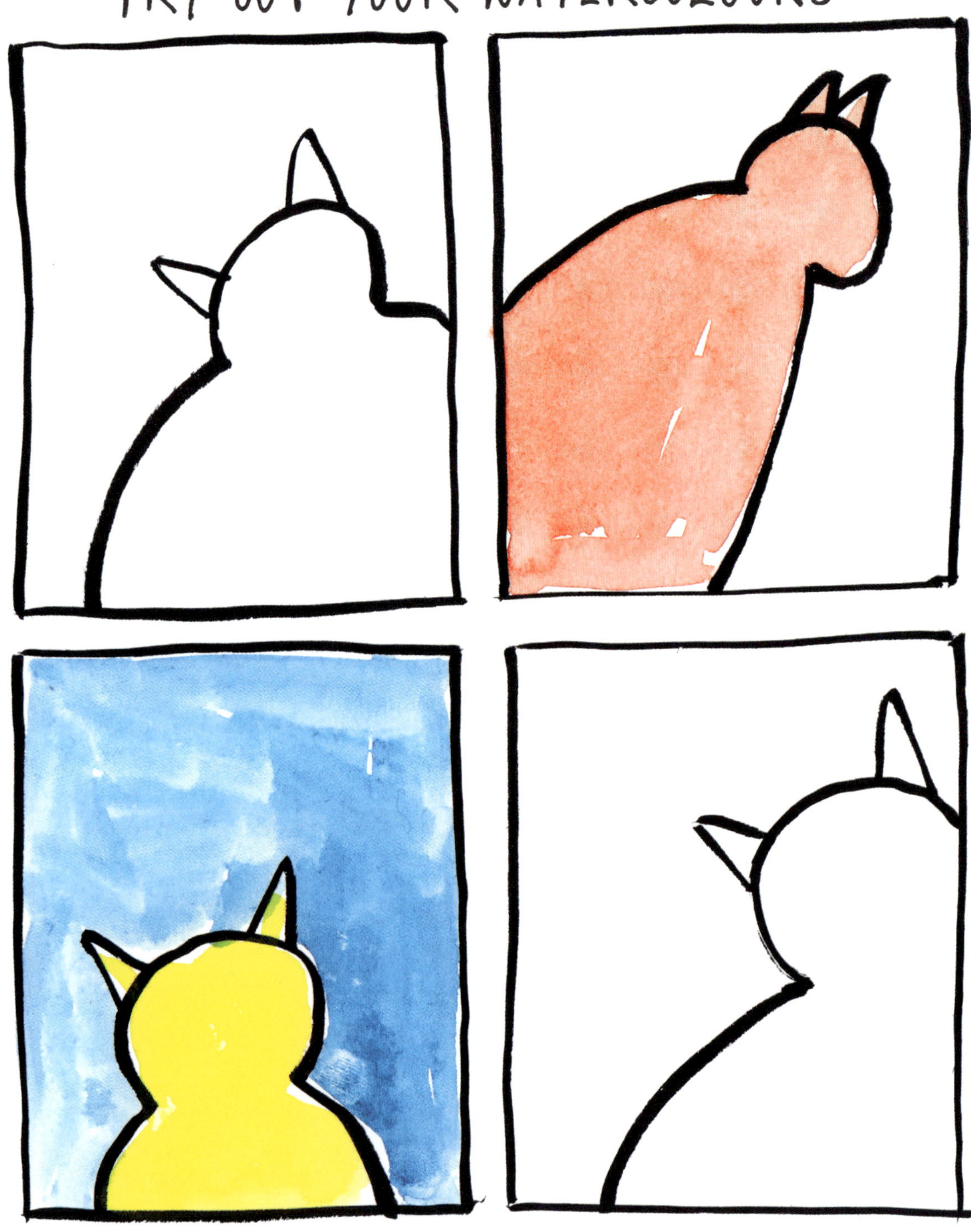

LIKE THIS ↑

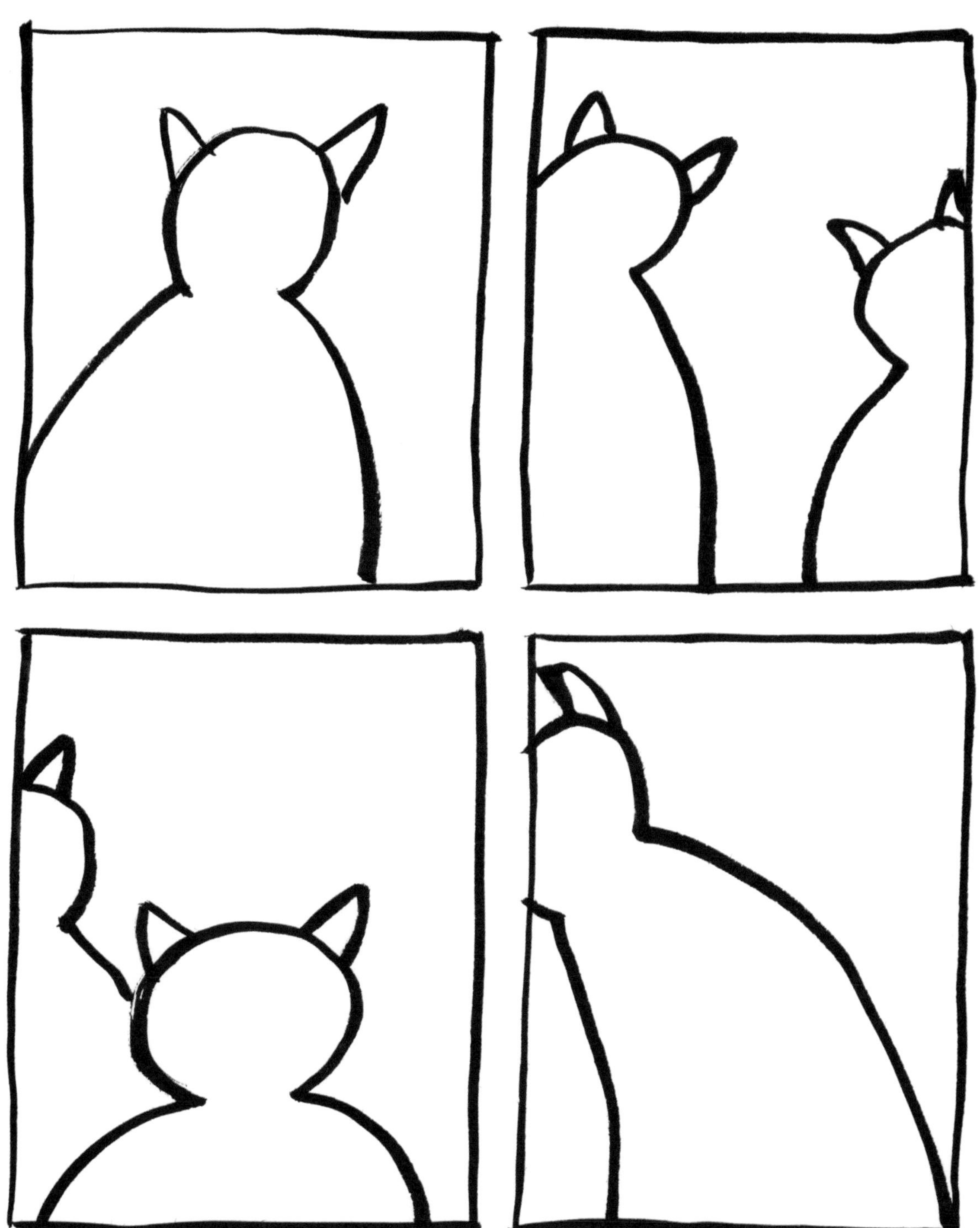

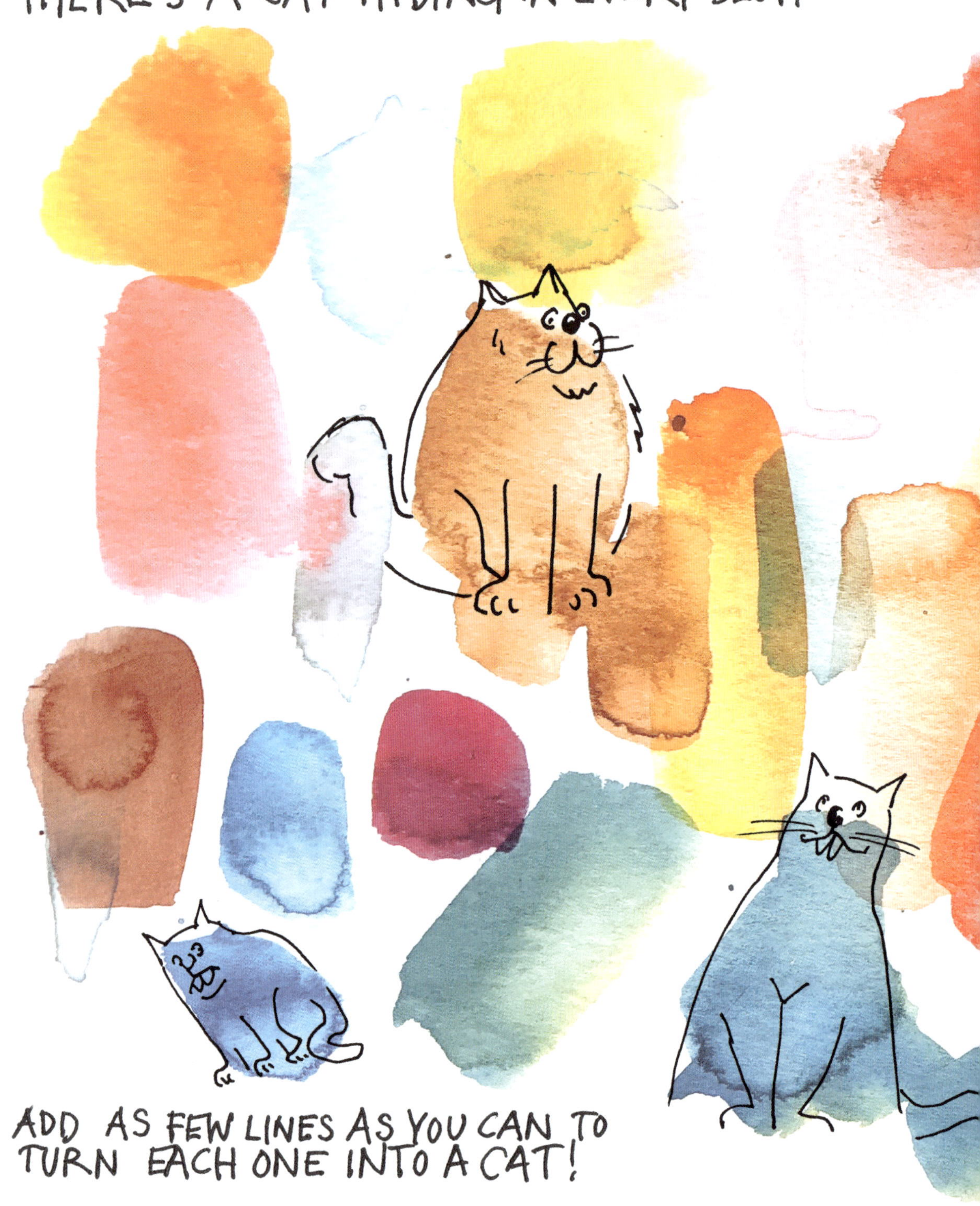

THERE'S A CAT HIDING IN EVERY BLOT.

ADD AS FEW LINES AS YOU CAN TO
TURN EACH ONE INTO A CAT!

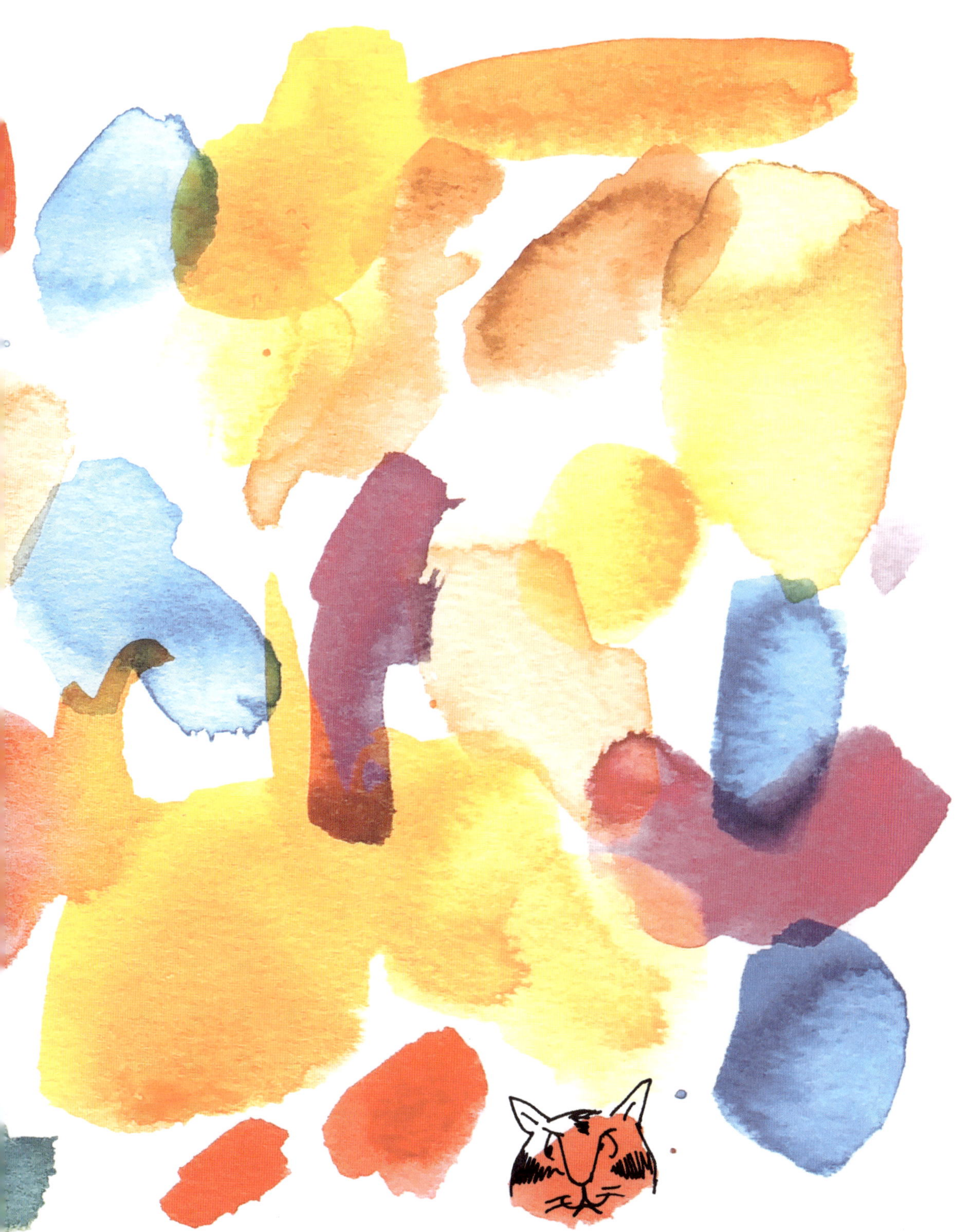

GROUP PORTRAITS

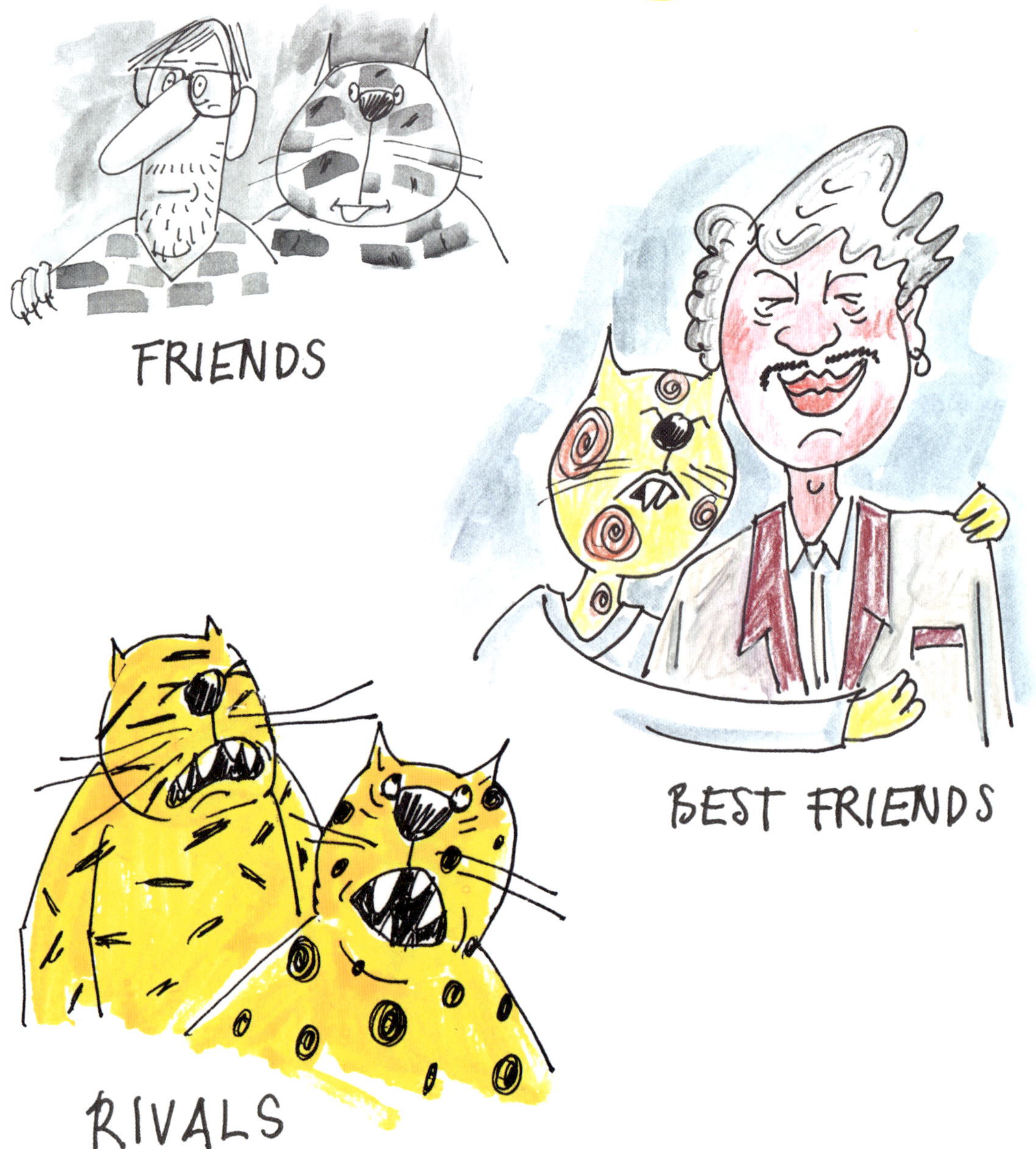

FRIENDS

BEST FRIENDS

RIVALS

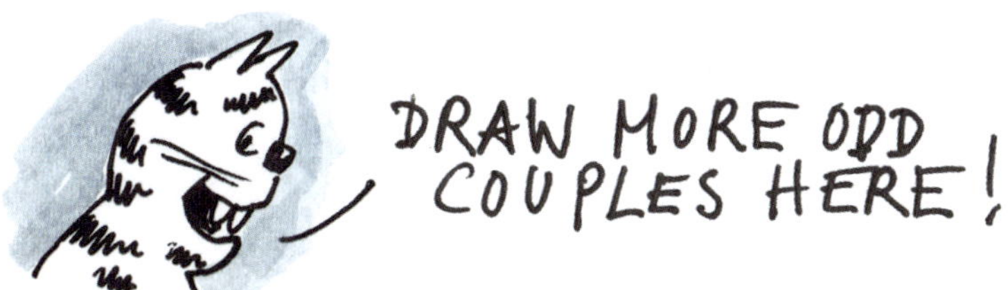
DRAW MORE ODD
COUPLES HERE!

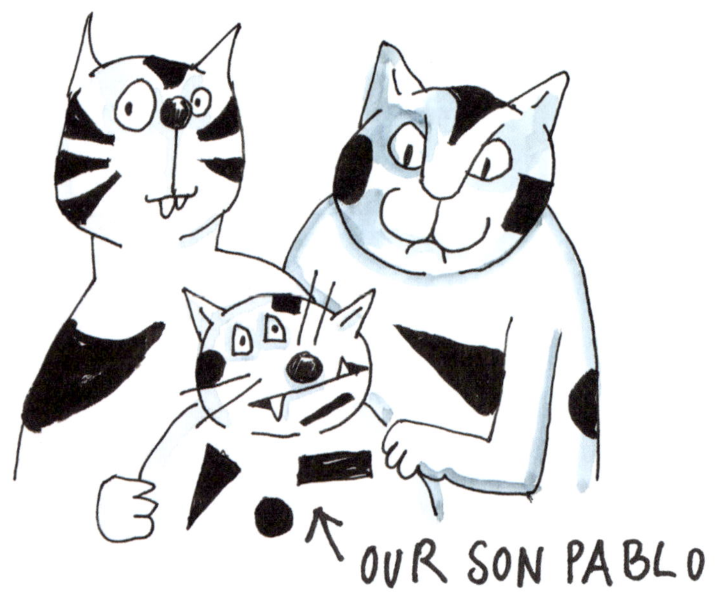

↑ DRAW THESE FAMILIES IN
A DIFFERENT POSE

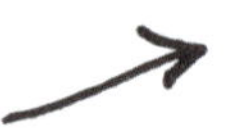

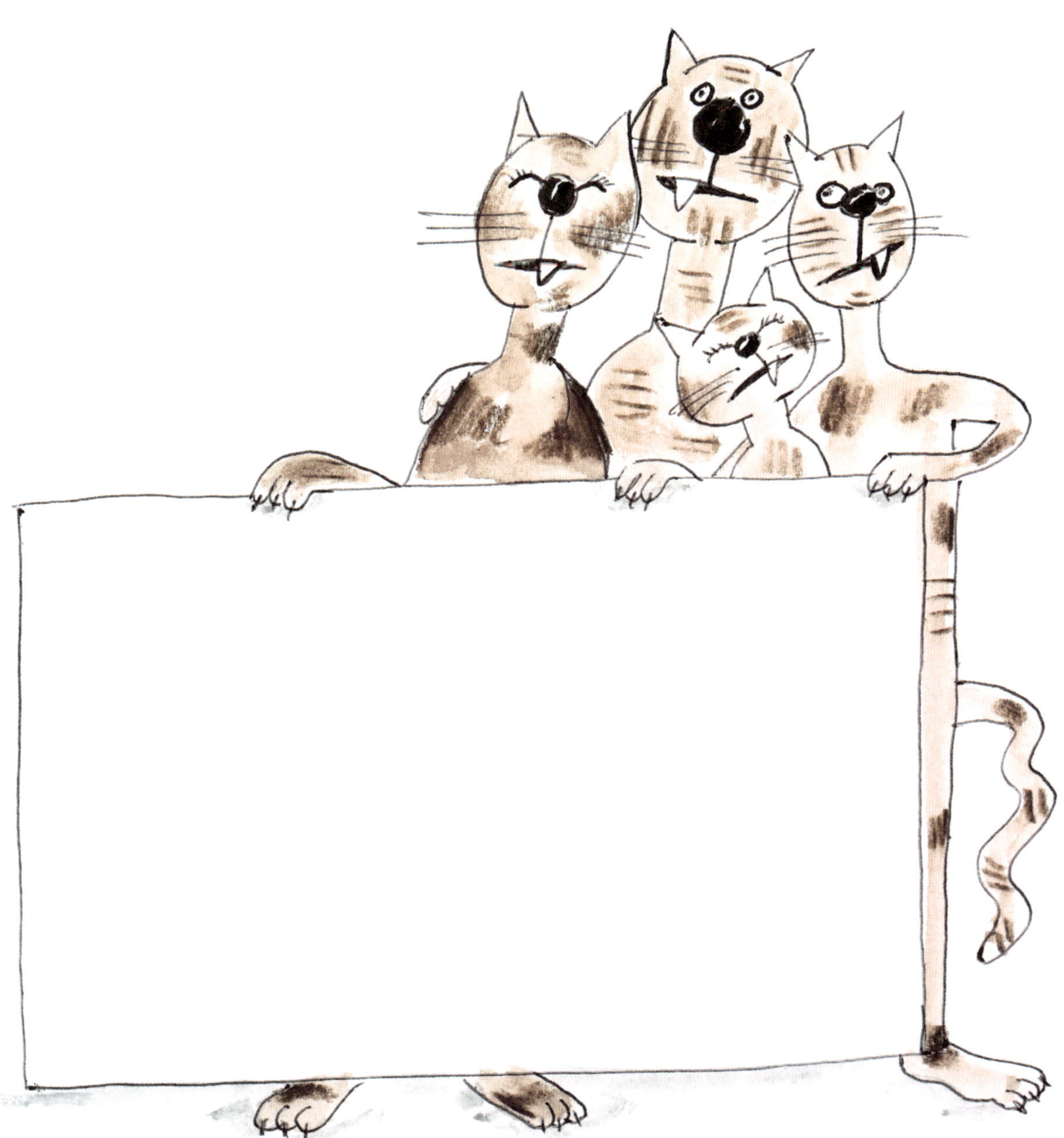

THEN FOUR ...

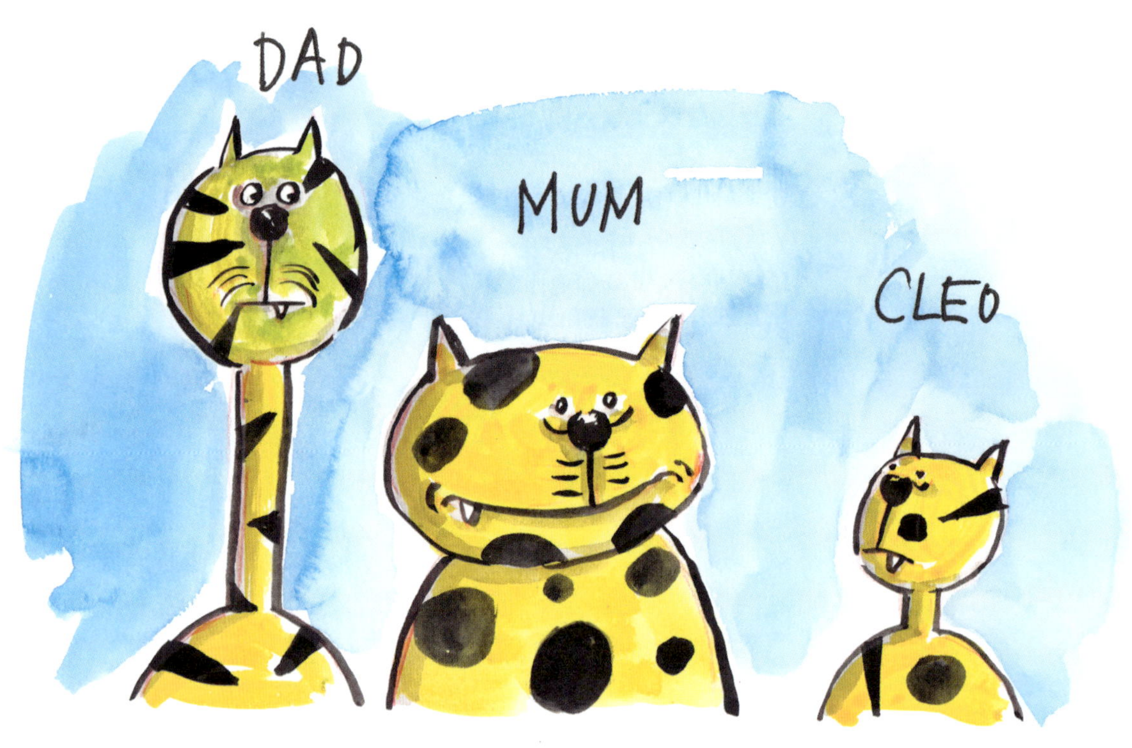

DRAW YOUR FRIENDS OR FAMILY IN
THIS STYLE AS CATS

...AND SOON YOU'LL HAVE A FULL HOUSE

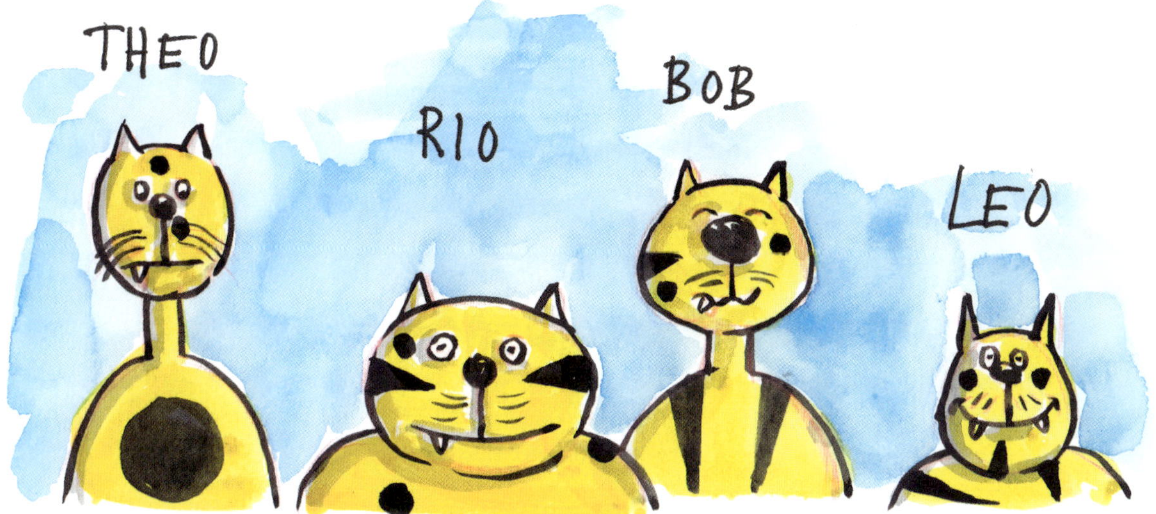
THEO
RIO
BOB
LEO

A FELINE FACE-OFF
TWO CROWDS OF CATS – NOW FINISH THEIR FACES!

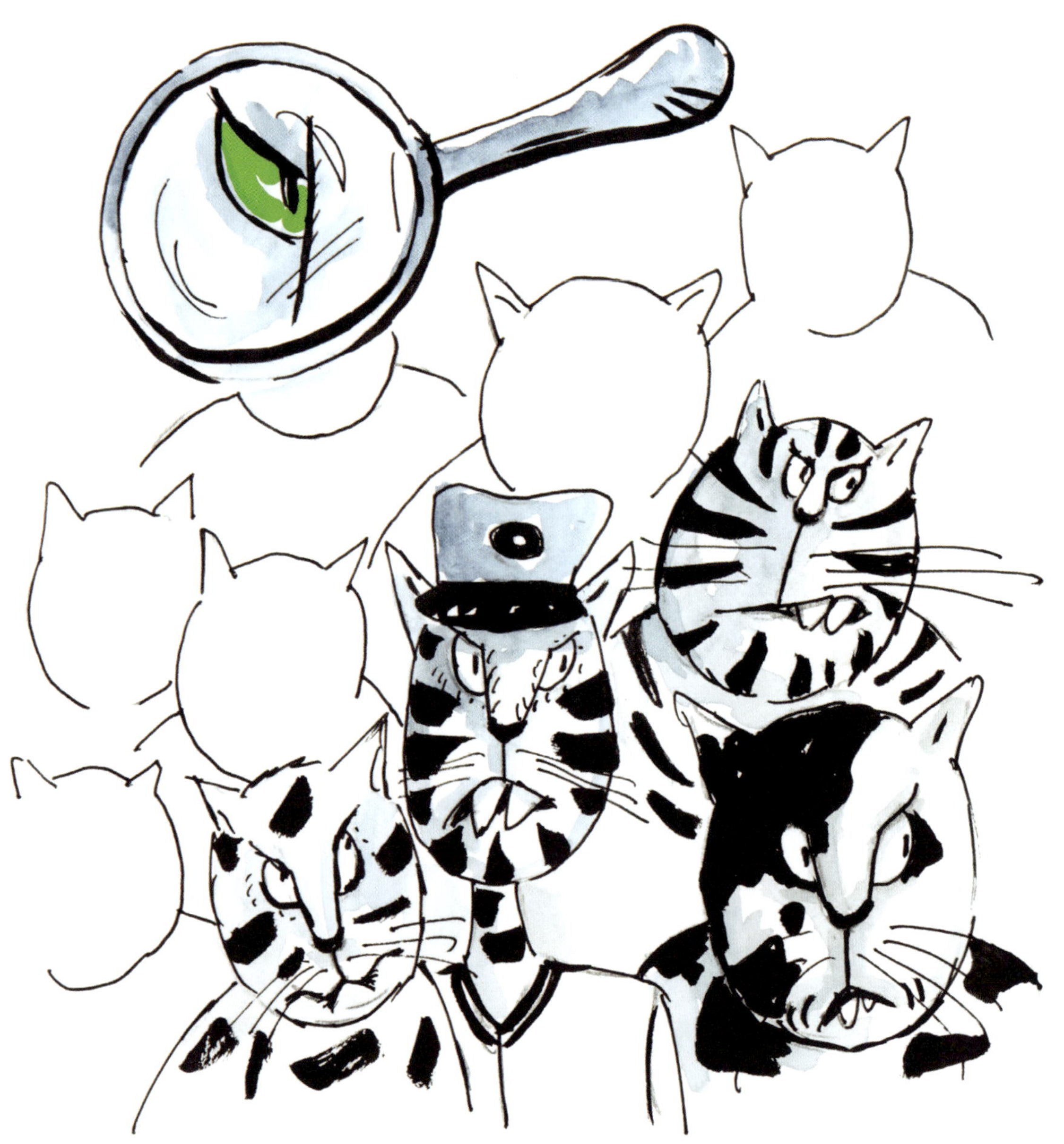

THE CATS ON THIS PAGE SHOULD LOOK
DISTRUSTFUL AND SUSPICIOUS...

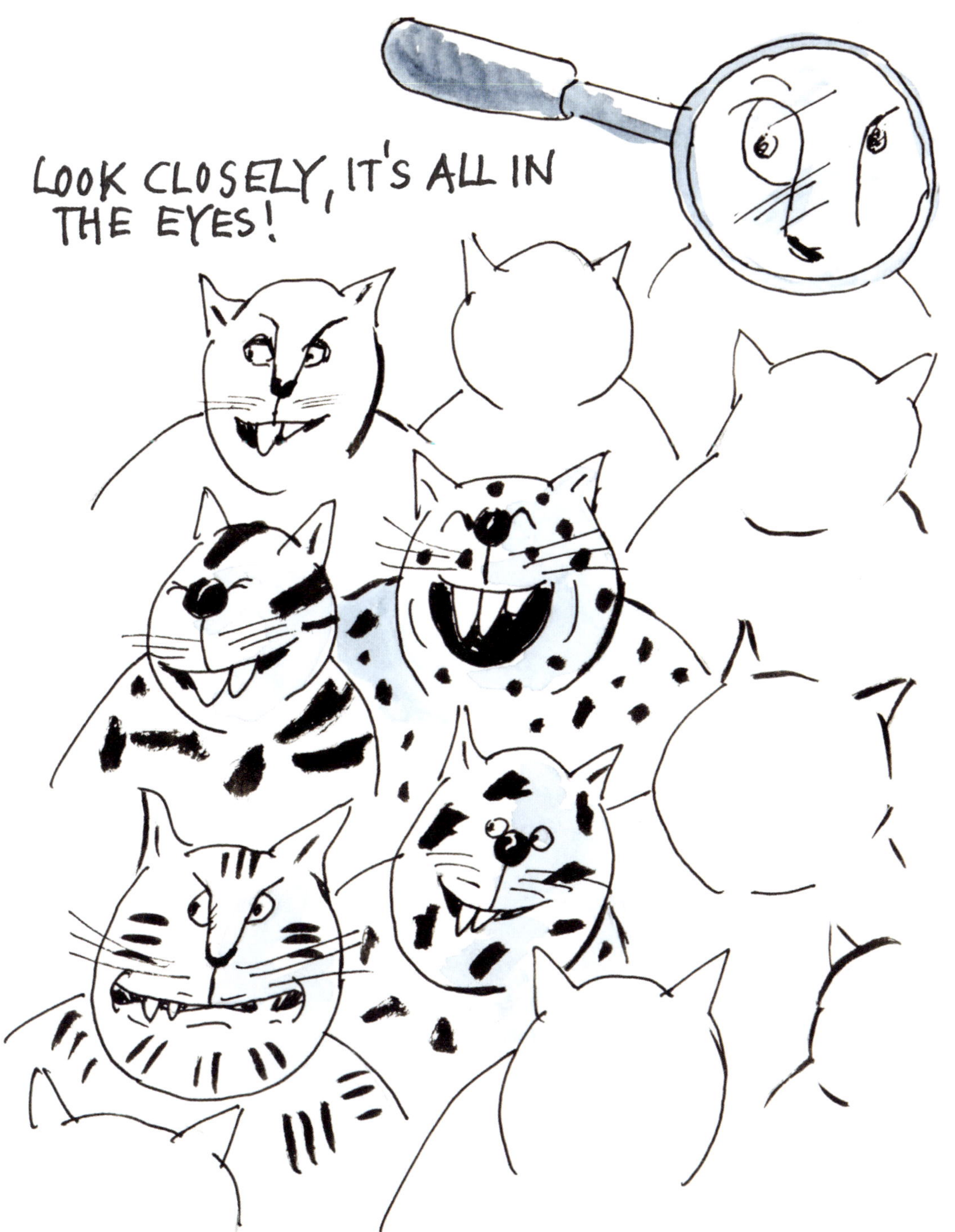

LOOK CLOSELY, IT'S ALL IN THE EYES!
THE CATS ON THIS PAGE THINK BEING GLARED AT IS THE FUNNIEST THING EVER.

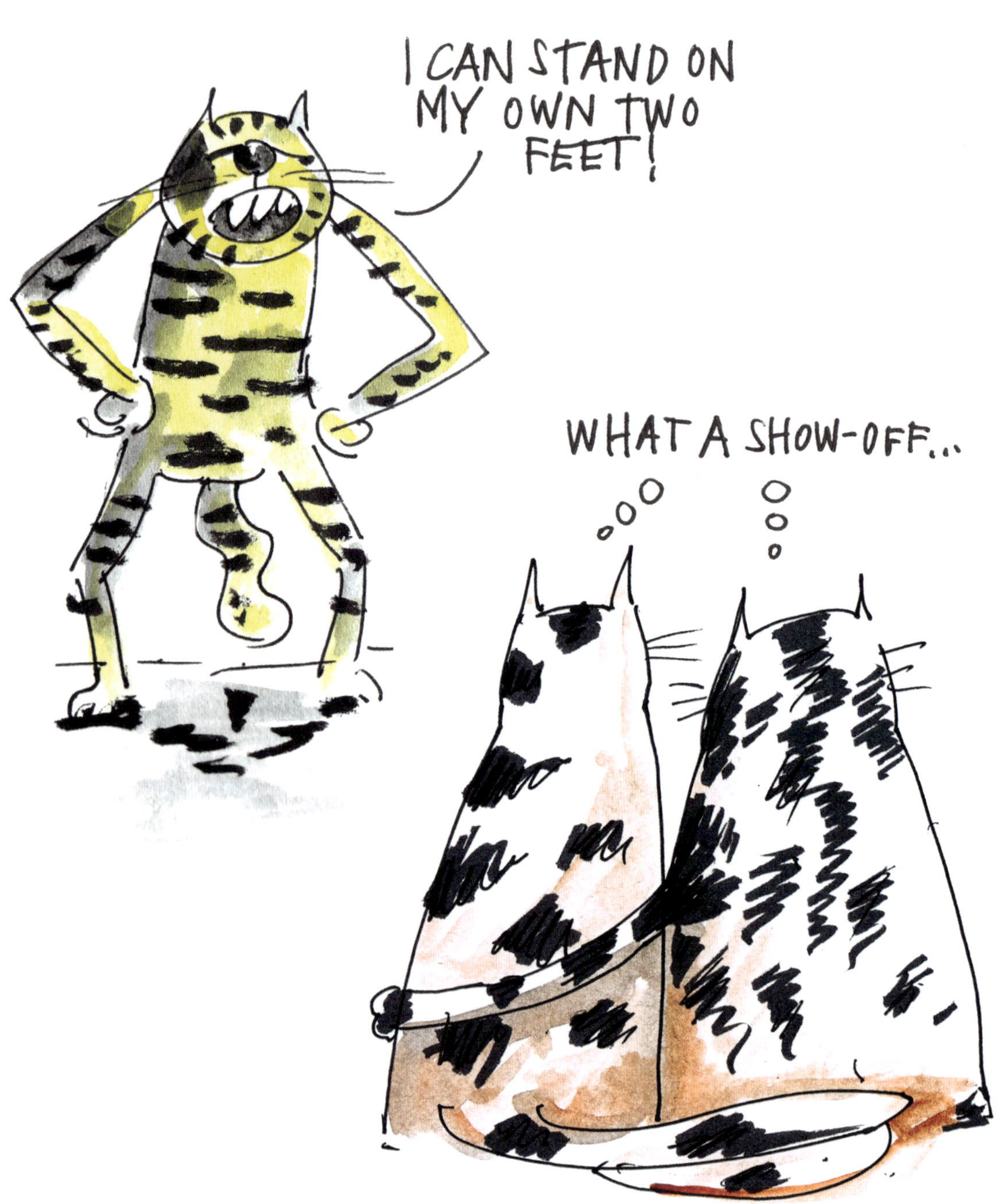

I CAN STAND ON MY OWN TWO FEET!

WHAT A SHOW-OFF...

HUMAN-STYLE CATS

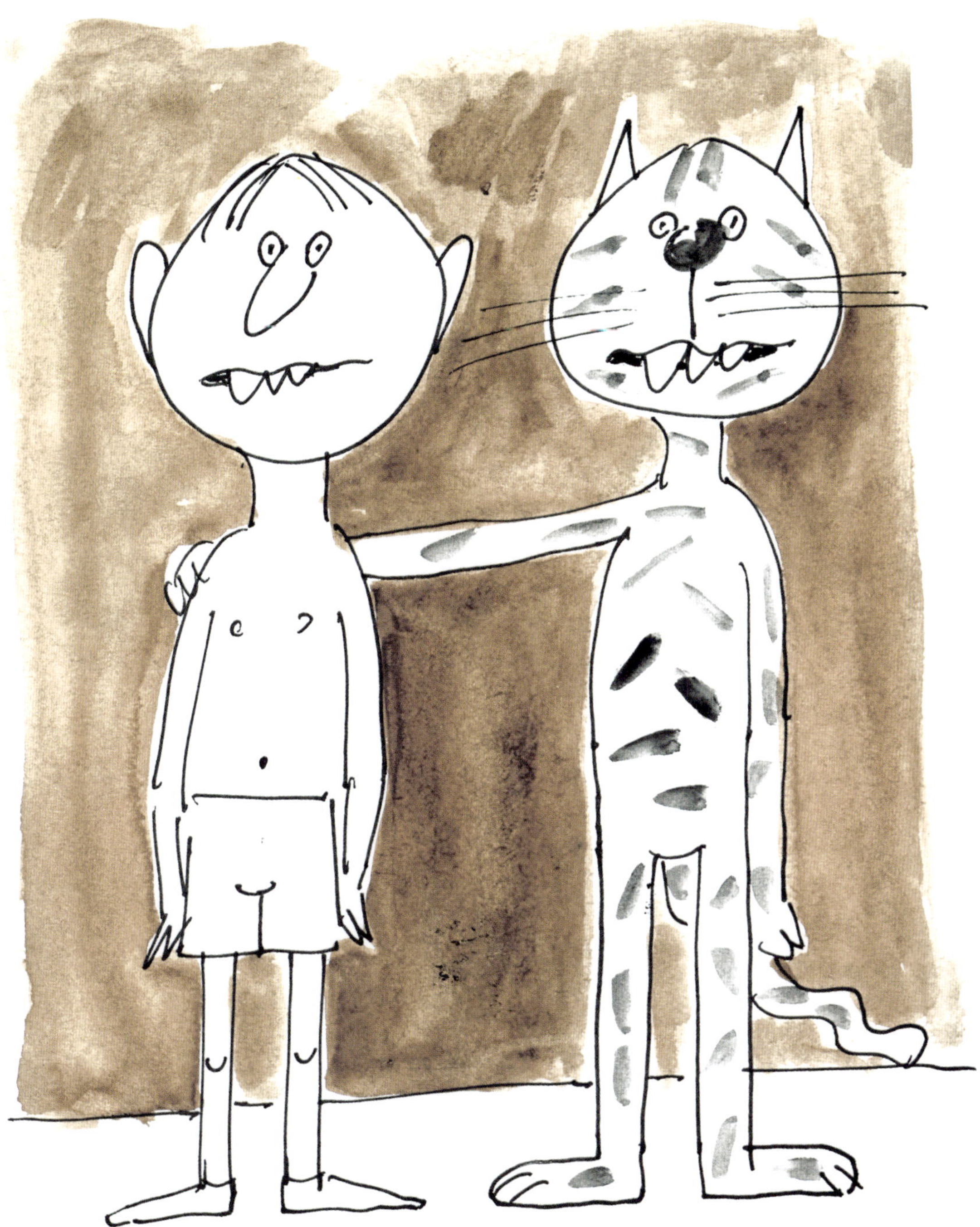

CATS WITH JOBS

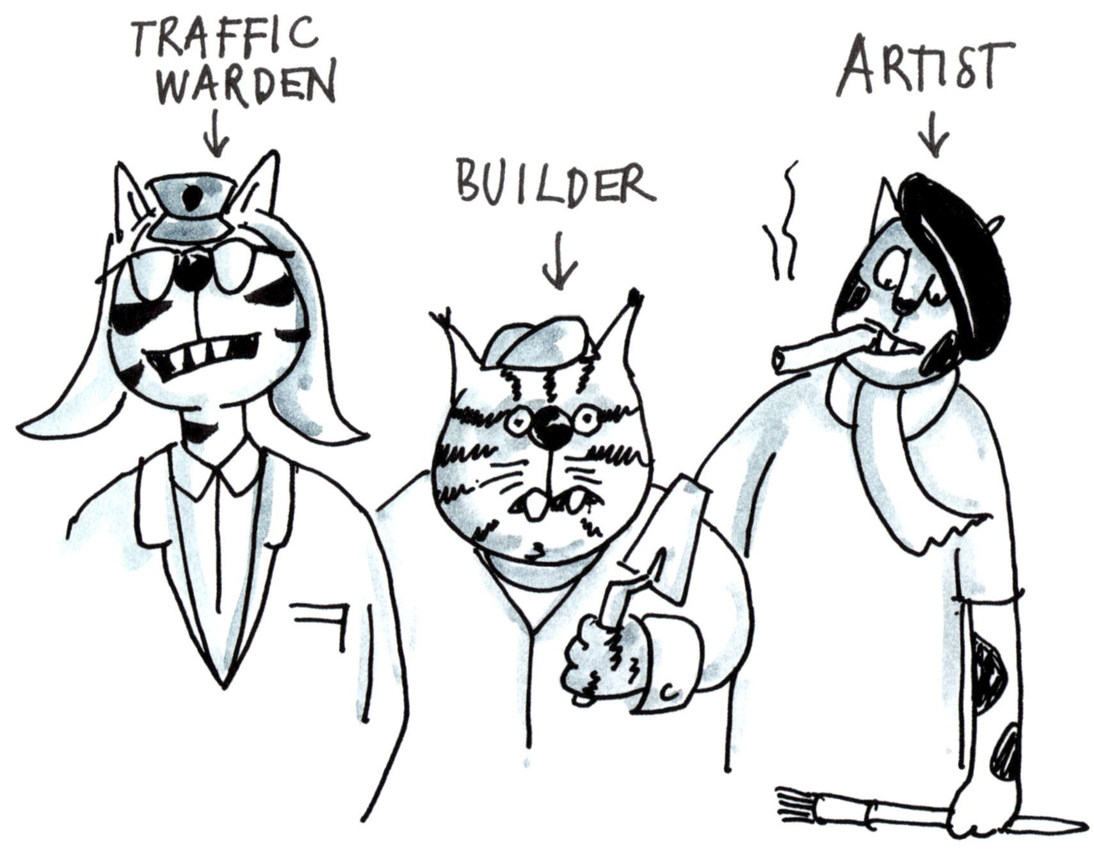

FILL IN THE BOTTOM HALF OF THEIR BODIES!

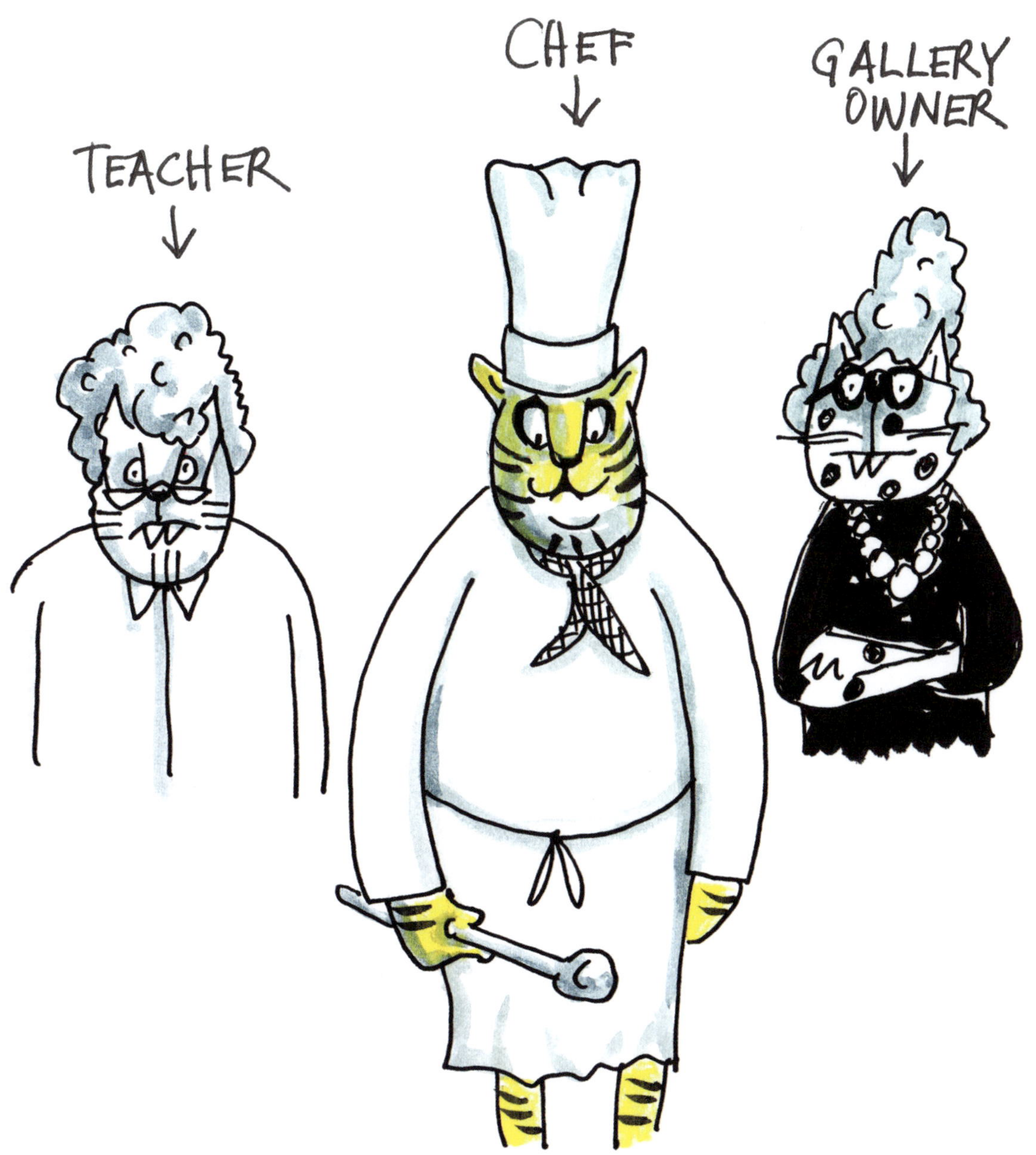

TEACHER
CHEF
GALLERY OWNER

CAT MUSIC

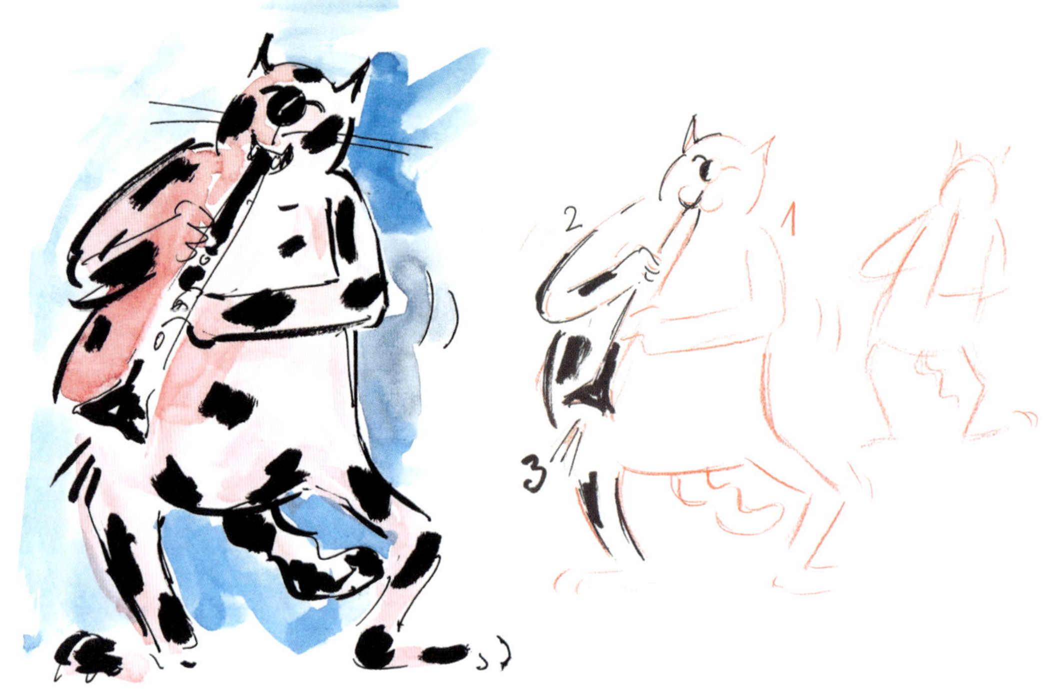

THIS BAND NEEDS MORE MUSICIANS!

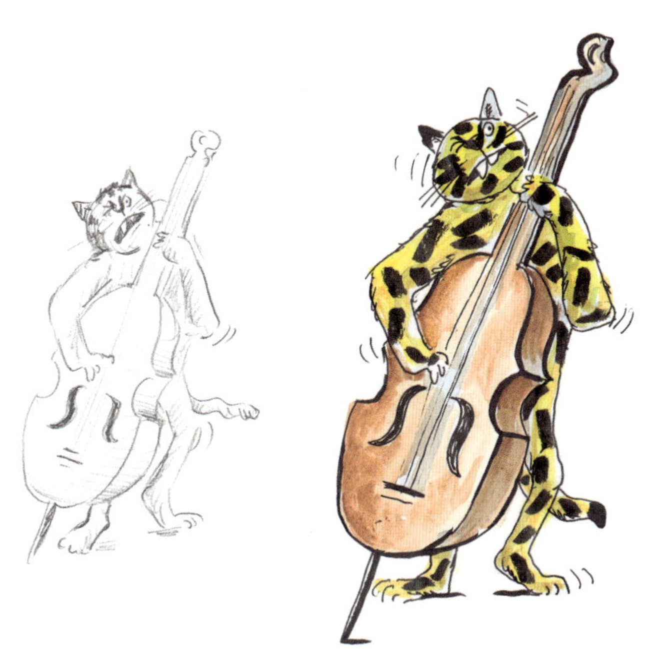

TRUMPET, TRIANGLE, DRUMS ... ADD
AS MANY AS YOU LIKE!

CAT SPORTS

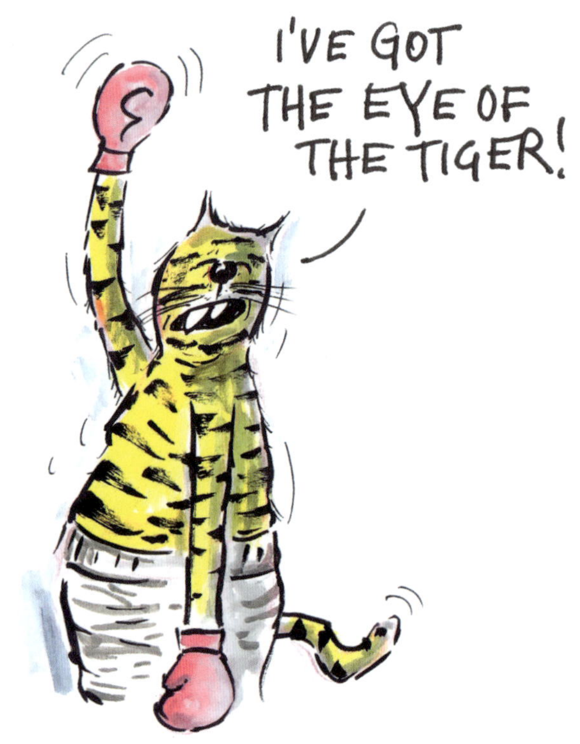

NOW IT'S YOUR TURN TO DRAW
MORE SPORTY CATS !

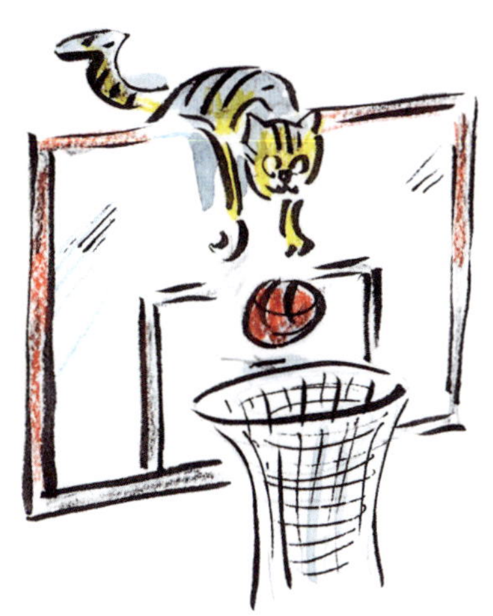

LOOKALIKES
CELEBRITY CATS

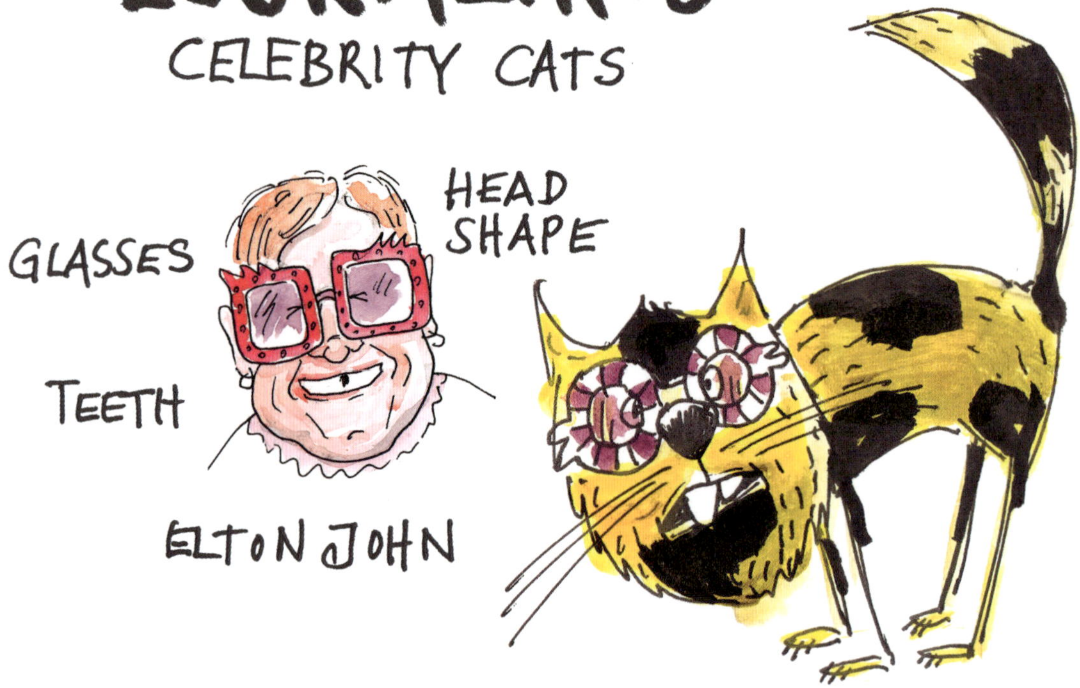

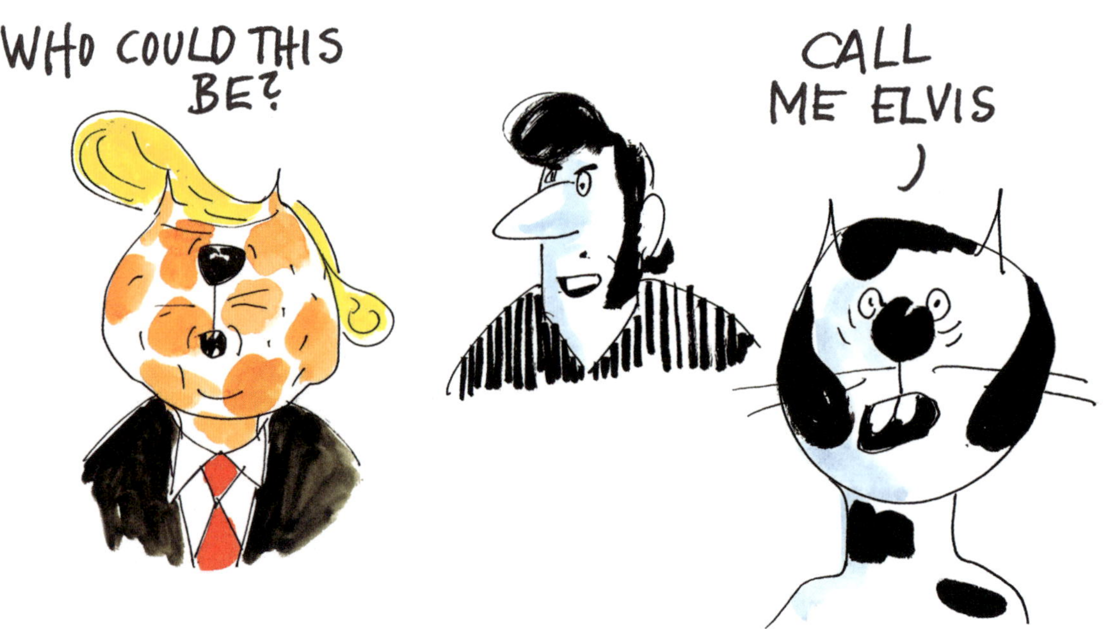

COME UP WITH CATS BASED ON OTHER CELEBRITIES, OR YOUR FRIENDS. CHOOSE PEOPLE WITH TWO OR THREE STRIKING FEATURES, TO MAKE YOUR CATS EASY TO RECOGNIZE.

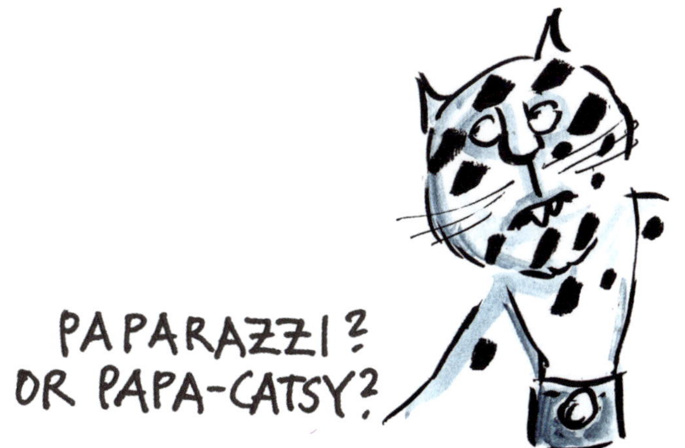

TYPICAL CATS
THEY'RE ALWAYS HANGING AROUND!

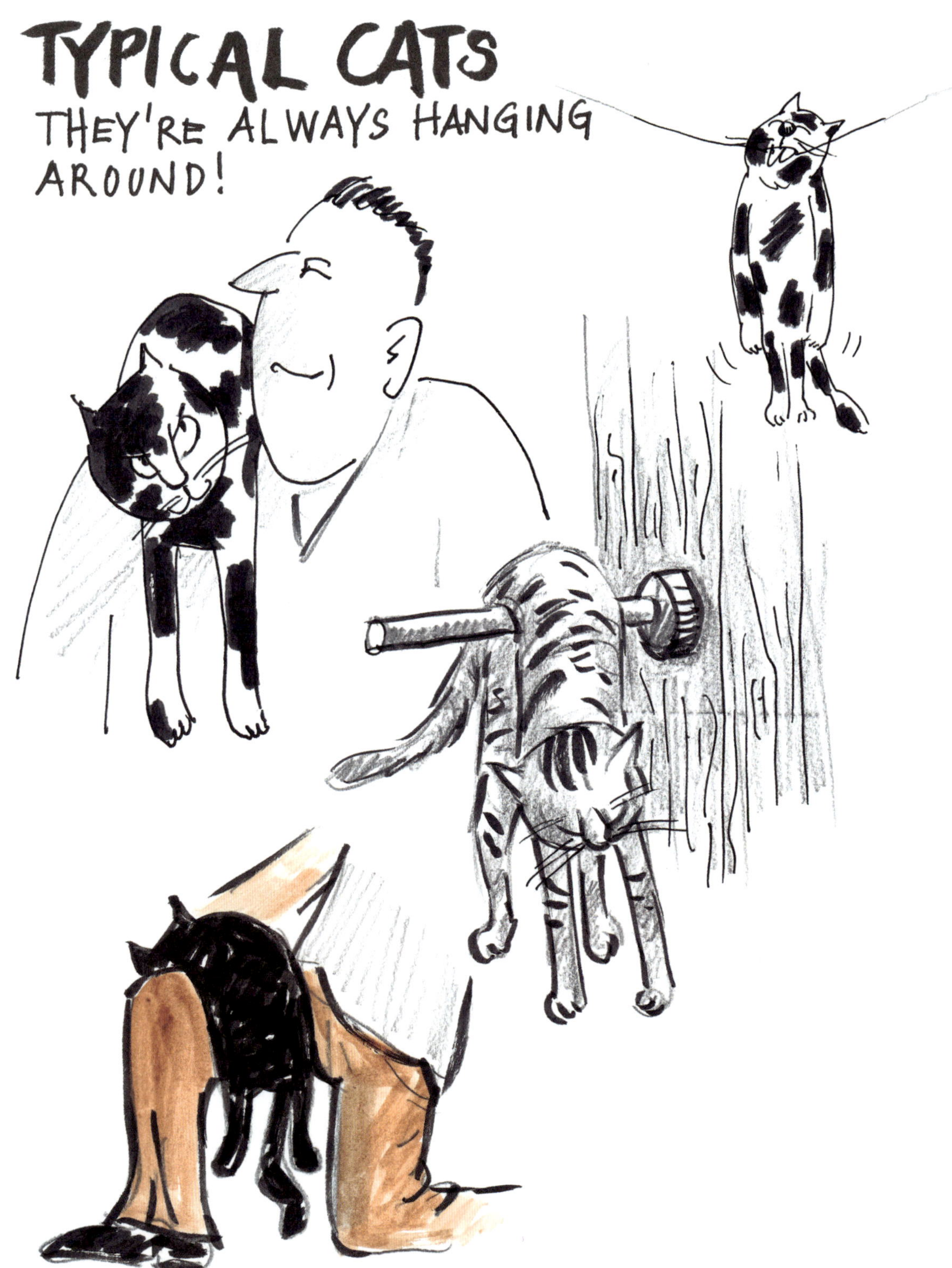

ADD SOME CATS HANGING
OVER THESE OBJECTS TOO.

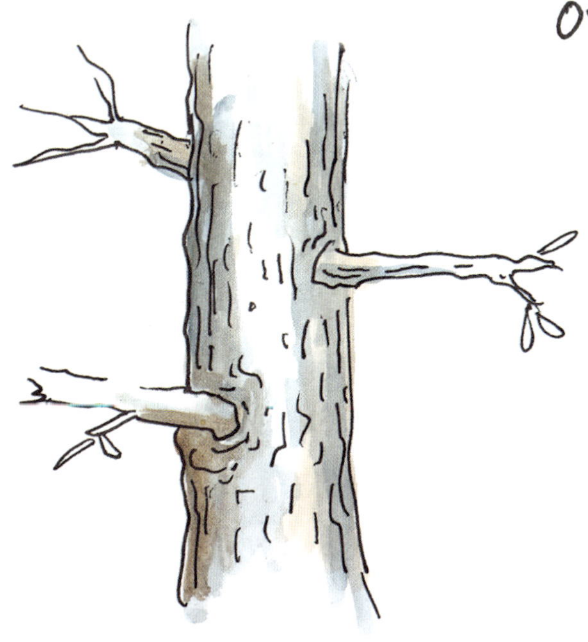

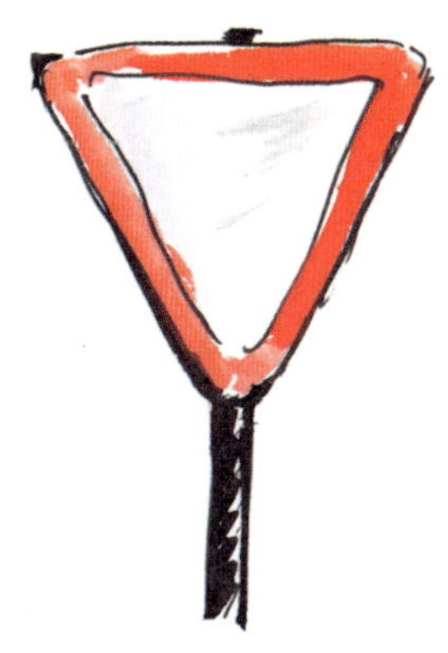

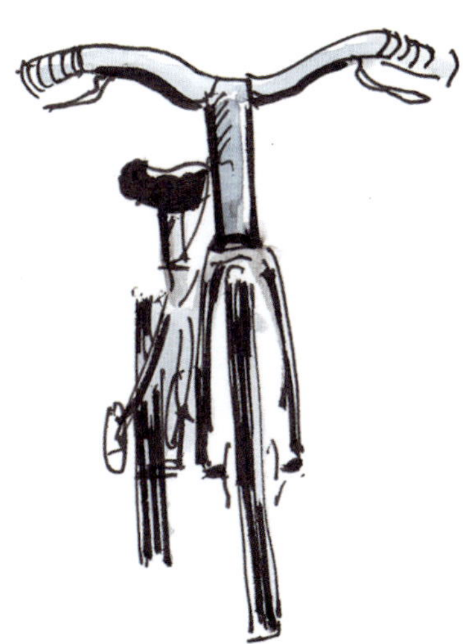

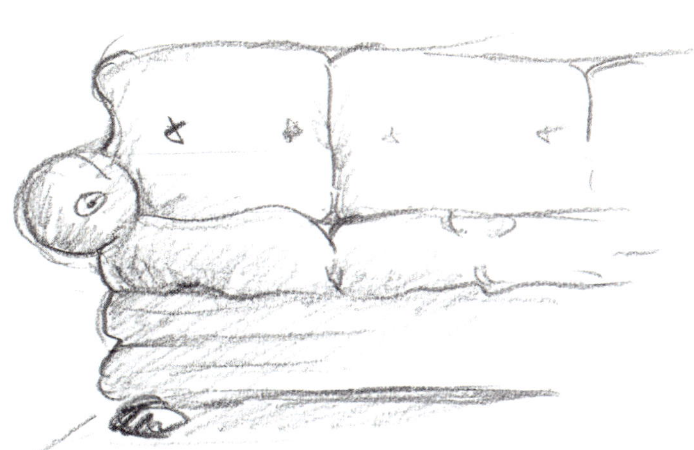

SOME CATS PREFER HIDE AND SEEK.

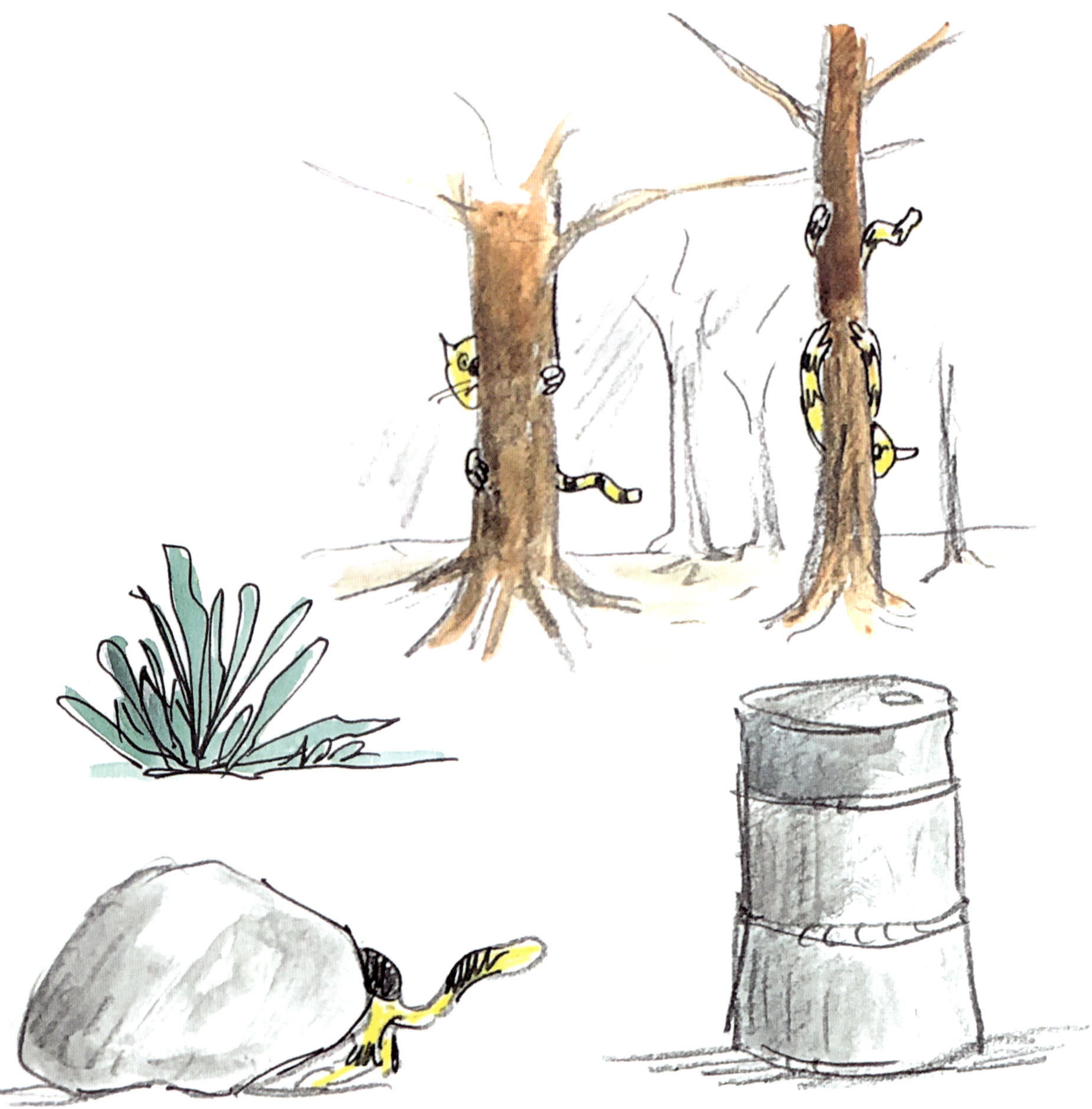

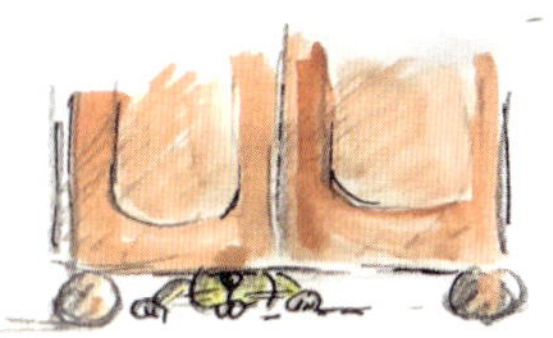

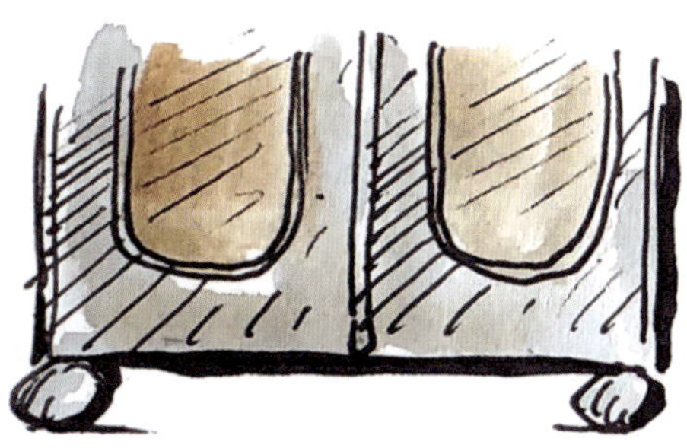

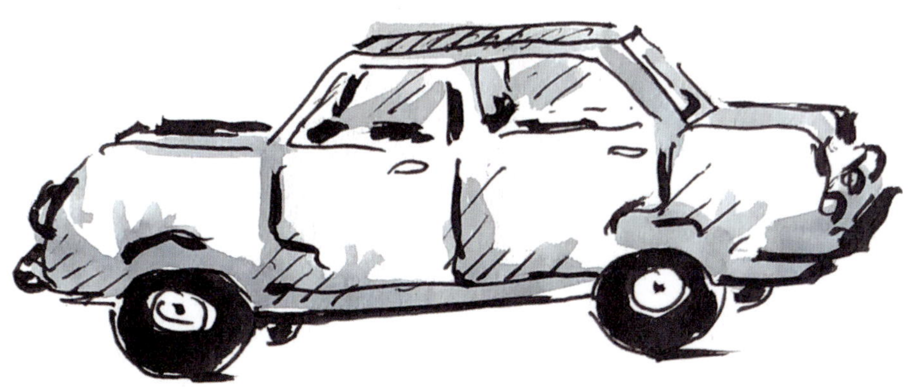

DRAW MORE CLEVERLY
CONCEALED CATS.

DANGEROUS PLACES TO HIDE

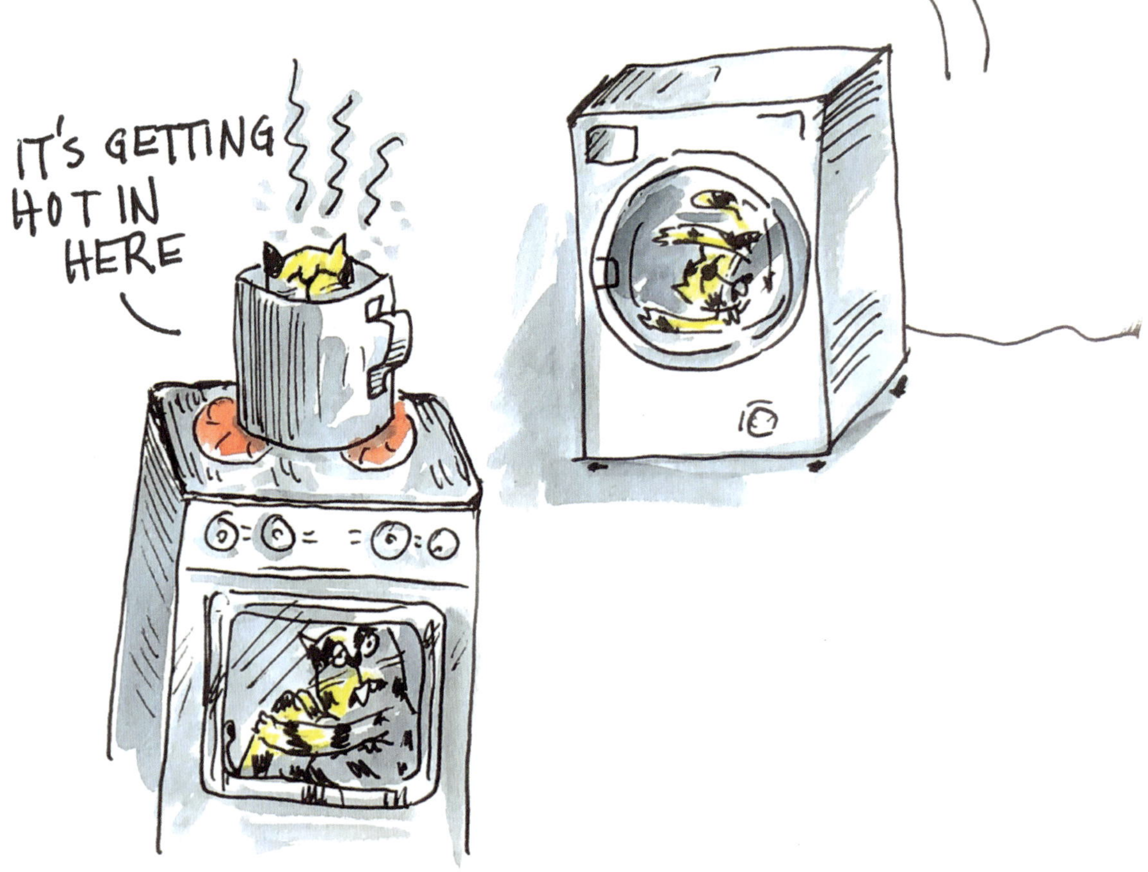

THINK OF MORE FORBIDDEN PLACES
WHERE CATS DEFINITELY SHOULDN'T GO!

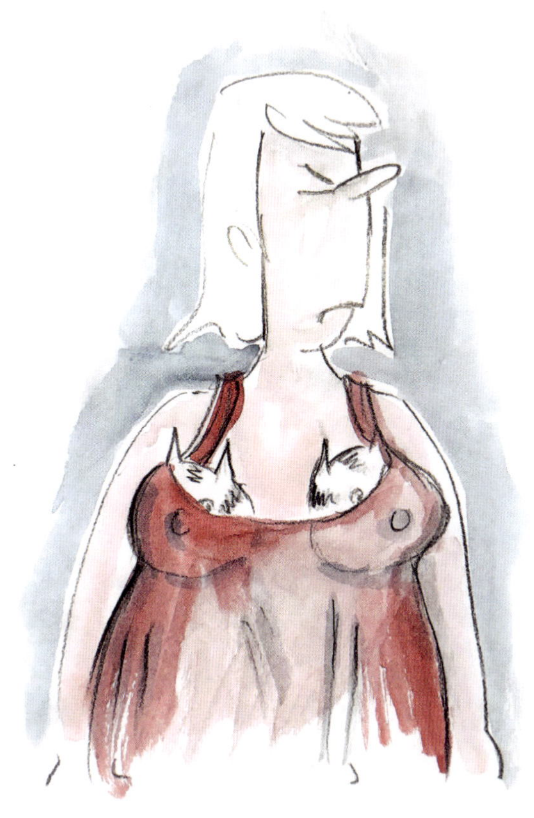

CATS IN THE WILD

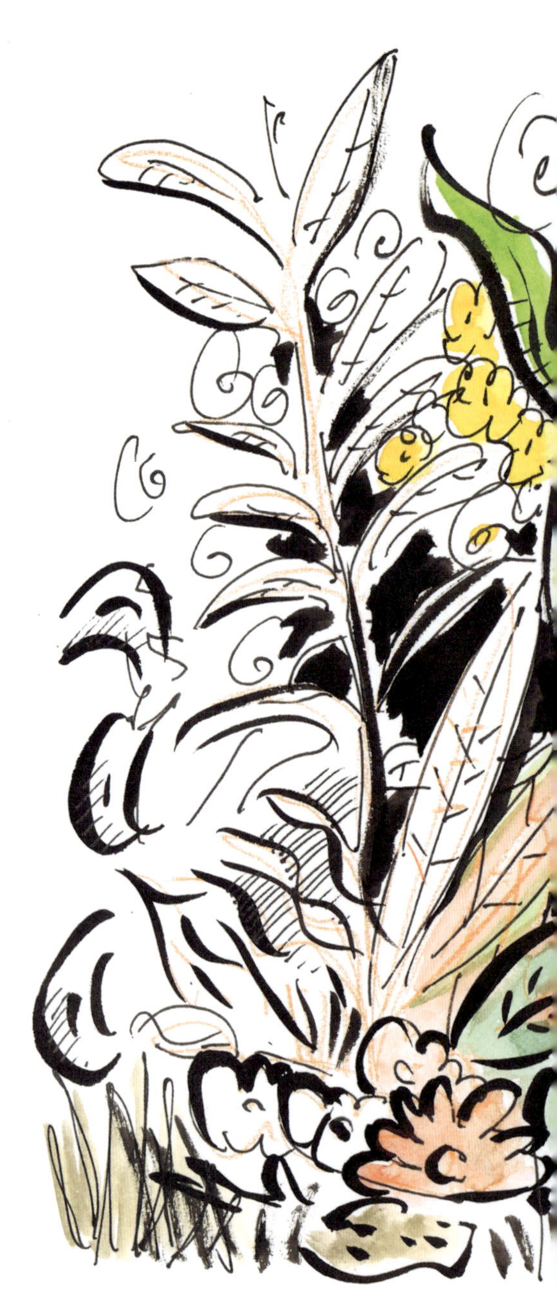

USE PENCILS, PENS AND FILL THESE
PAGES COMPLETELY

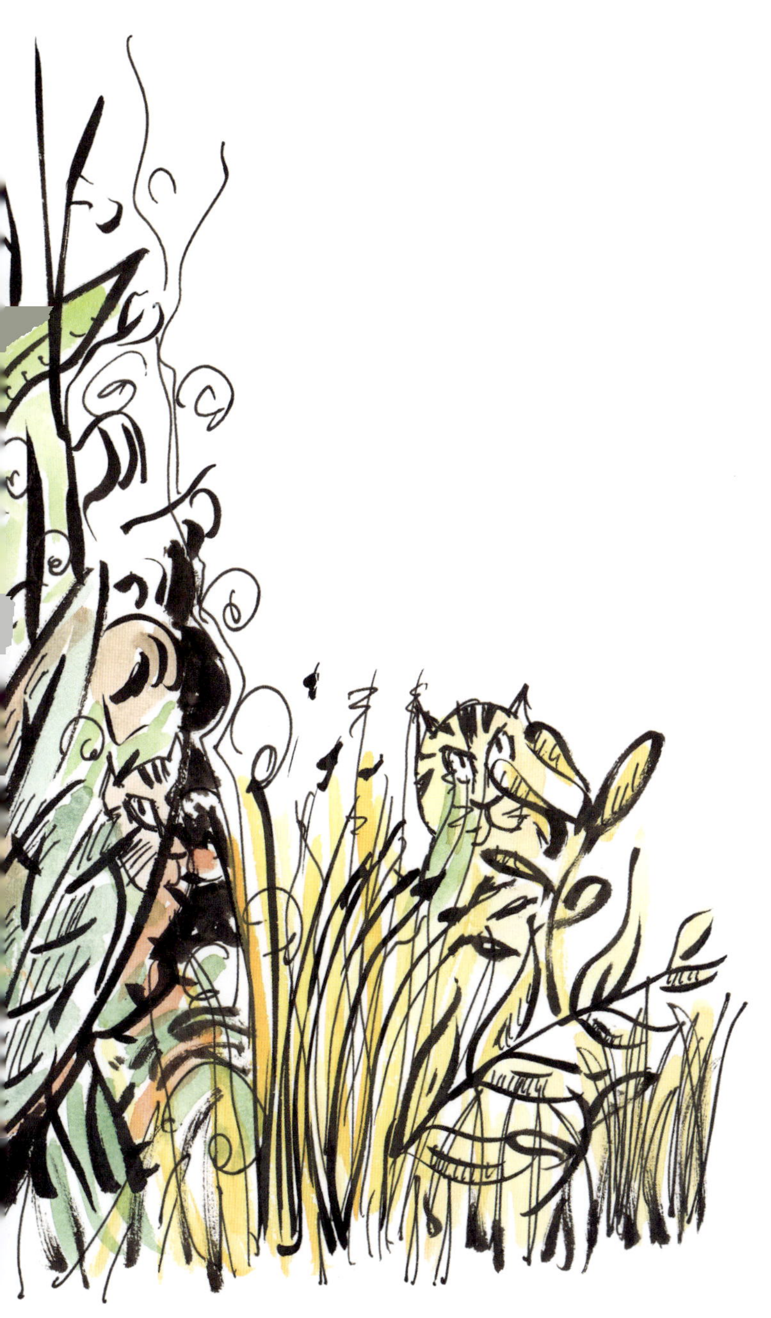

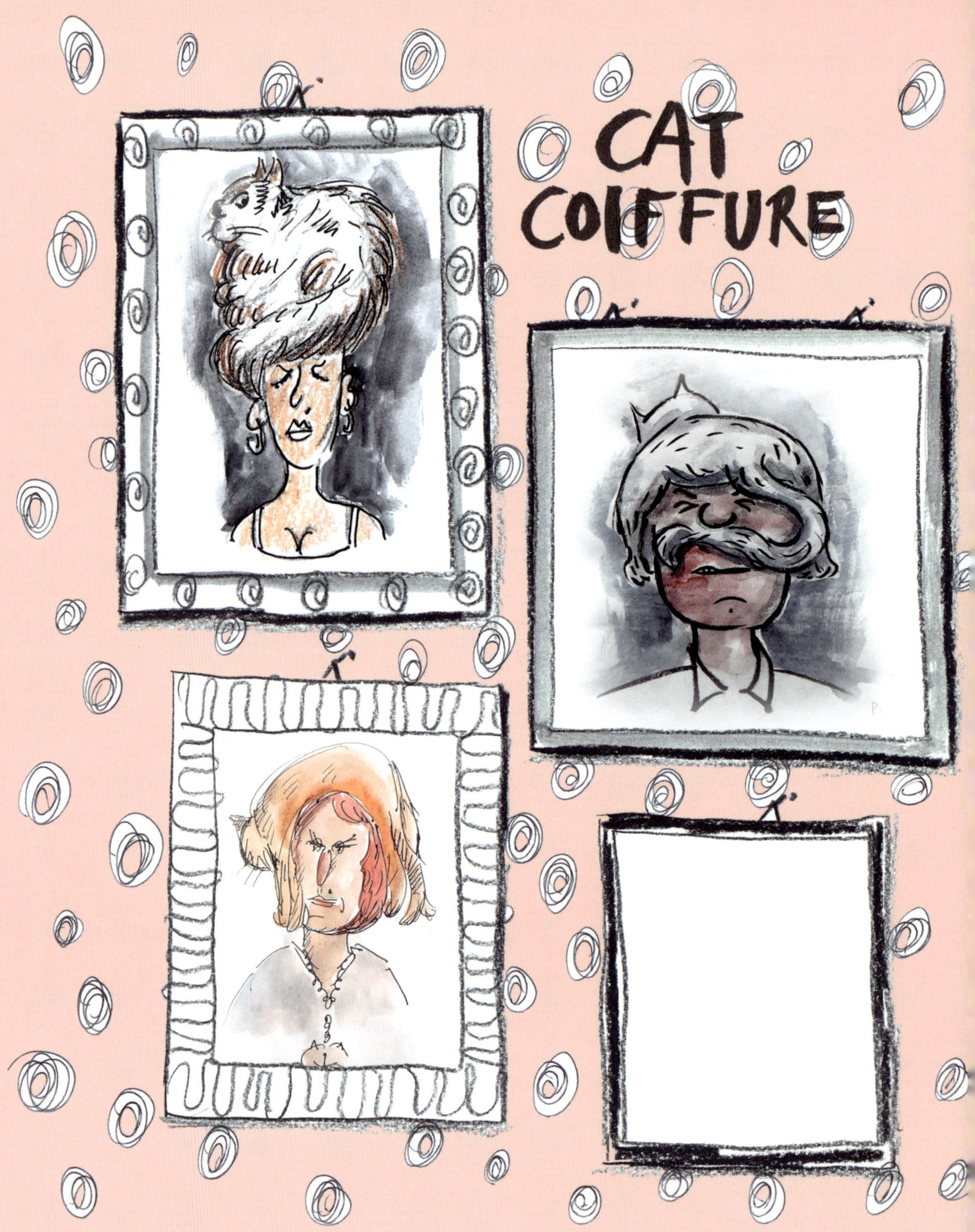

CAT
COIFFURE

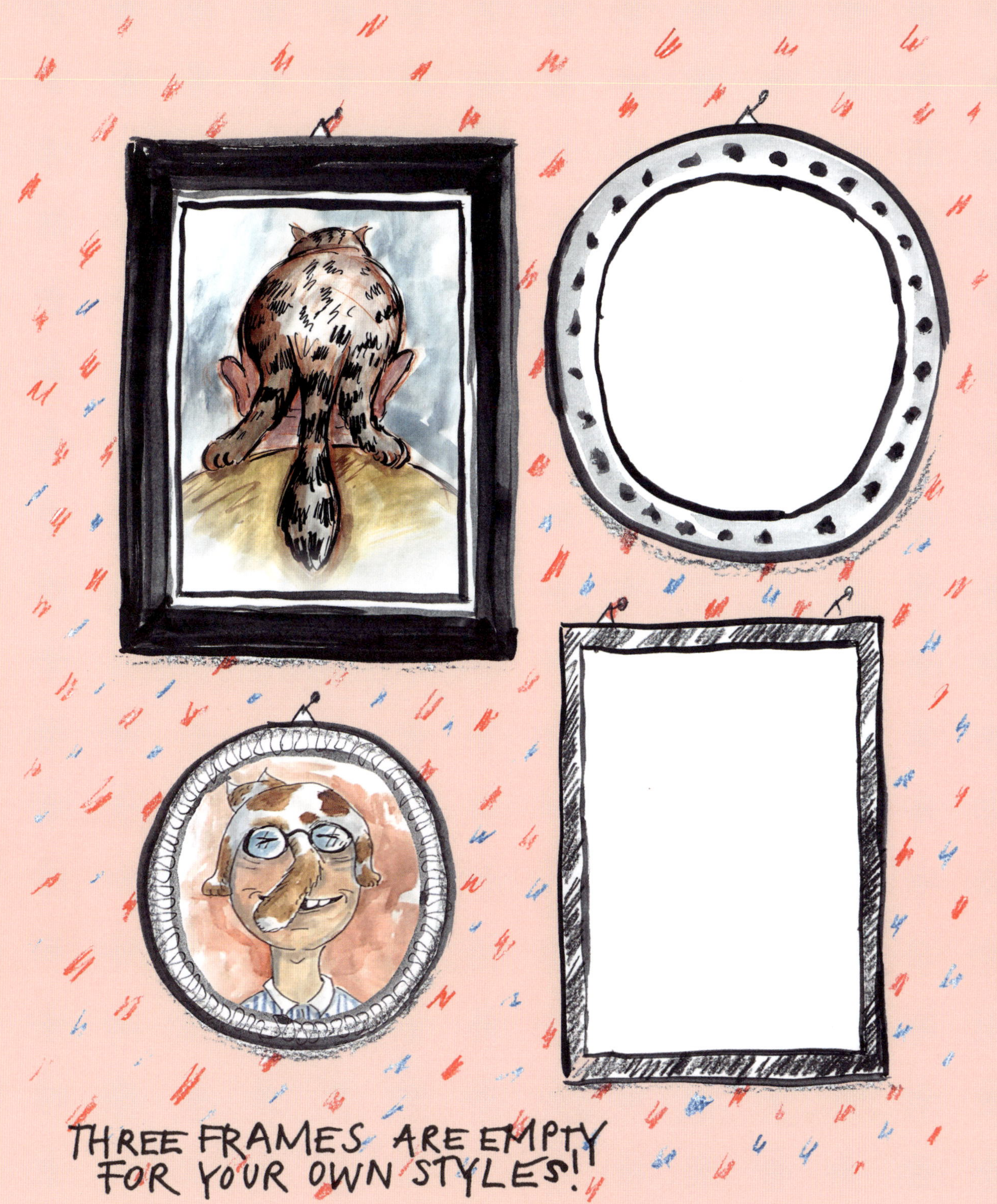

THREE FRAMES ARE EMPTY
FOR YOUR OWN STYLES!

CAT TATTOOS

THESE PEOPLE WANT TO COVER THEMSELVES IN CATS!

COME UP WITH TATTOO IDEAS OF YOUR OWN!

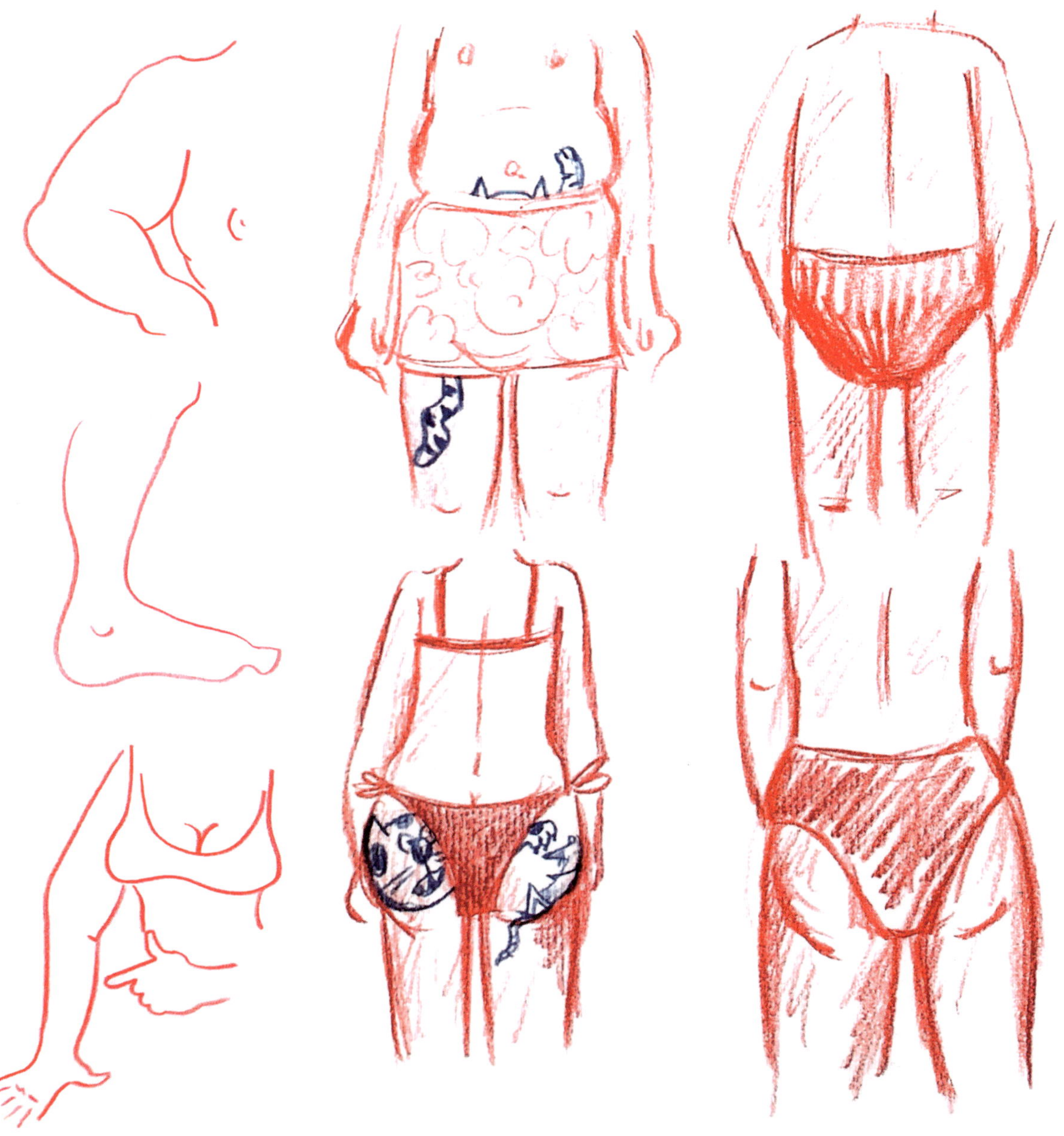

CAT AND MOUSE

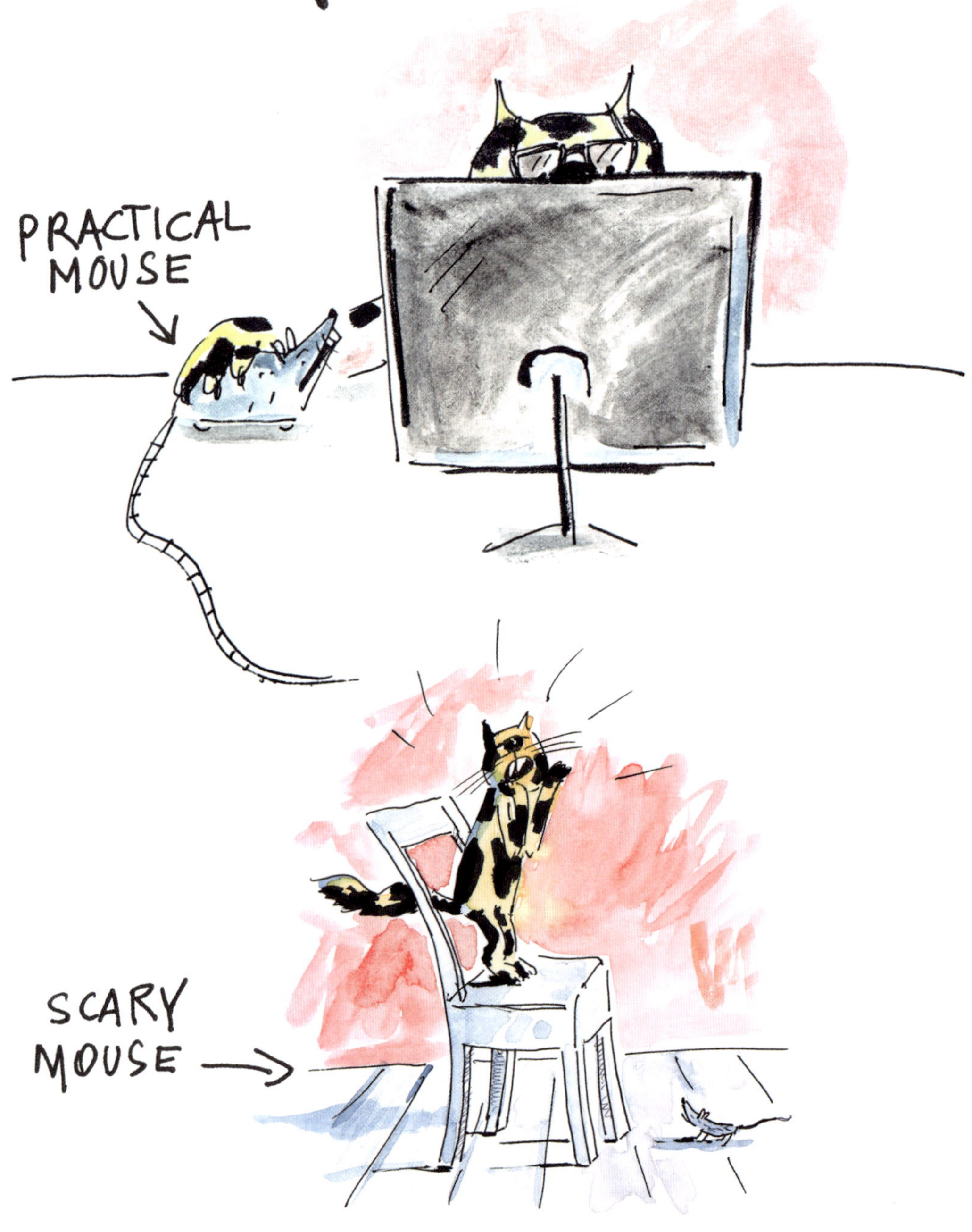

DRAW MORE CAT AND MOUSE PAIRS!

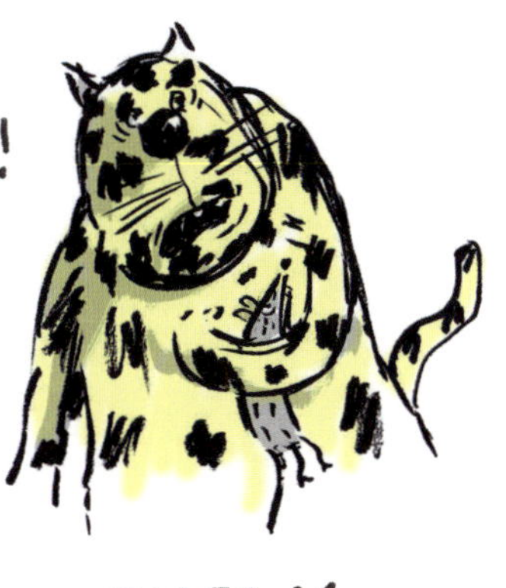

CUDDLY
MOUSE

HERE'S HOW TO DRAW MICE

CATS LOVE BIRDS
IT'S A WELL-KNOWN FACT

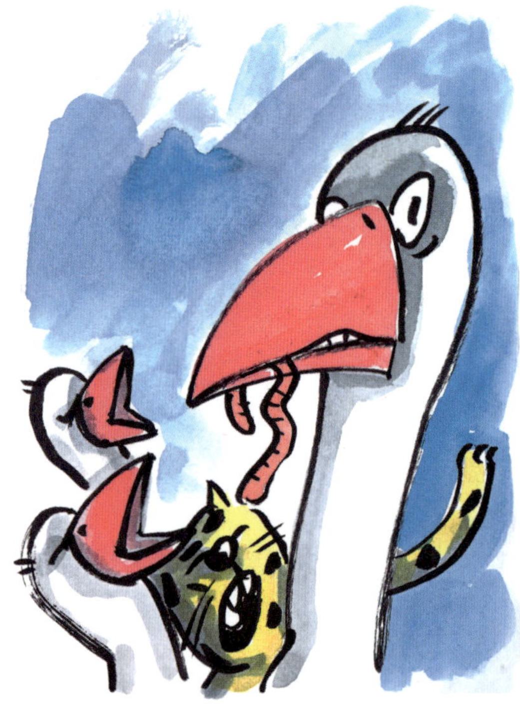

CUCKOO
CAT

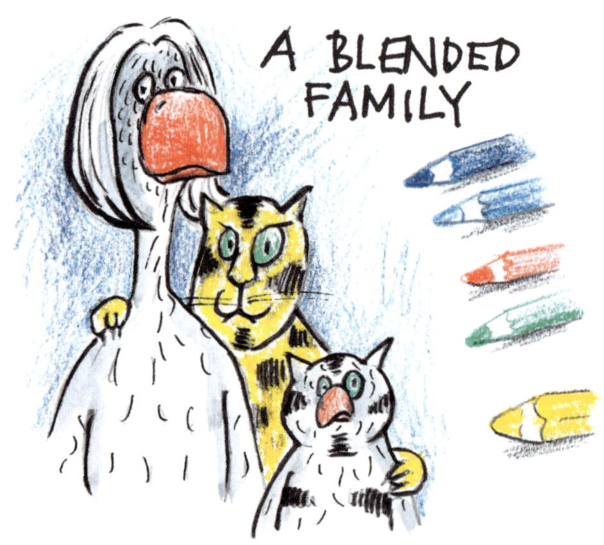

A BLENDED
FAMILY

DRAW MORE LOVE STORIES...

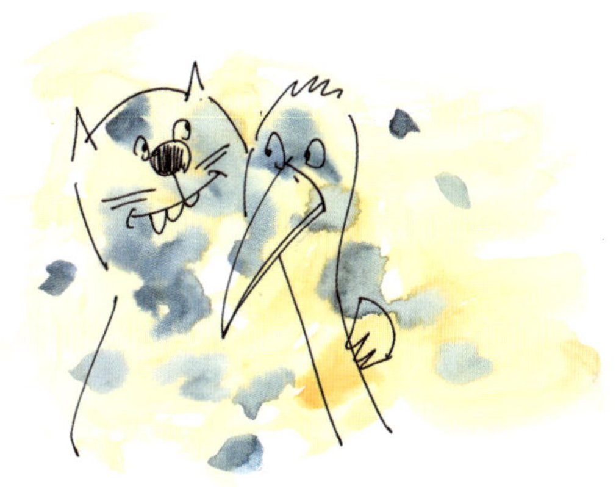

BIRDS AREN'T HARD TO DRAW:

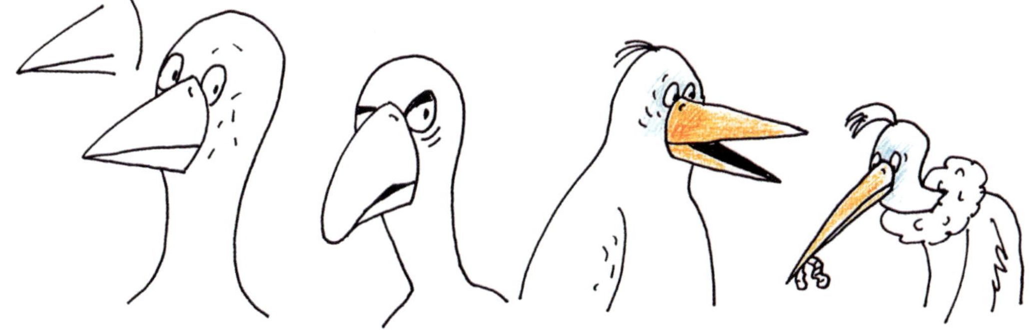

THIS BEAR LOVES CATS

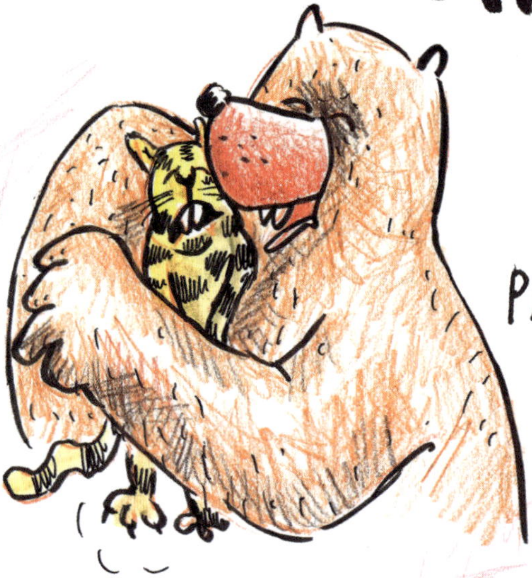

PERHAPS...

A LITTLE TOO MUCH!

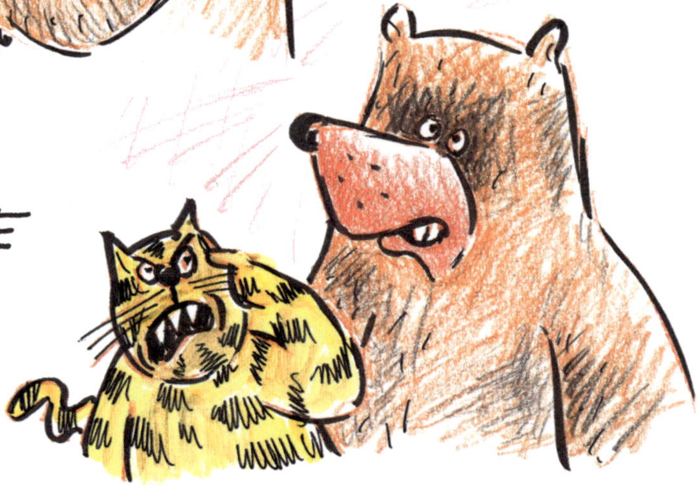

A BEAR LOOKS LIKE THIS...

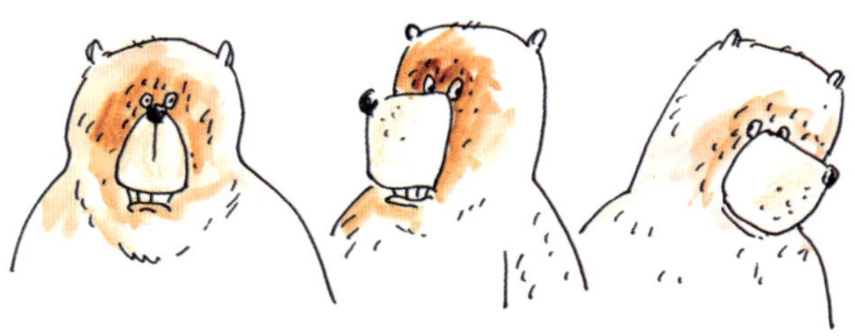

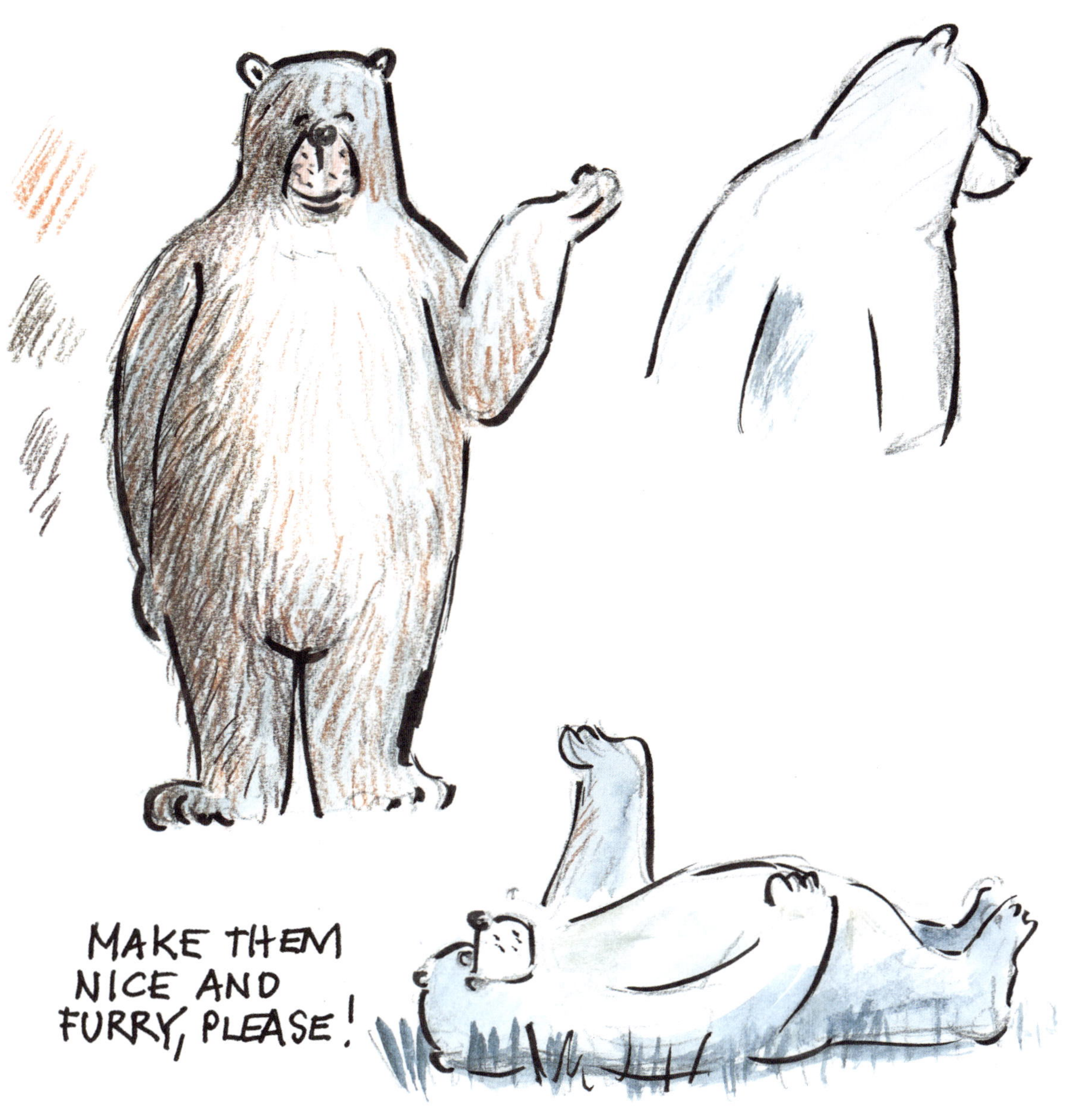

HERE ARE SOME SPACES WHERE CATS COULD FIT.

MAKE THEM NICE AND FURRY, PLEASE!

LIKE CAT AND DOG
THIS CLASSIC COUPLE DON'T HAVE TO HATE EACH OTHER!

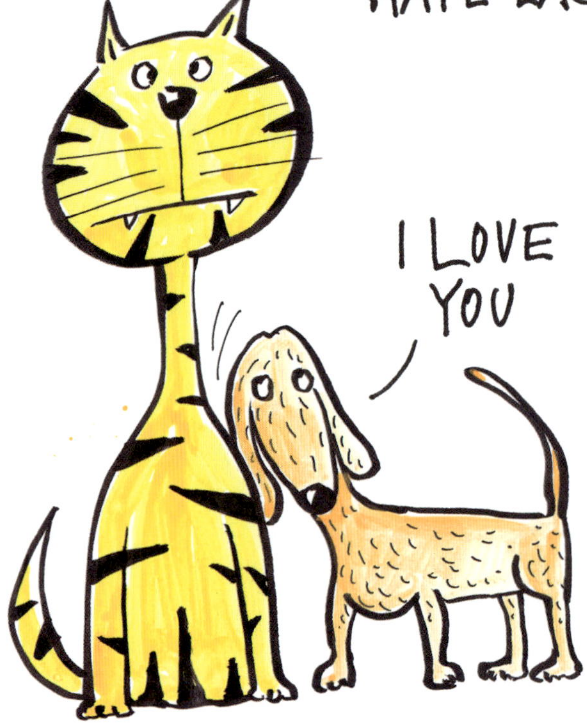

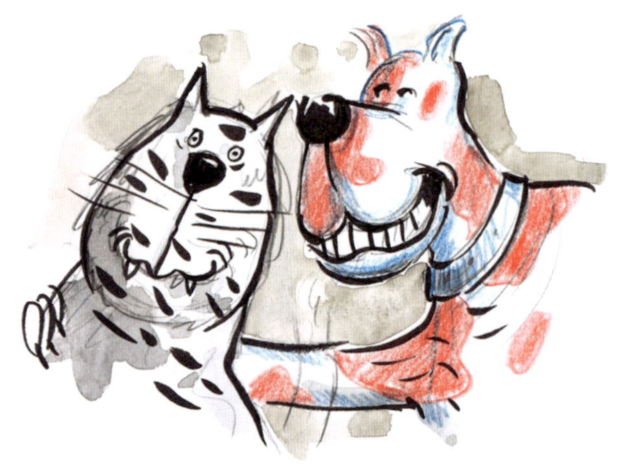

HERE'S SOME SPACE FOR YOUR OWN IDEAS!

AND HERE'S HOW TO DRAW A DOG

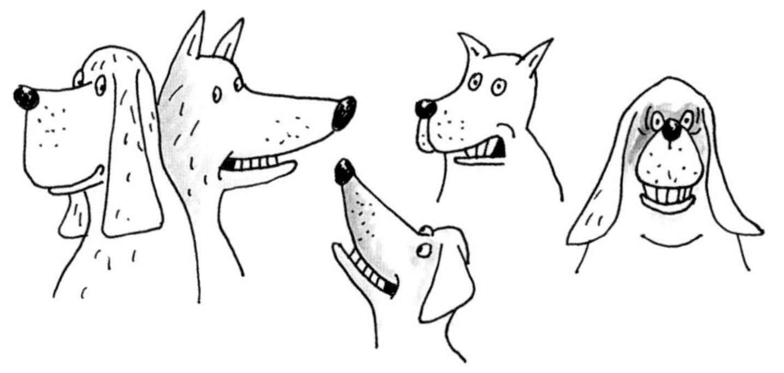

FAMOUS RELATIONS
LIONS AND TIGERS — REALISTIC OR SIMPLE

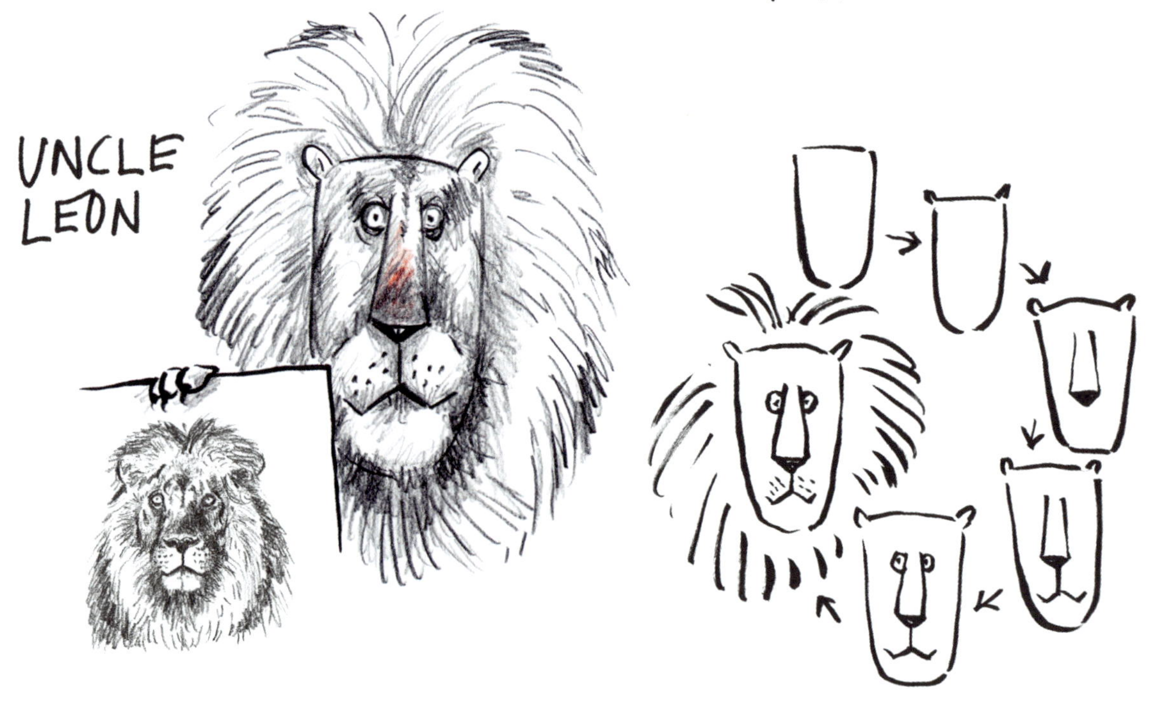

DRAW A LION'S HEAD HERE...

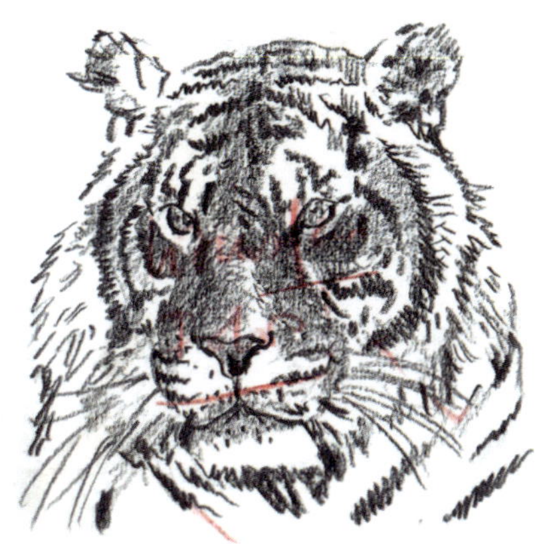

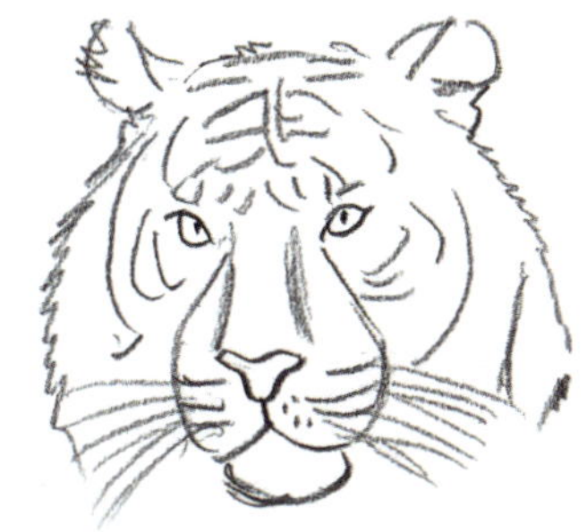

AUNTY
TINA

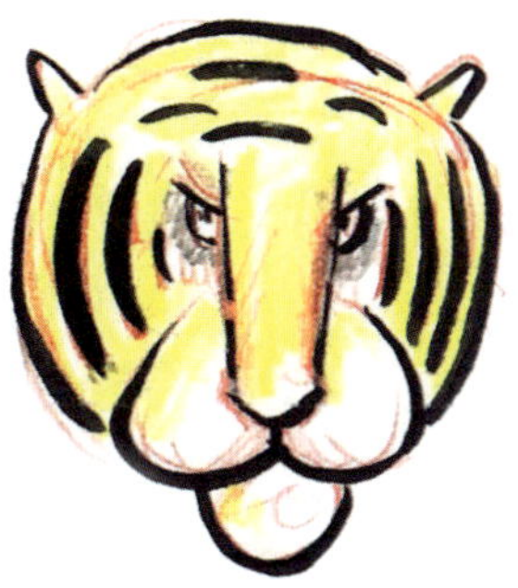

AND A TIGER'S HEAD HERE!

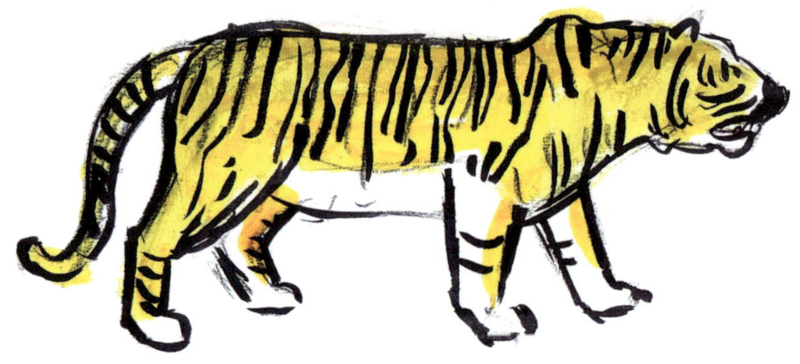

YOU CAN ALSO MAKE THE SHAPES
MORE SIMPLE — TRY IT AND SEE!

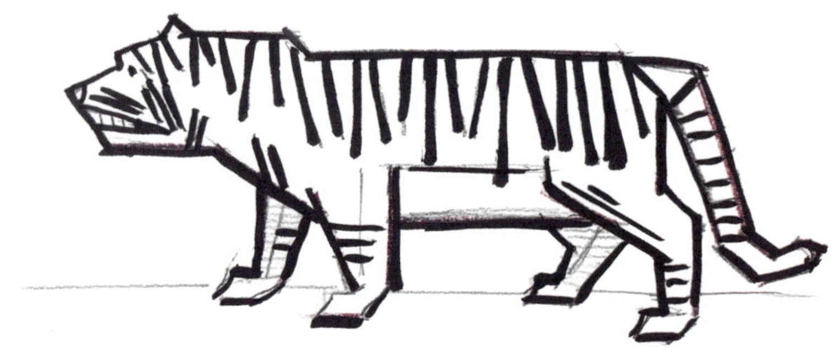

FILL IN THE MISSING BODY PARTS...

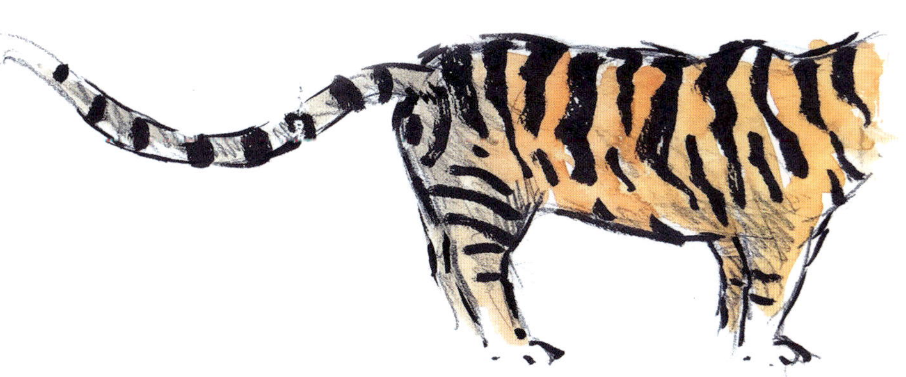

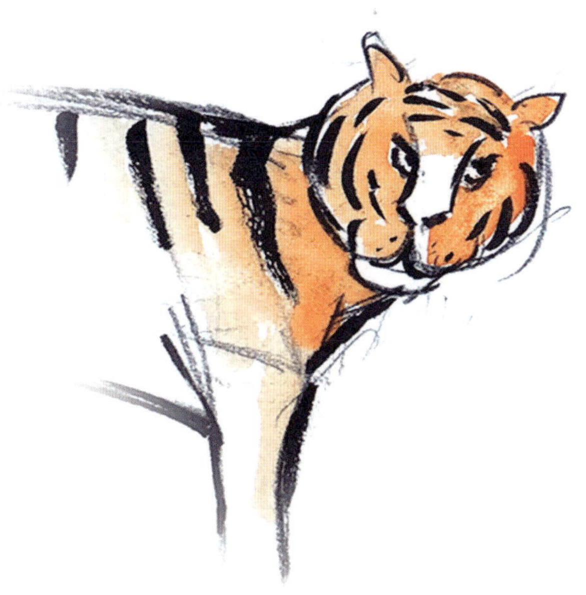

HOW TO DRAW CARTOONS

① FIRST YOU NEED A SUBJECT, FOR INSTANCE, THE IDEA THAT PEOPLE LOOK LIKE THEIR PETS.

② NOW YOU NEED TO COME UP WITH A FUNNY IDEA. THIS PART'S NOT ALWAYS EASY! HERE ARE THREE EXAMPLES.

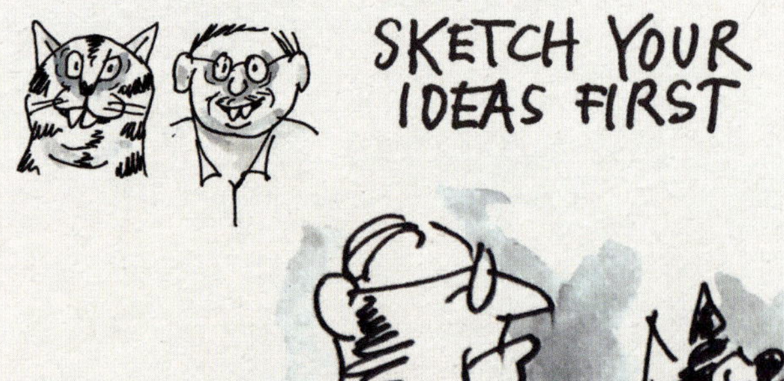

SKETCH YOUR IDEAS FIRST

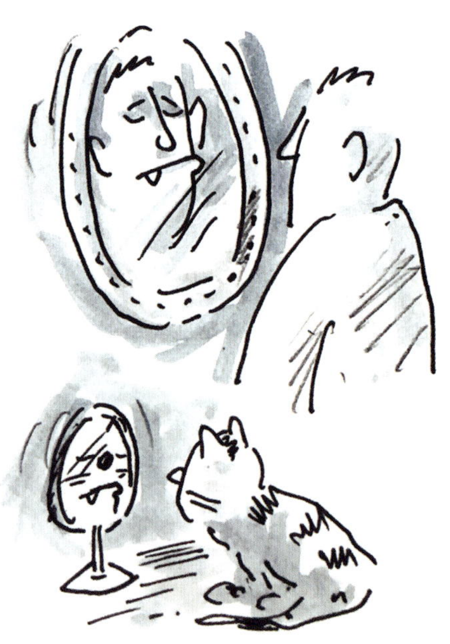

• BOTH LOOKING IN THE MIRROR

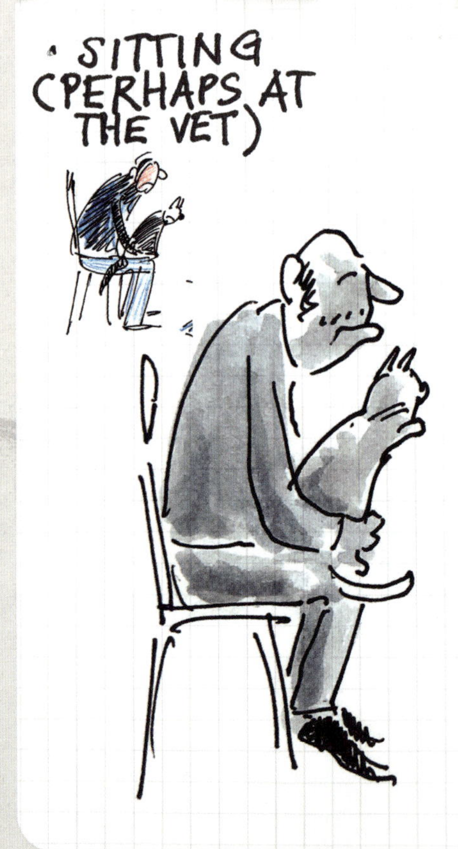

• SITTING (PERHAPS AT THE VET)

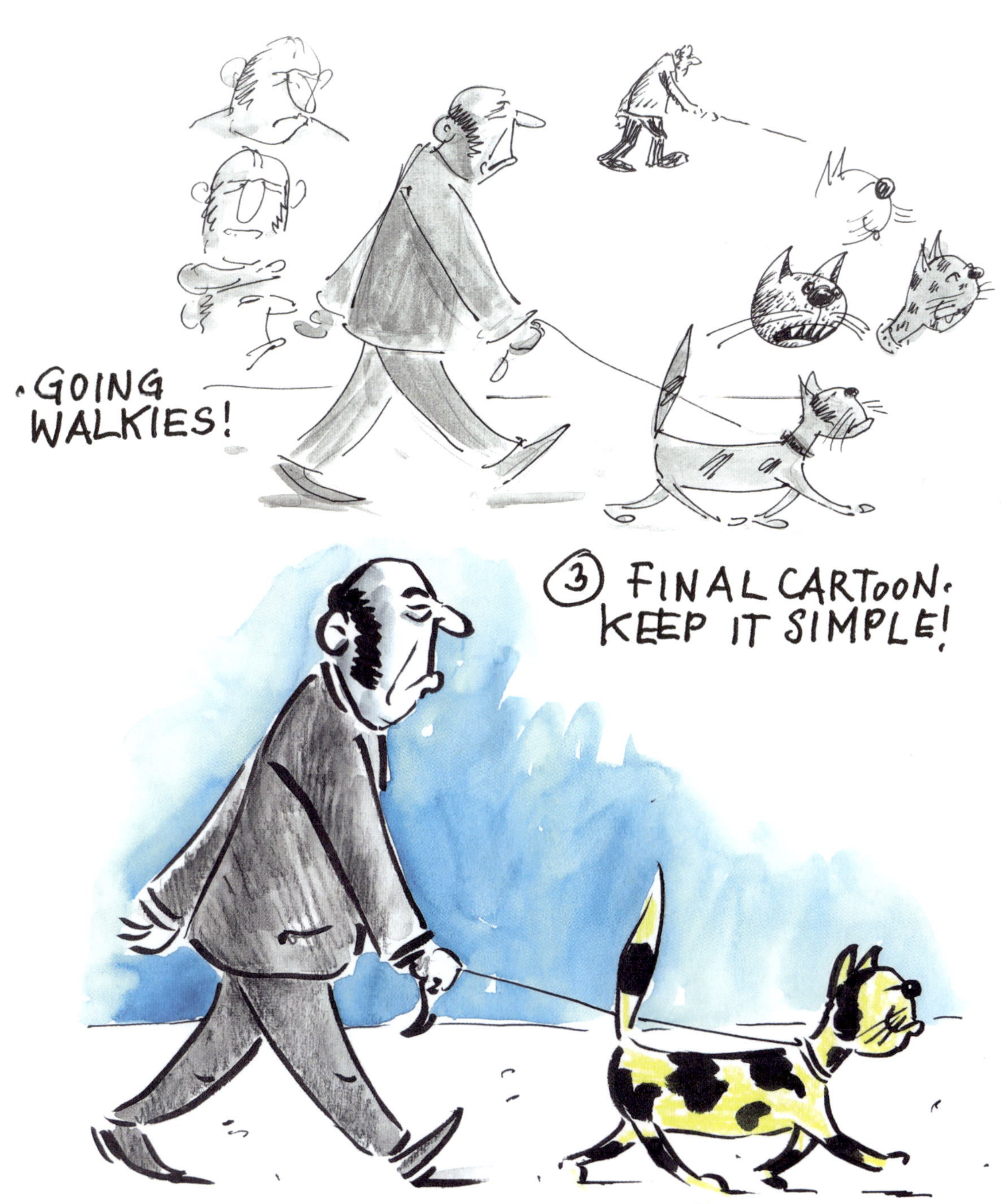
GOING
WALKIES!

3 FINAL CARTOON.
KEEP IT SIMPLE!

THIS CARTOON DOESN'T NEED ANY TEXT.

PENG'S SKETCHBOOK

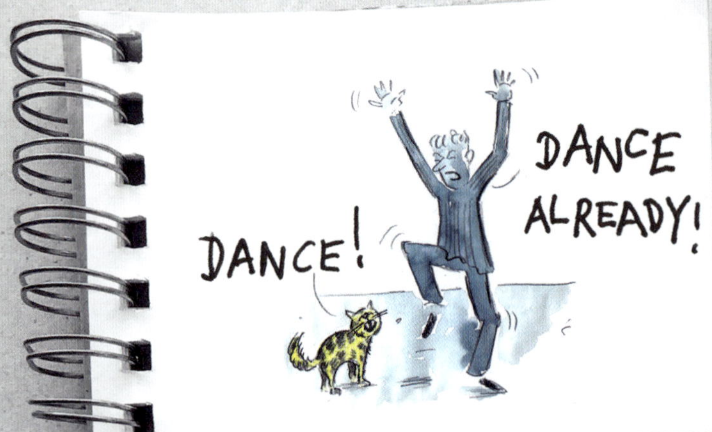

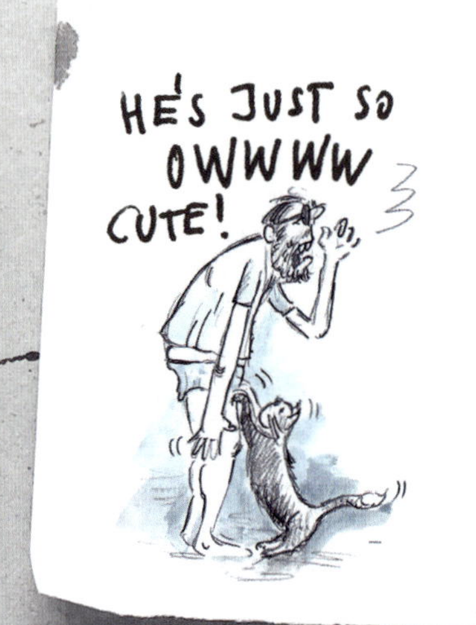

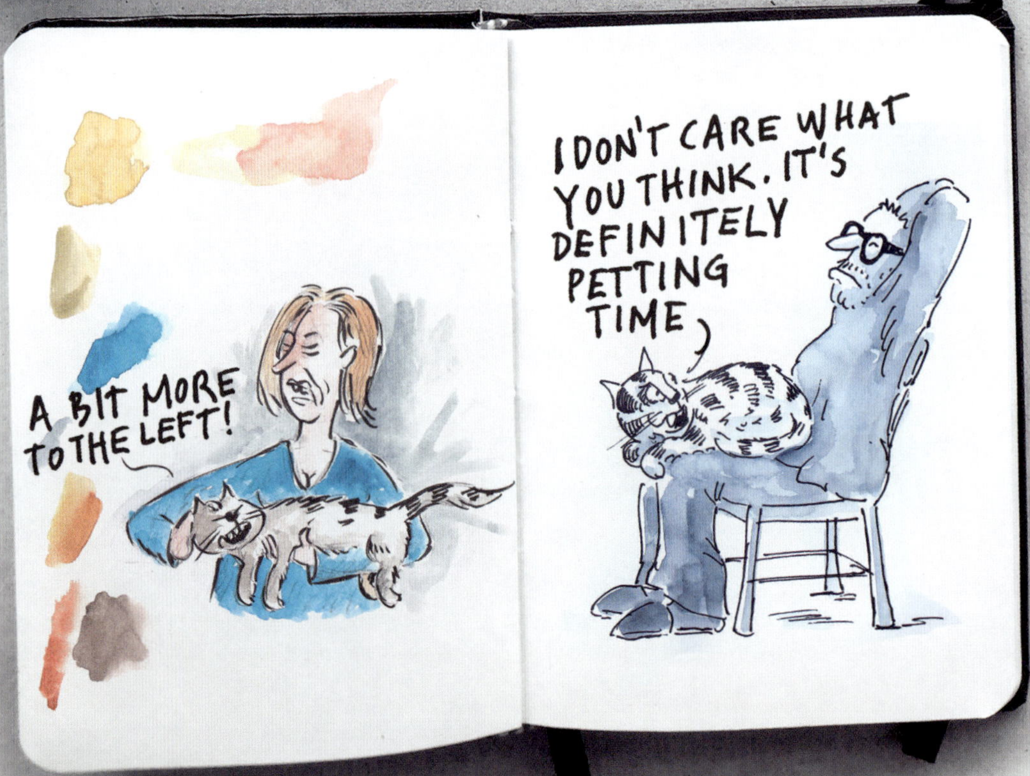

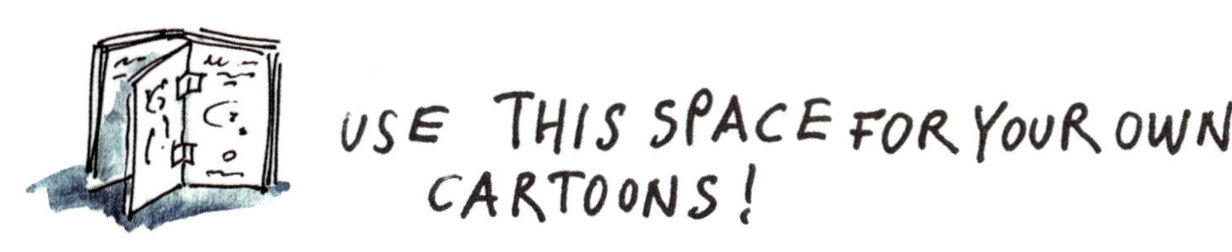

USE THIS SPACE FOR YOUR OWN CARTOONS!

PICTURE POSTCARDS
TO COPY

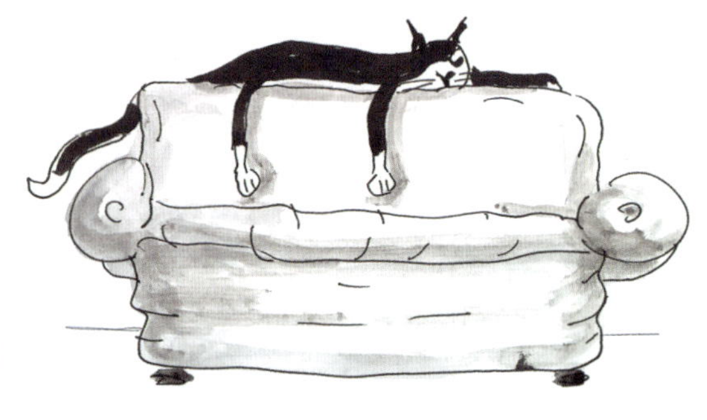

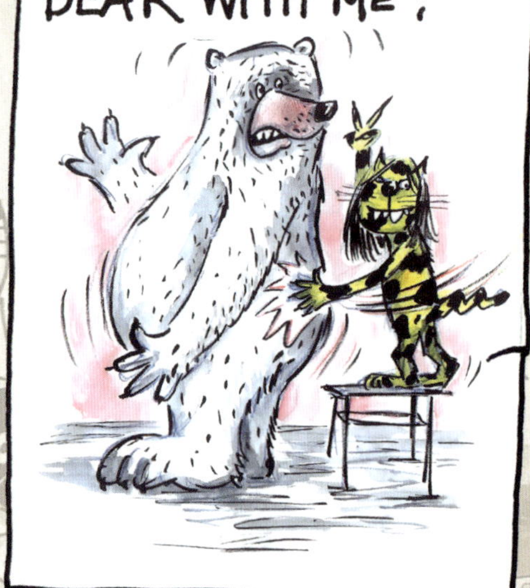

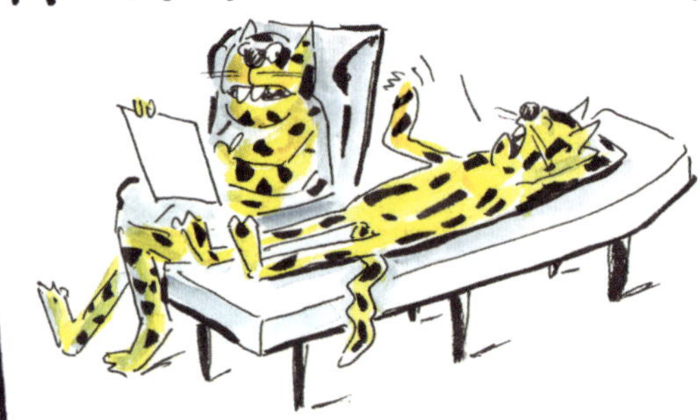

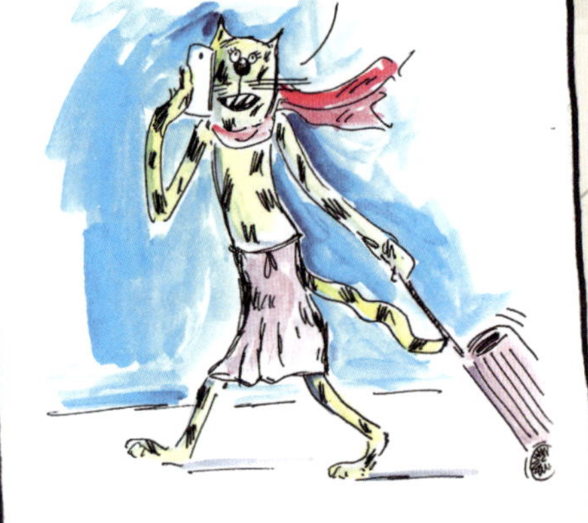

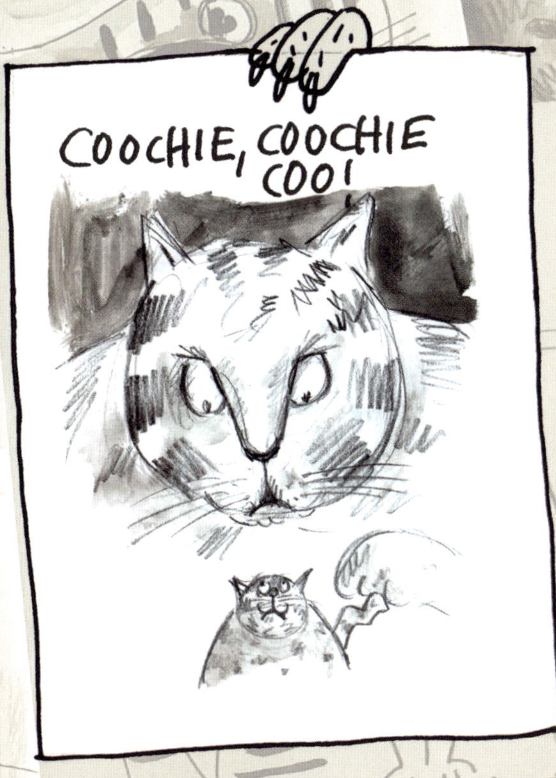

COOCHIE, COOCHIE COO!

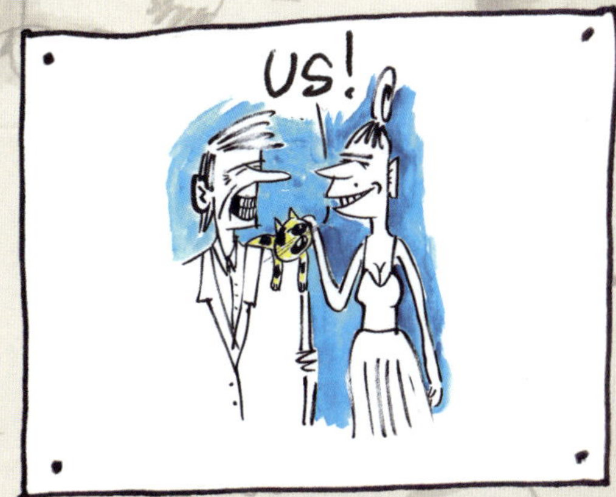

US!

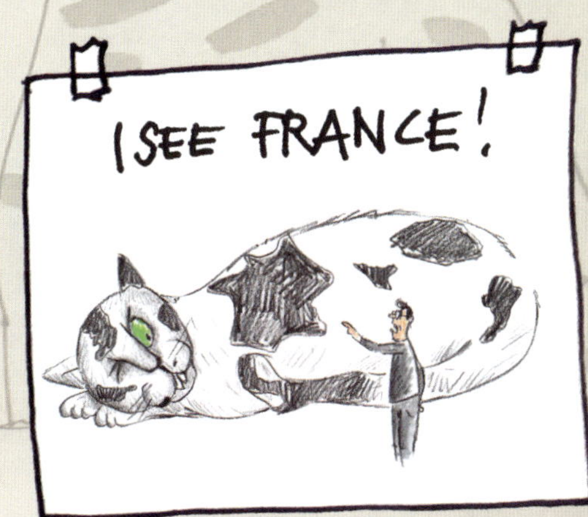

I SEE FRANCE!

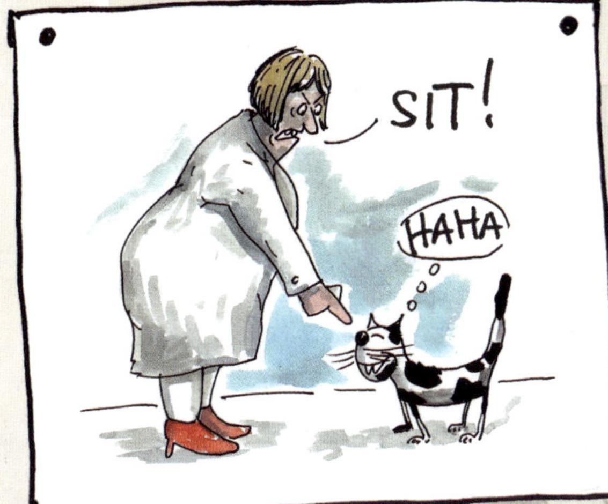

SIT!
HAHA

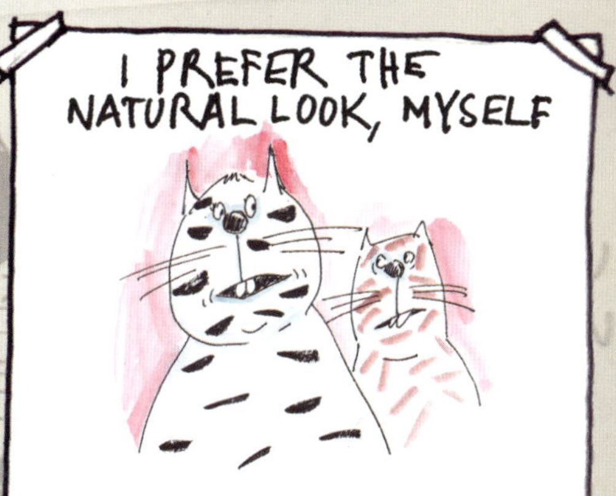

I PREFER THE NATURAL LOOK, MYSELF

CAT MASKS

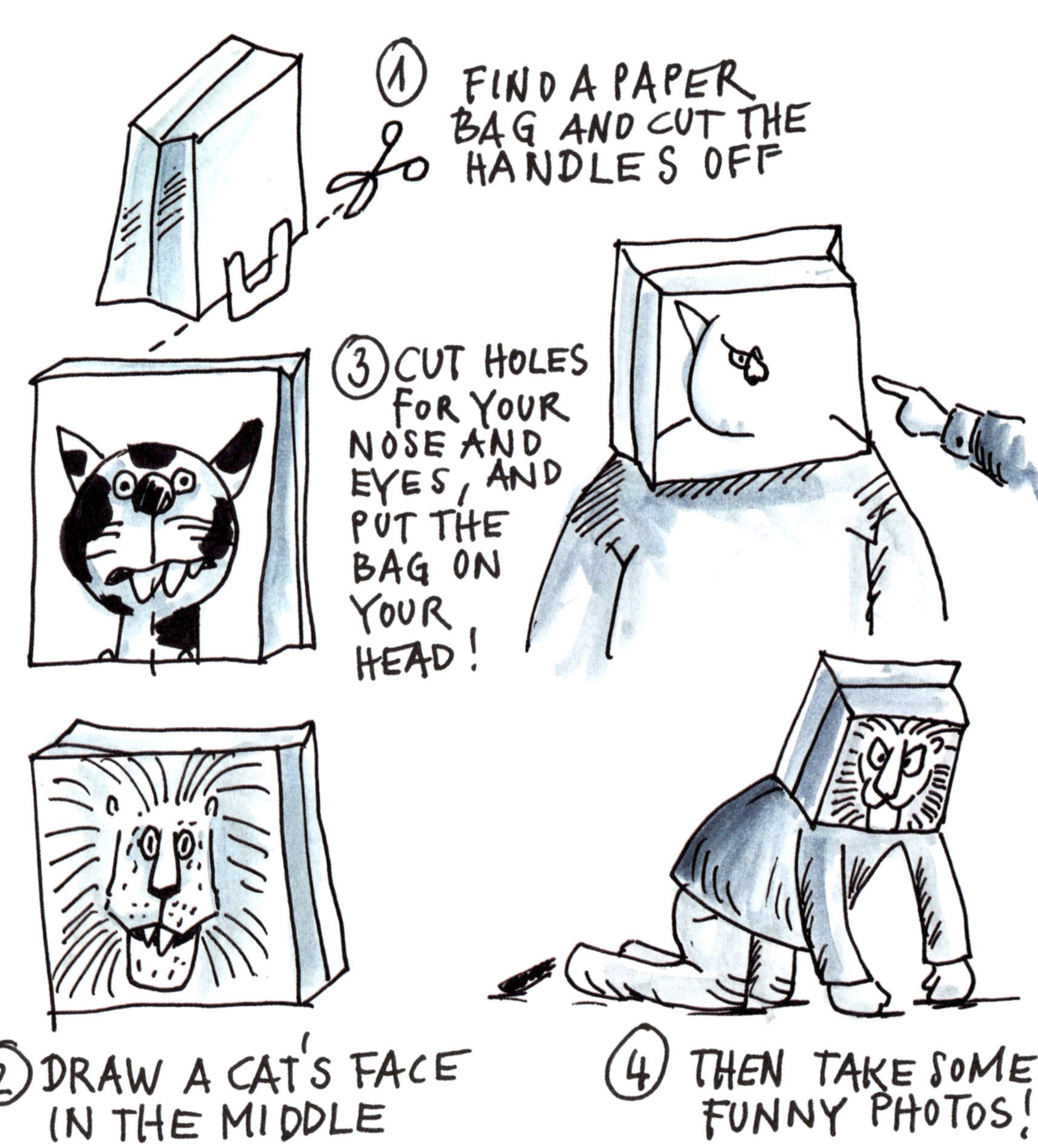

1 FIND A PAPER BAG AND CUT THE HANDLES OFF
3 CUT HOLES FOR YOUR NOSE AND EYES, AND PUT THE BAG ON YOUR HEAD!
2 DRAW A CAT'S FACE IN THE MIDDLE
4 THEN TAKE SOME FUNNY PHOTOS!

IF YOU'VE GOT LONG HAIR, TRY CUTTING SOME SLITS IN THE TOP AND THREADING YOUR HAIR THROUGH.

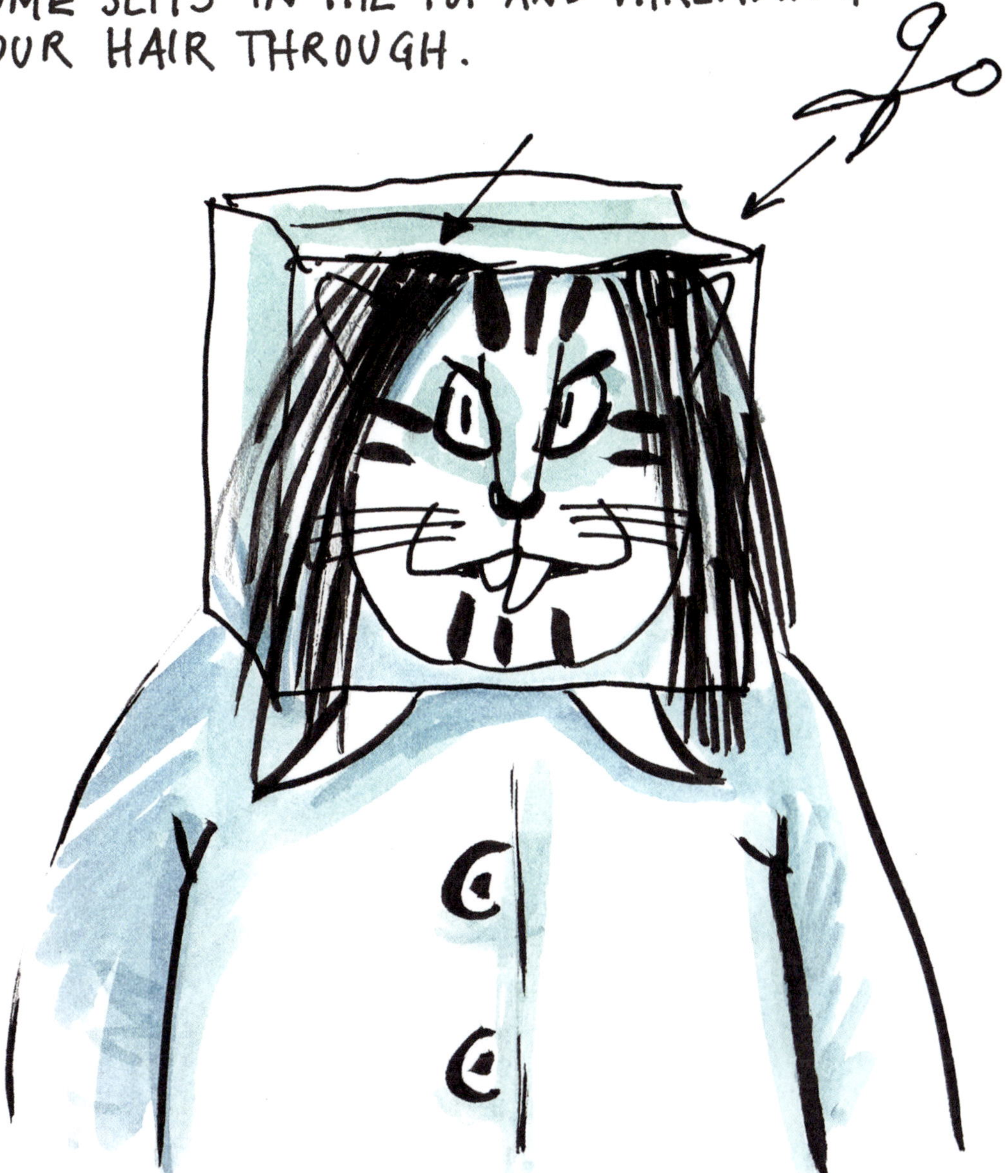

A TALKING CAT

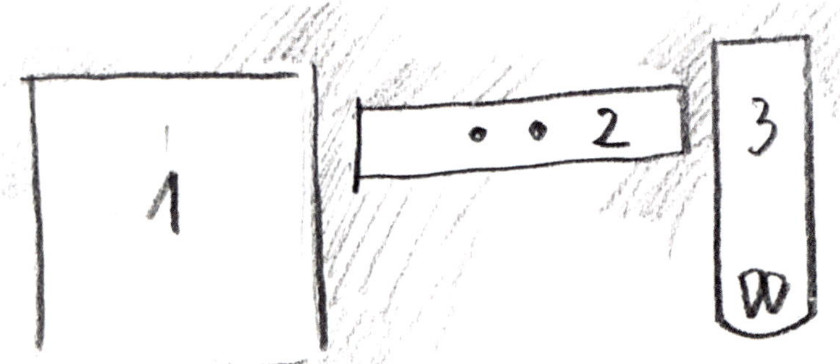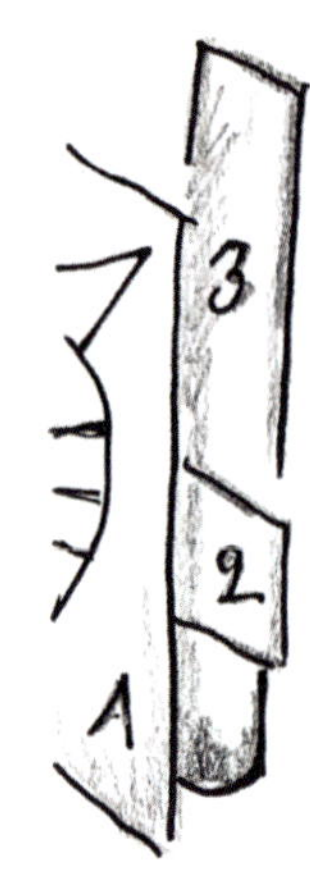

YOU WILL NEED: THICK PAPER CUT INTO THREE PIECES (1, 2, 3)

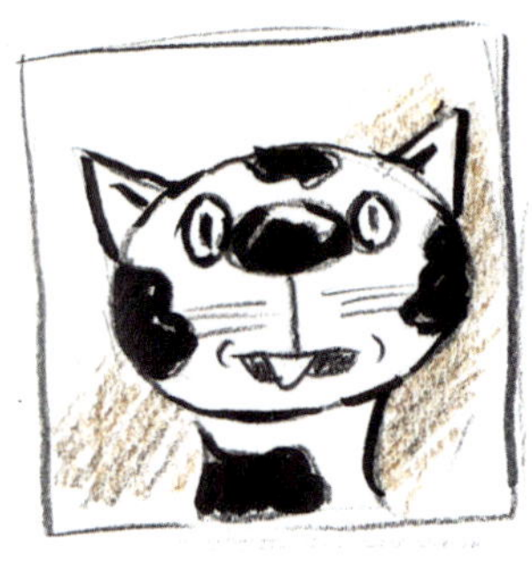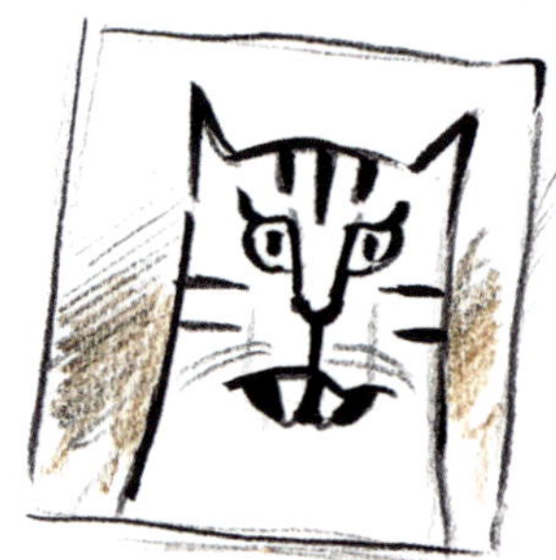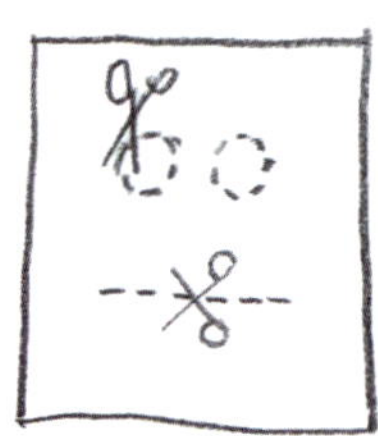

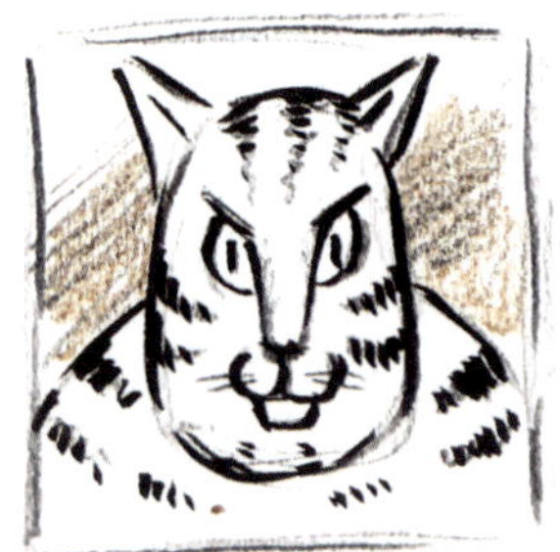

↑ EXAMPLES

INSTRUCTIONS:
- DRAW A CAT'S HEAD ON PIECE 1
- CUT OUT THE EYE HOLES
- CUT OUT A SLIT RIGHT UNDER THE NOSE FOR THE TOP LIP
- STRIPS OF PAPER (2 AND 3) ARE THE MOVING PARTS
- DRAW THE PUPILS ON PIECE 2 AND THE TOP OF THE LIP ON PIECE 3.

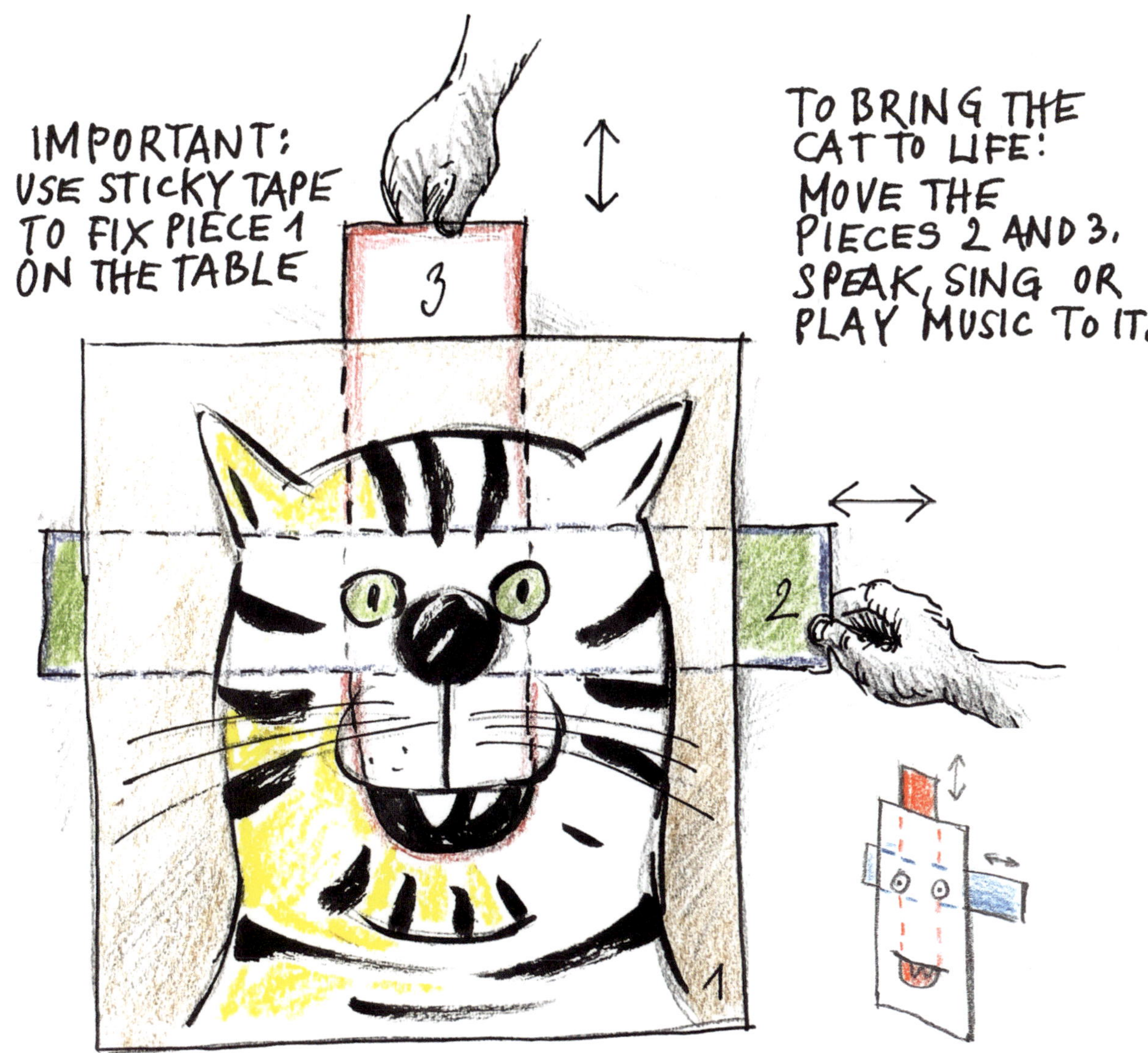

IMPORTANT:
USE STICKY TAPE
TO FIX PIECE 1
ON THE TABLE

TO BRING THE
CAT TO LIFE!
MOVE THE
PIECES 2 AND 3.
SPEAK, SING OR
PLAY MUSIC TO IT.

3

2

1

YOU COULD USE A PHONE
TO FILM YOUR CAT!
YOU'LL PROBABLY
NEED A SECOND
PERSON TO
HELP.

CHAPTER 3
THE ART OF CATS

BECOMING A MASTER CAT PAINTER

DRAWING REALISTIC CATS
IS A BIG CHALLENGE,
BUT LOTS OF FUN!

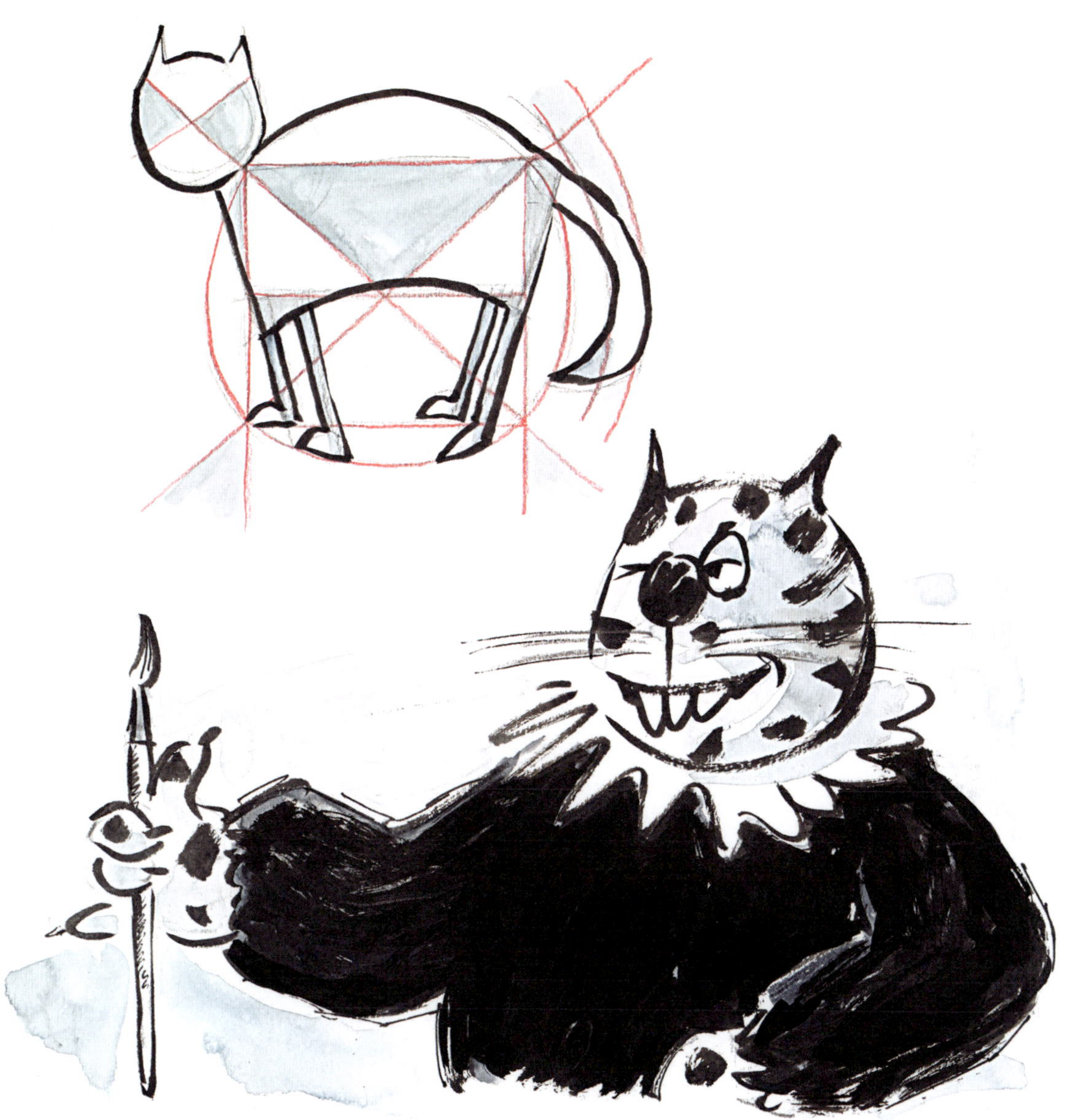

SKETCHING
AN IMPORTANT FIRST STEP

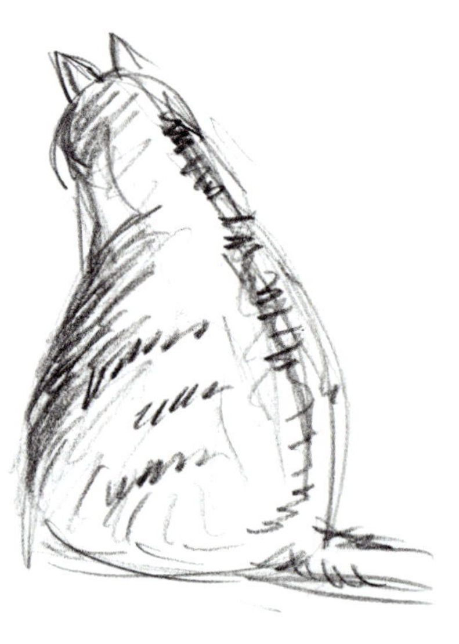

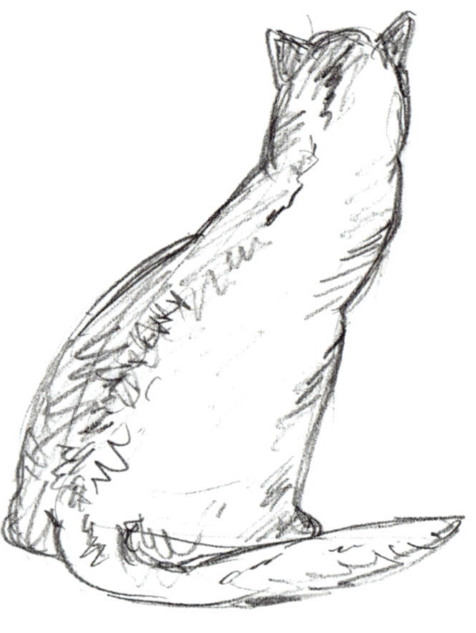

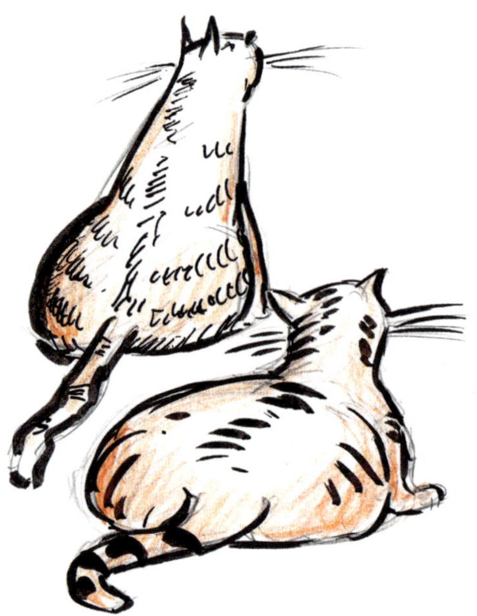

THIS IS WHAT YOU NEED TO DO:

- LOOK CLOSELY
- TRY TO GET THE GENERAL SHAPE OF THE CAT FIRST
- THEN ADD THE DETAILS

TRY NOT TO RUSH, AND PRACTISE AS MUCH AS YOU CAN! YOU CAN PASTE IN YOUR ⟶ FAVOURITE SKETCHES HERE

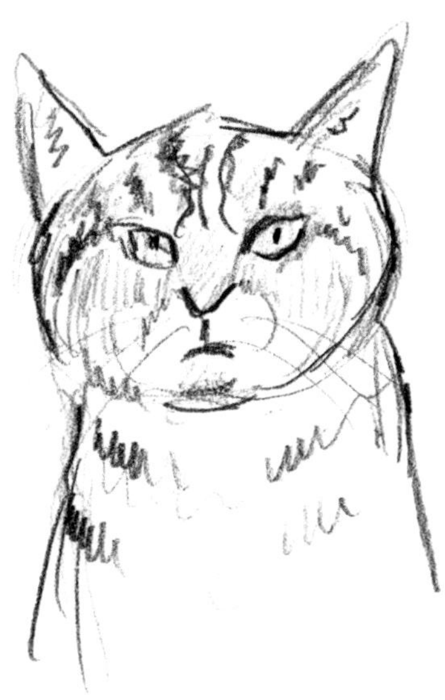

NOW TRY SOME FAST, LOOSE, ROUGHLY DRAWN SKETCHES!

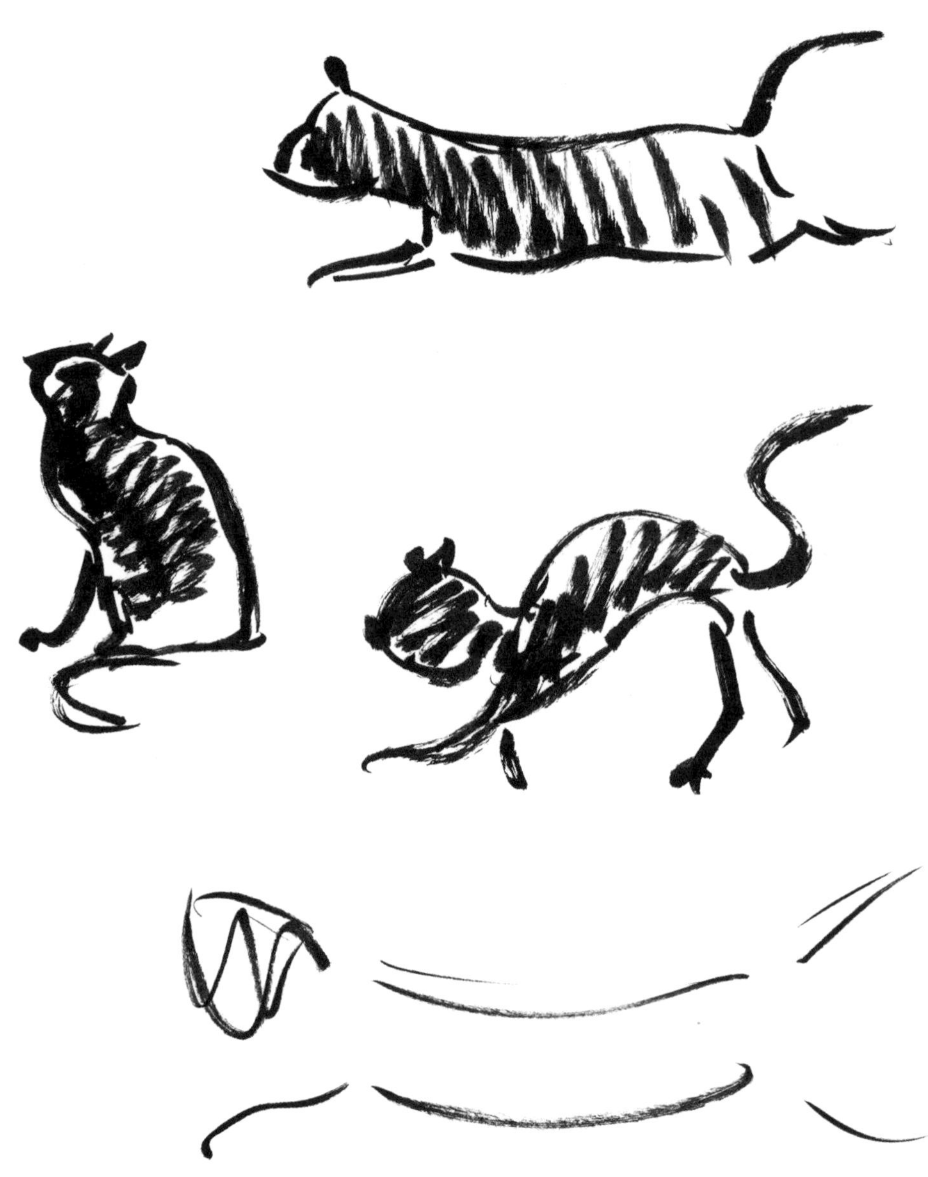

A FINE PAINTBRUSH OR FELT-TIP PEN
IS GOOD FOR THIS (AS SEEN ON THE
OPPOSITE PAGE)

PAINTING ON CARDBOARD

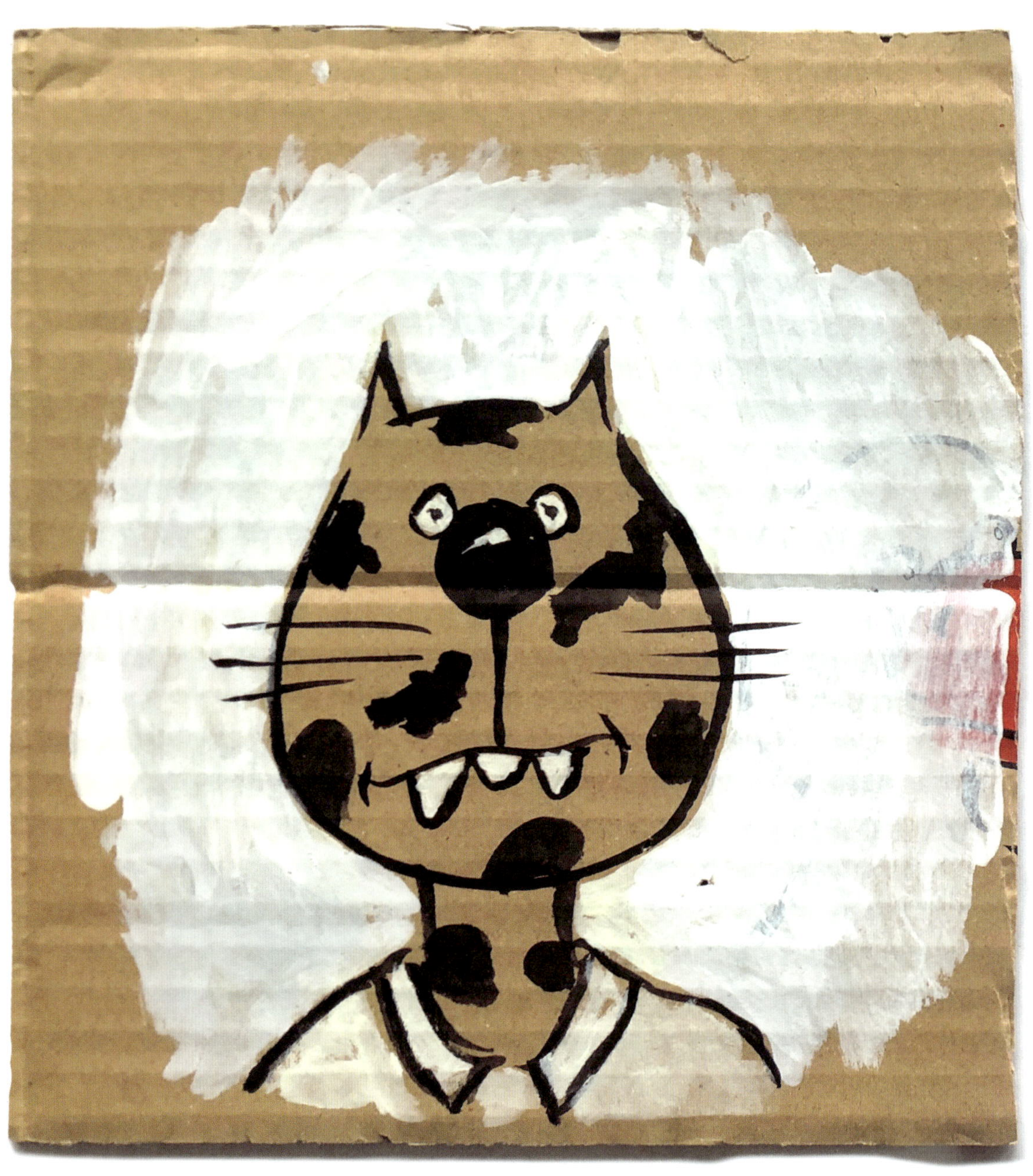

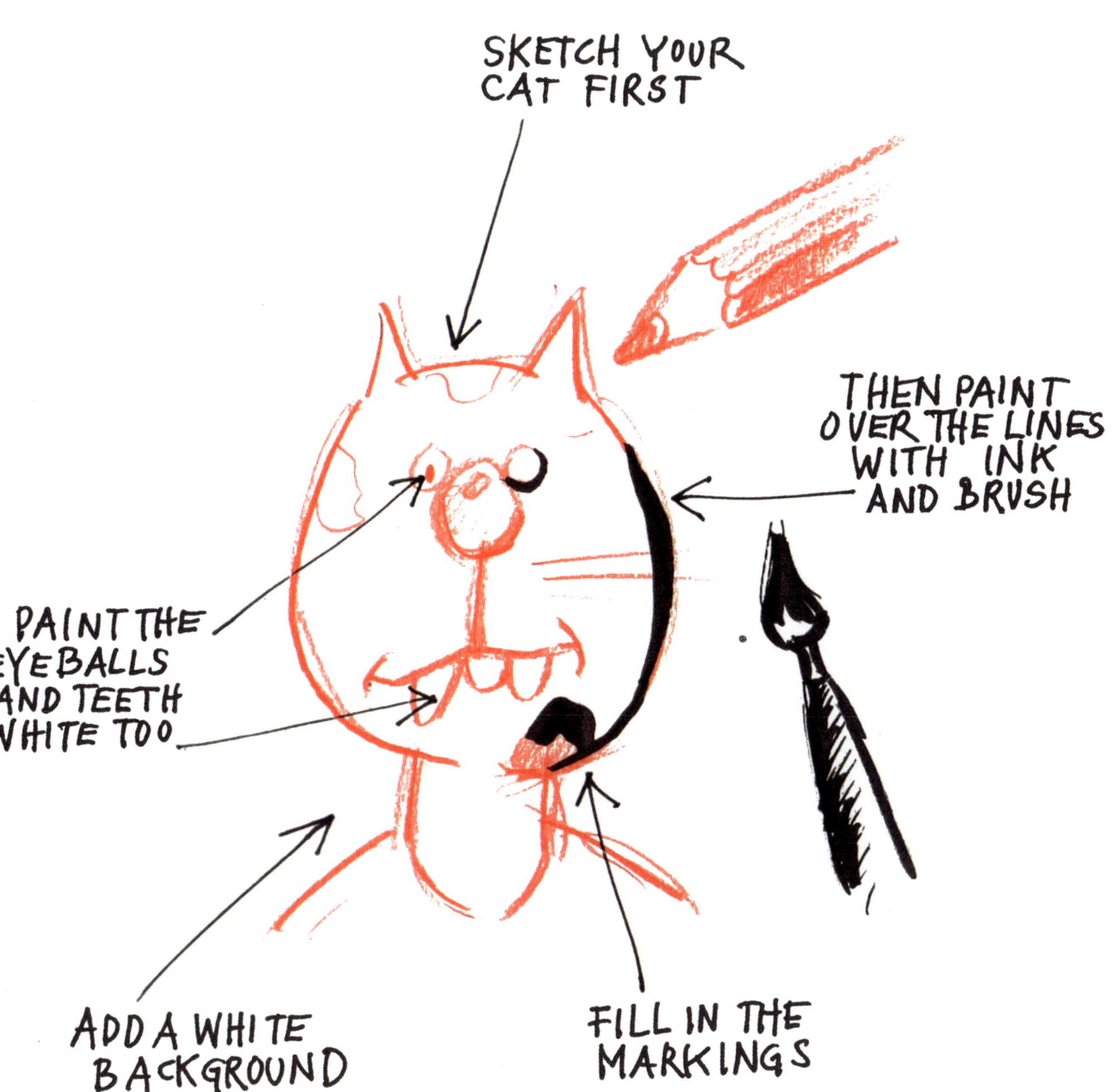

YOU WILL NEED:
CARDBOARD, INK, A BRUSH, WHITE ACRYLIC PAINT
SKETCH YOUR CAT FIRST
THEN PAINT OVER THE LINES WITH INK AND BRUSH
PAINT THE EYEBALLS AND TEETH WHITE TOO
ADD A WHITE BACKGROUND
FILL IN THE MARKINGS

PAINTING LIKE AN OLD MASTER
FROM DARK TO LIGHT

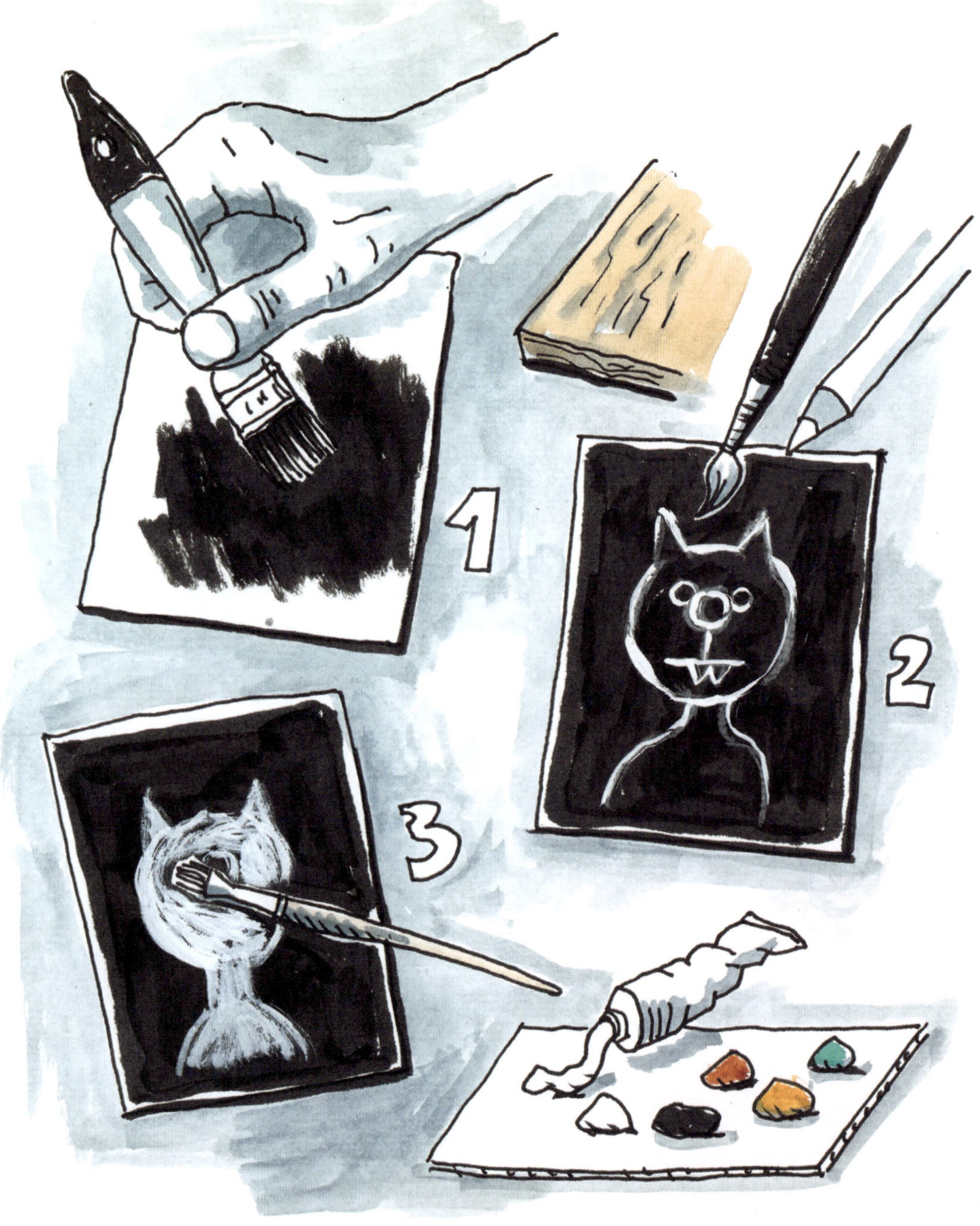

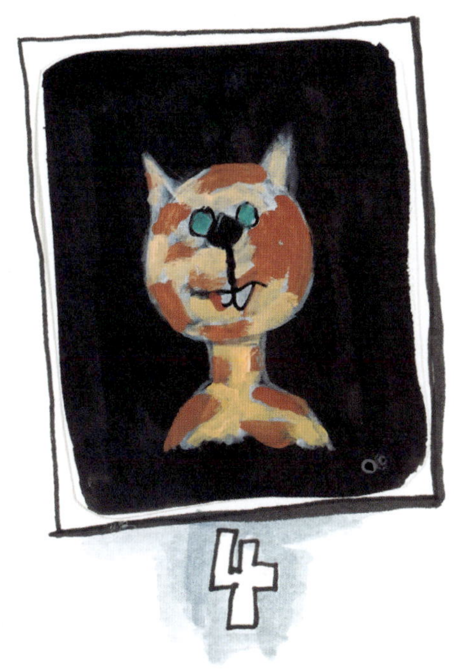

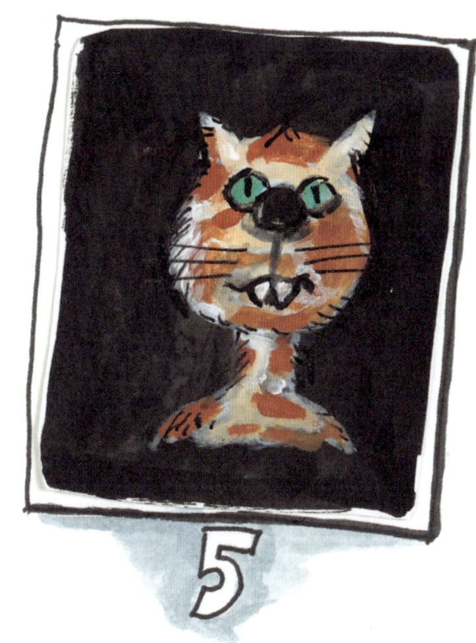

1. PAINT THE BACKGROUND BLACK AND LEAVE IT TO DRY.
2. SKETCH THE OUTLINES IN WHITE PAINT.
3. NOW PAINT WITH THE MID TONES.
4. ADD PATCHES OF OTHER COLOURS.
5. GO OVER THE DETAILS IN BLACK
   (NOSE, WHISKERS)

6 FINE TUNING
WHEN THE PAINT IS DRY

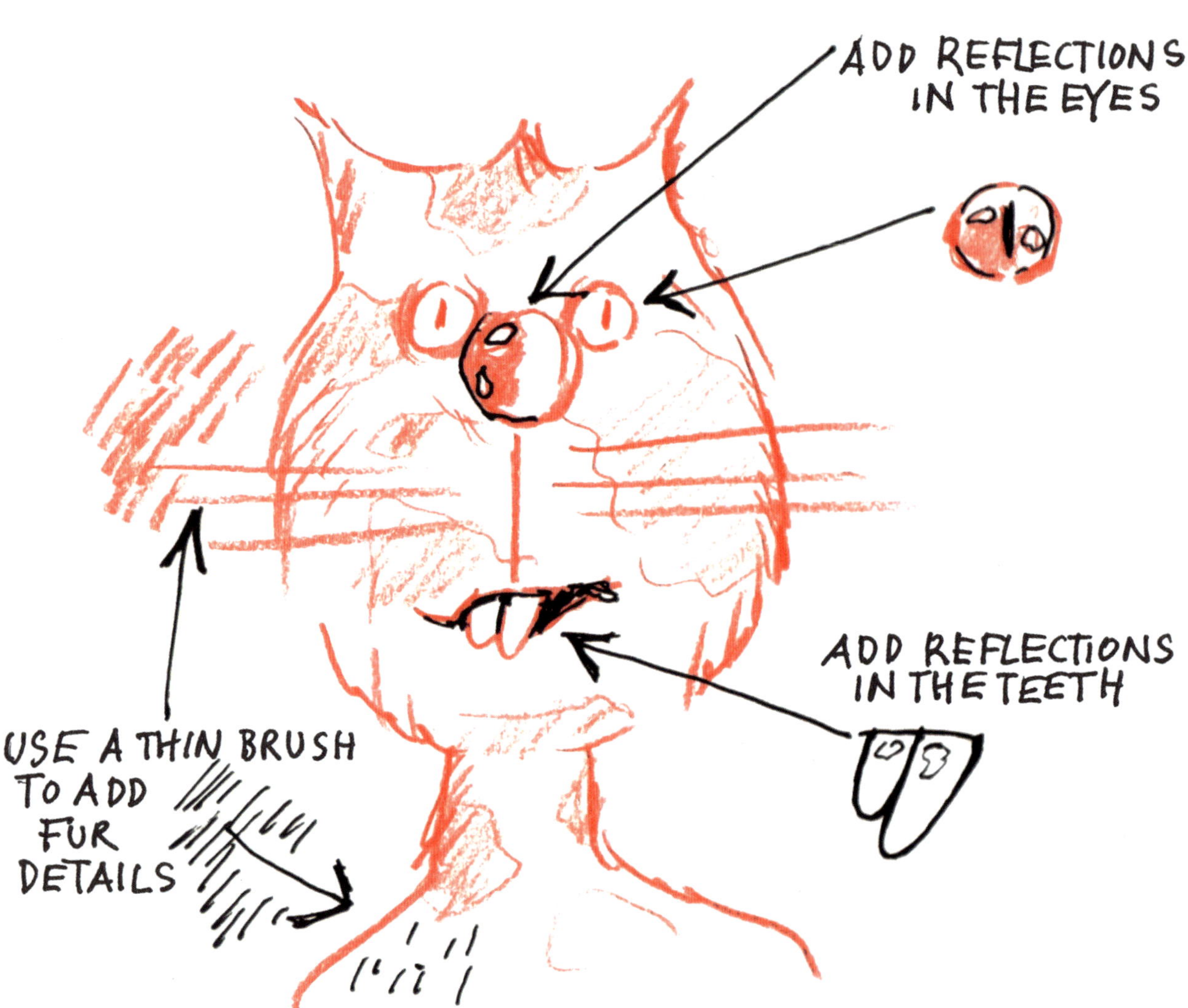

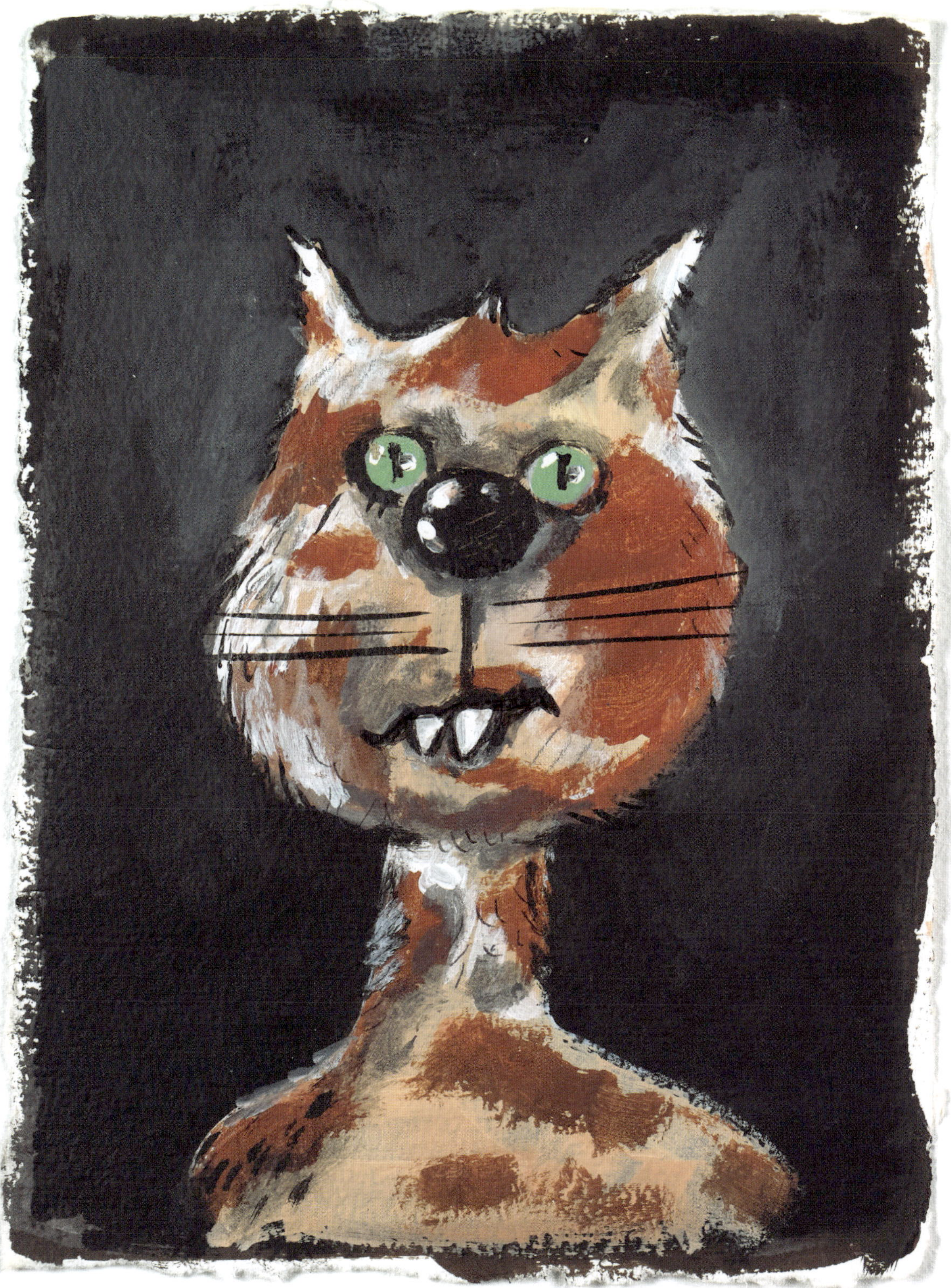

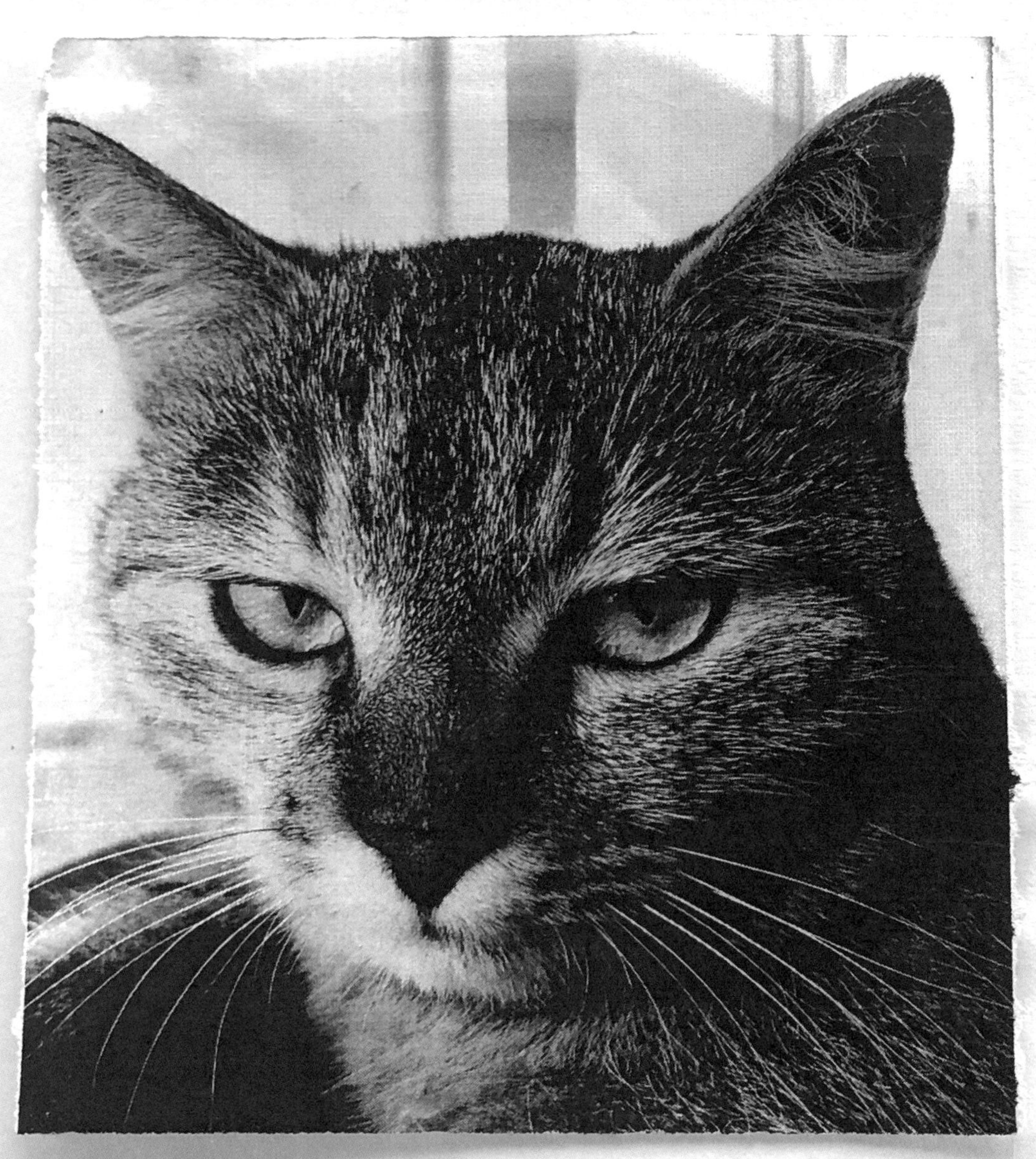

BEGIN IN THE MIDDLE AND WORK OUTWARDS.
USE THE DARK AREAS AND LIGHT AREAS AS A GUIDE.
DRAW THE LINES FOR THE FUR, FOLLOWING THE
DIRECTION OF THE COAT. A BLACK AND WHITE
PHOTO MAKES A GREAT SOURCE PICTURE.

PHOTO STUDIES
THIS IS A GOOD WAY TO GET READY FOR THE NEXT STEP!

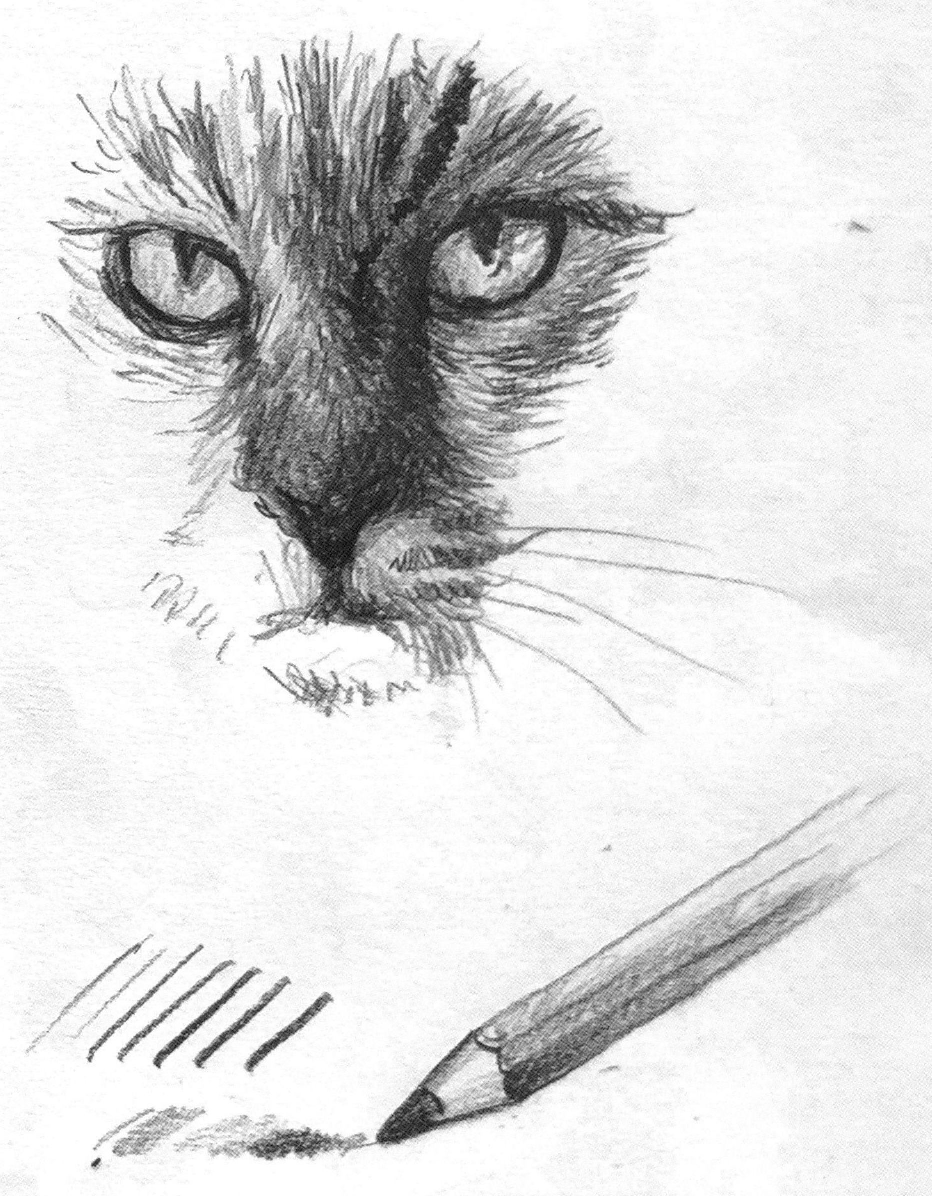

YOUR PRACTICE PAGE

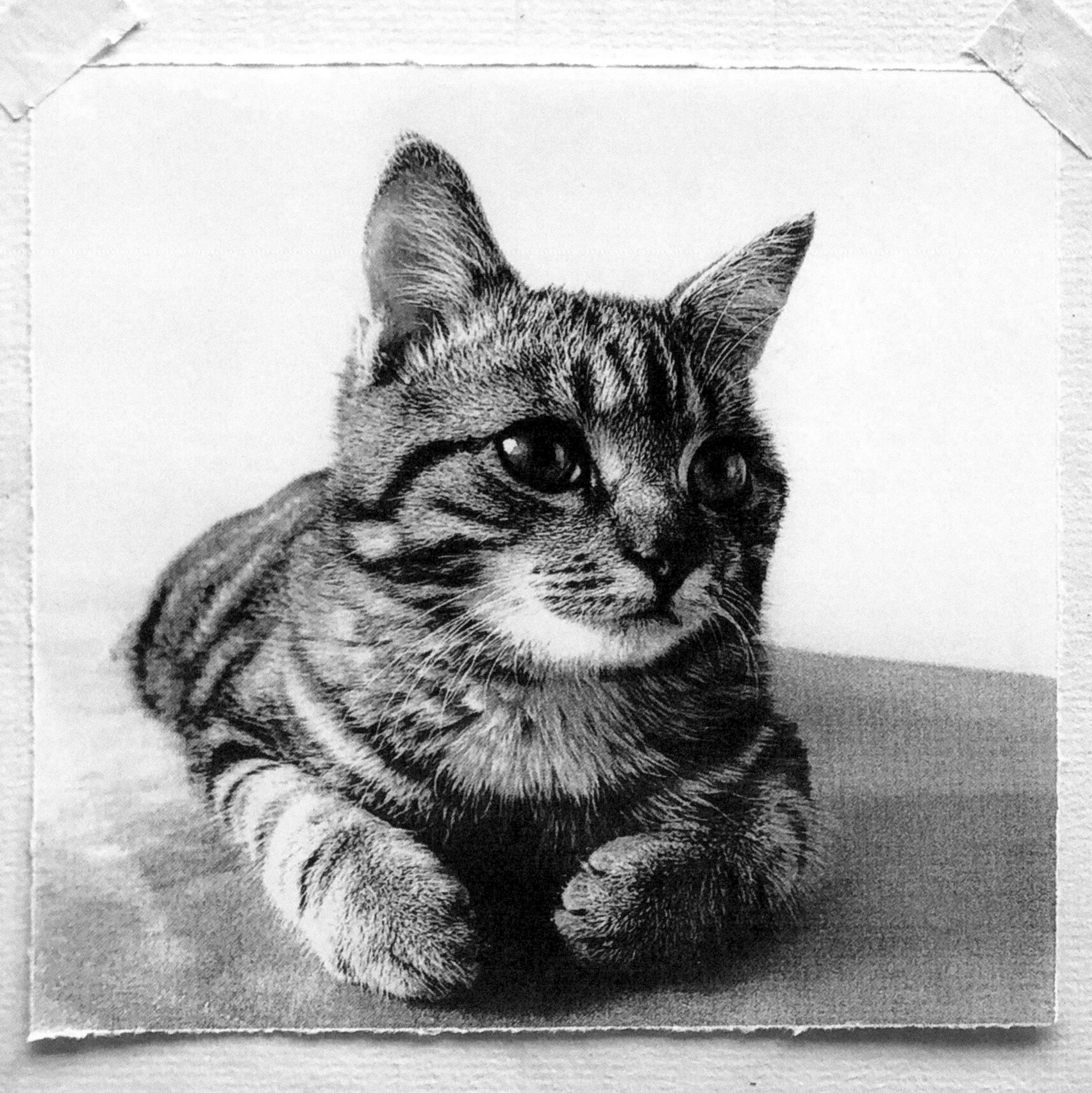

YOUR MASTERPIECE
A CAT PORTRAIT ON WOOD

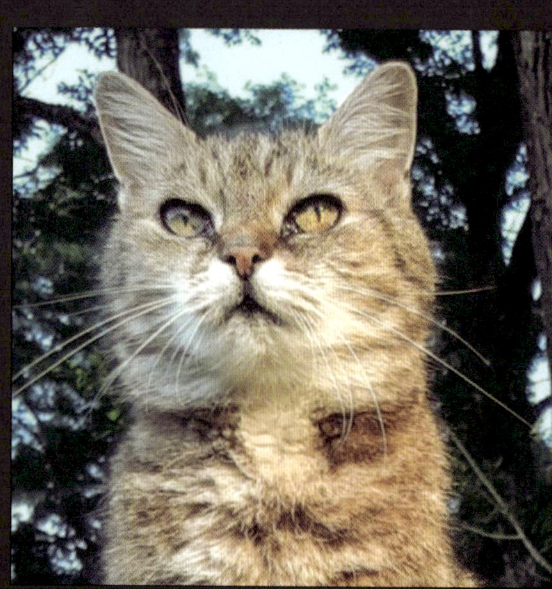

YOU WILL NEED:
- A SMALL WOODEN OR PLYWOOD BOARD (AROUND 15×20 CM)
- SANDPAPER
- ACRYLIC PAINTS (BLACK, WHITE, RED, BROWN, YELLOW OCHRE, ETC.)
- A RANGE OF BRUSHES
- A SOURCE PICTURE (PHOTO OR PHOTOCOPY)

INSTRUCTIONS:
- START BY MAKING SKETCHES OF YOUR SOURCE PICTURE
- SAND DOWN THE SURFACE OF YOUR WOODEN BOARD
- COVER IT WITH BLACK PAINT TO FORM THE BACKGROUND
- LET IT DRY
- DRAW THE OUTLINES OF THE HEAD ON THE BACKGROUND USING A BRUSH AND WHITE PAINT (1)
- KEEP ADDING WHITE PAINT, LAYER BY LAYER (2-4)
- YOU'LL SOON SEE YOUR PICTURE STARTING TO TAKE SHAPE. DON'T LOSE HEART DURING THE EARLY STAGES!

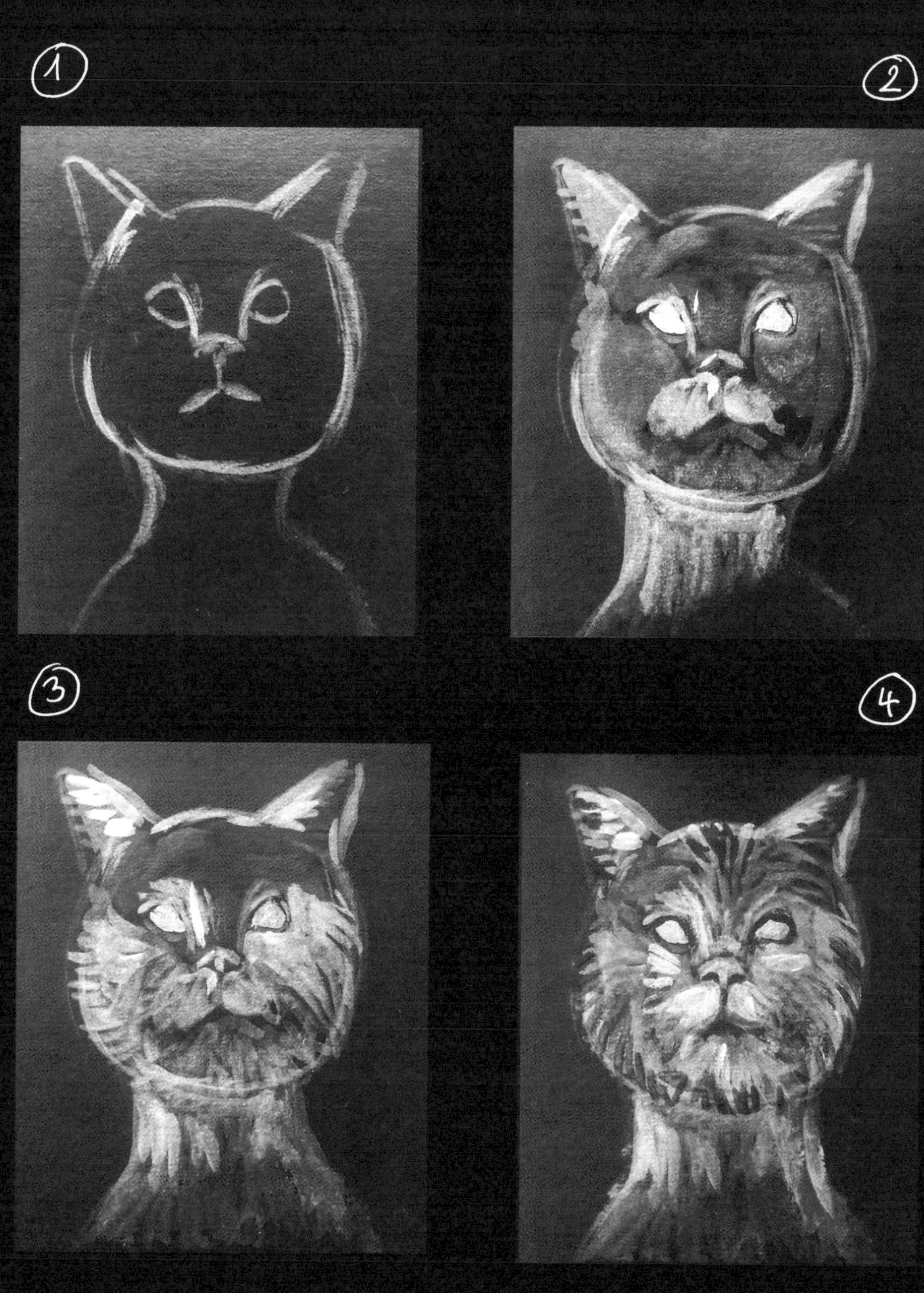

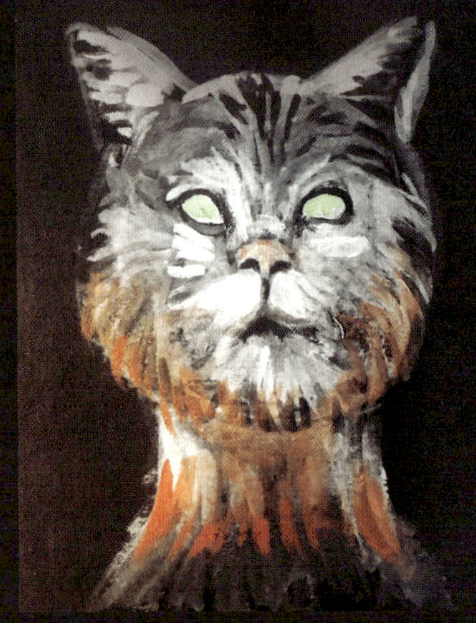

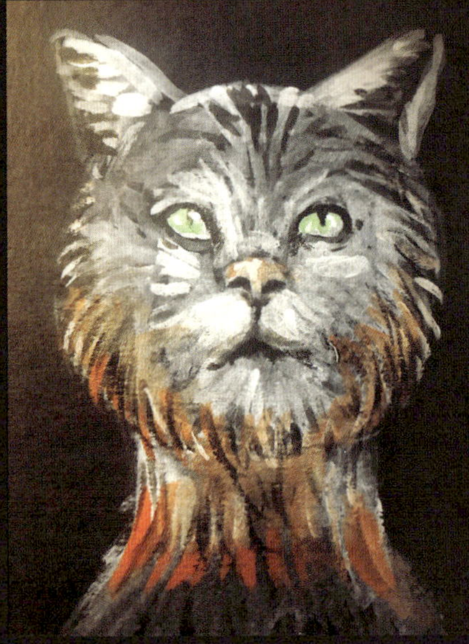

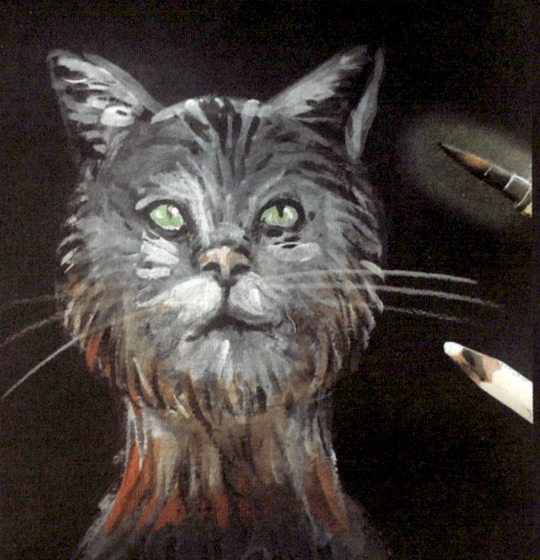

• NOW START TO ADD OTHER COLOURS — BROWN OR YELLOW OCHRE, FOR EXAMPLE (5-7) KEEP LOOKING CLOSELY AT YOUR SOURCE PICTURE AS YOU WORK, IT'S REALLY FUN TO SEE YOUR PAINTING COMING TO LIFE!

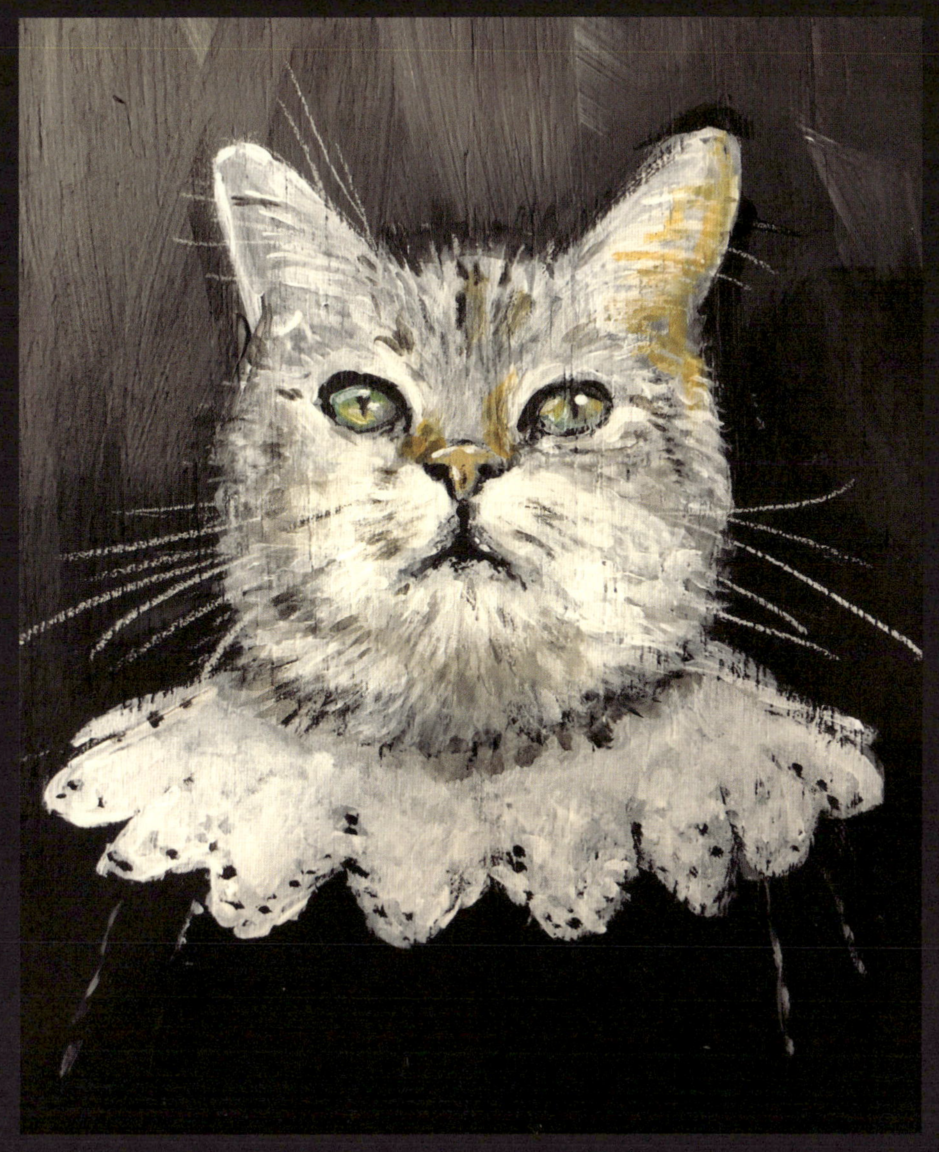

LAST STAGE:
· ADD THE FINAL DETAILS AND FINISH WITH
  WHITE HIGHLIGHTS TO SHOW REFLECTIONS

THE IDEA FOR THE LACE COLLAR COMES
FROM HISTORICAL PORTRAITS AND GIVES
YOUR PORTRAIT A DISTINCTIVE TOUCH.

FINISHED!

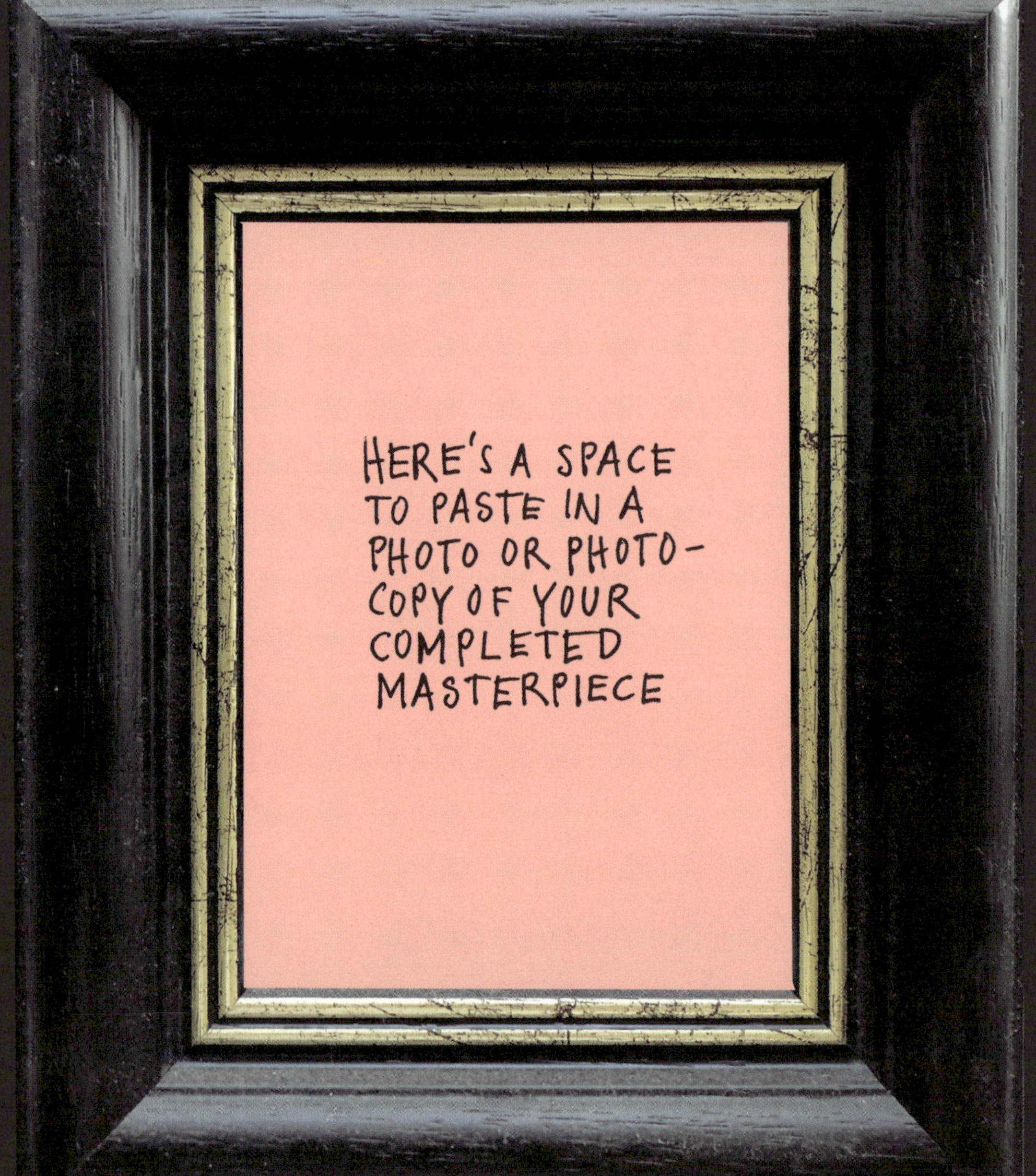

HERE'S A SPACE
TO PASTE IN A
PHOTO OR PHOTO-
COPY OF YOUR
COMPLETED
MASTERPIECE

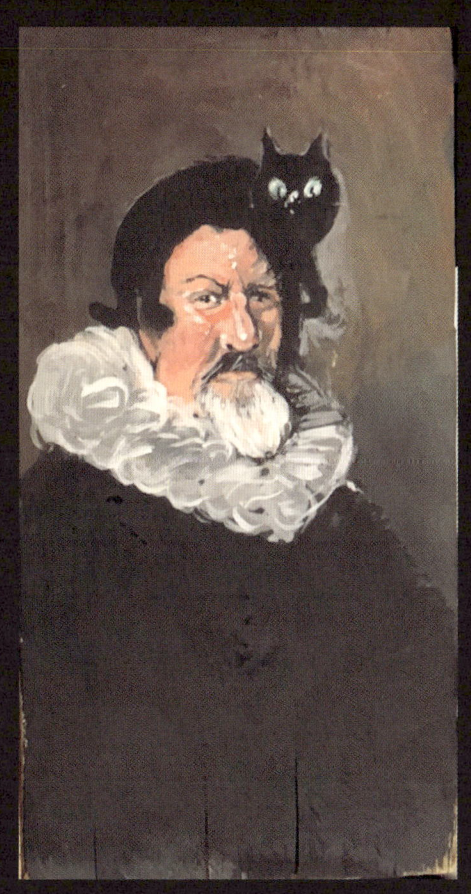

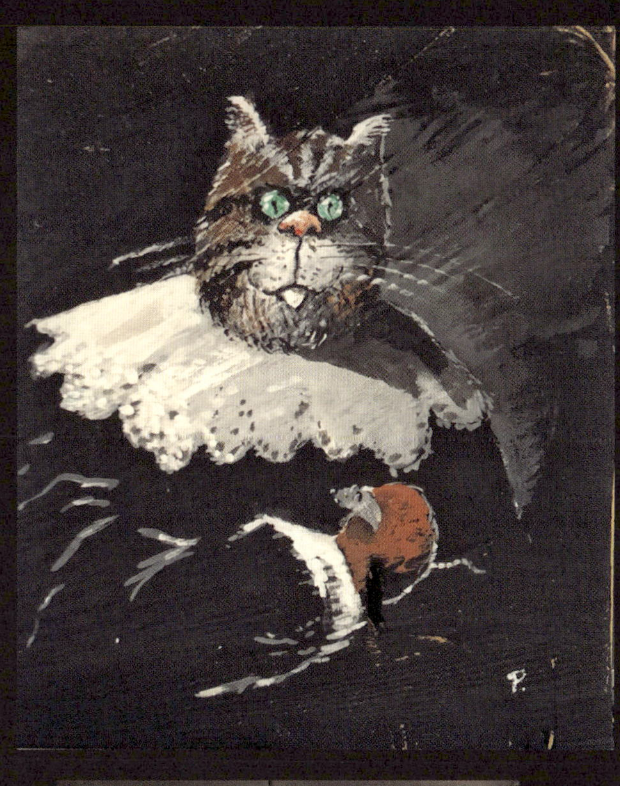

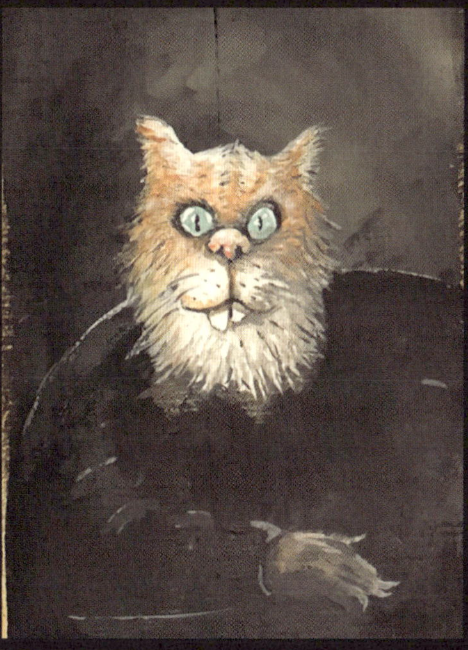

A FEW EXAMPLES
FOR INSPIRATION—
YOU COULD ALSO
USE THEM AS
SOURCE PICTURES!

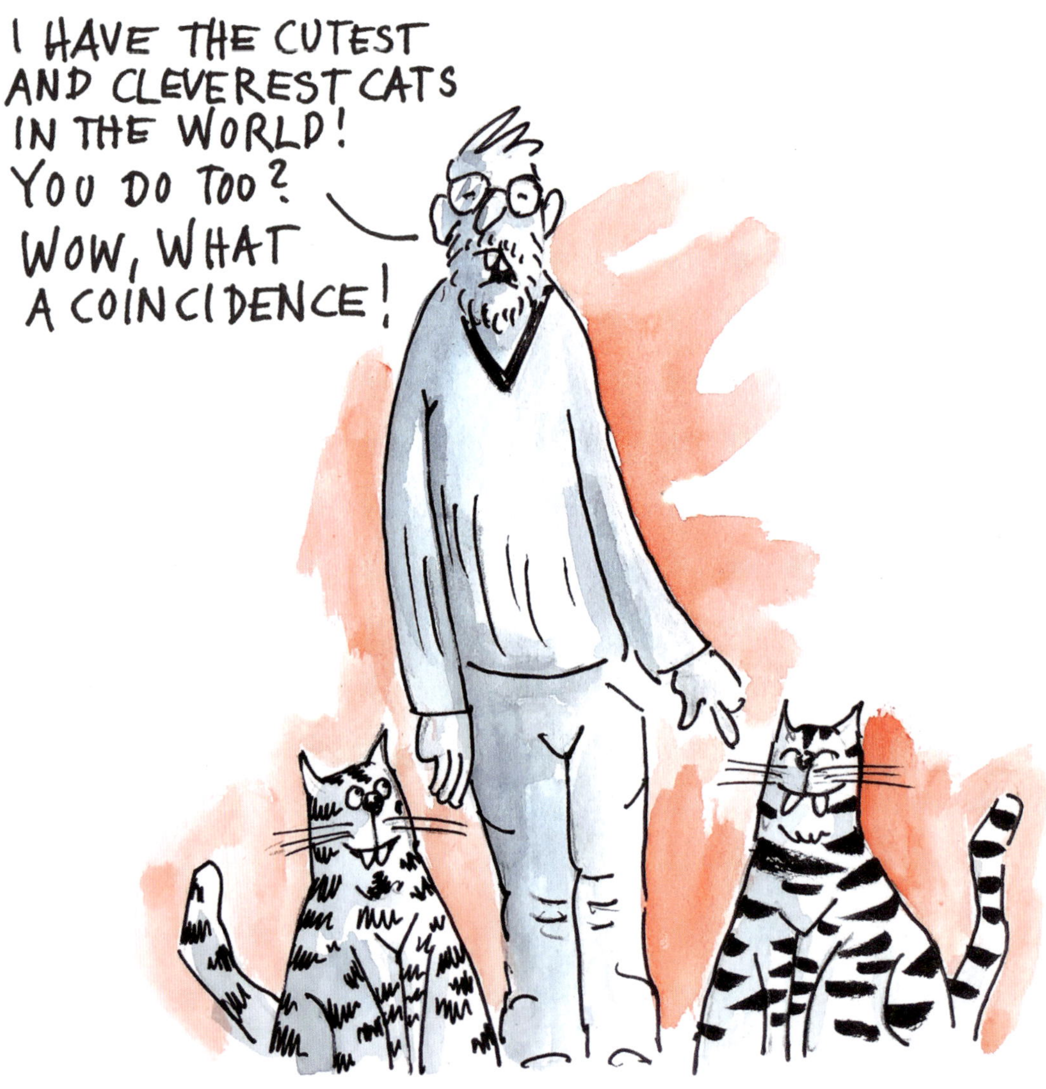

THAT'S IT!
NOW IT'S TIME TO KEEP PRACTISING ON YOUR OWN.
HAVE FUN!

I HAVE THE CUTEST AND CLEVEREST CATS IN THE WORLD!
YOU DO TOO?
WOW, WHAT A COINCIDENCE!

ABOUT THE AUTHOR

PENG IS AN ILLUSTRATOR FROM THE ALPS IN AUSTRIA.
HIS STUDIO IS IN A CUL-DE-SAC CLOSE TO A WOOD,
WHICH IS IDEAL FOR HIS BELOVED CATS MOMO AND
COSIMA — LOTS OF MICE AND NOT A LOT OF TRAFFIC.

HIS PREVIOUS BOOK <u>I CAN DRAW</u> WAS ALSO PUBLISHED
BY THAMES + HUDSON AND WON A BRITISH BOOK
DESIGN AND PRODUCTION AWARD.

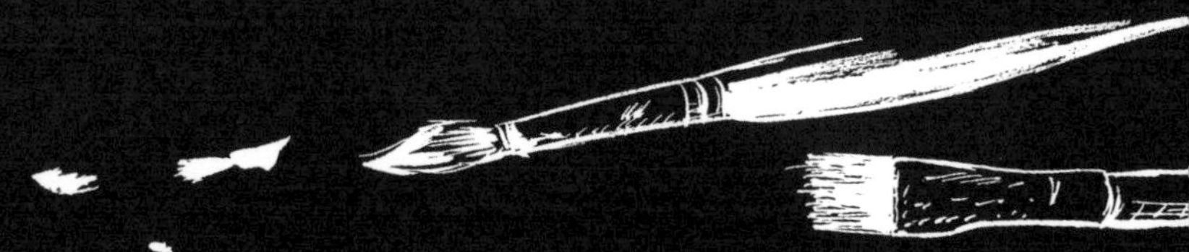

ALSO AVAILABLE

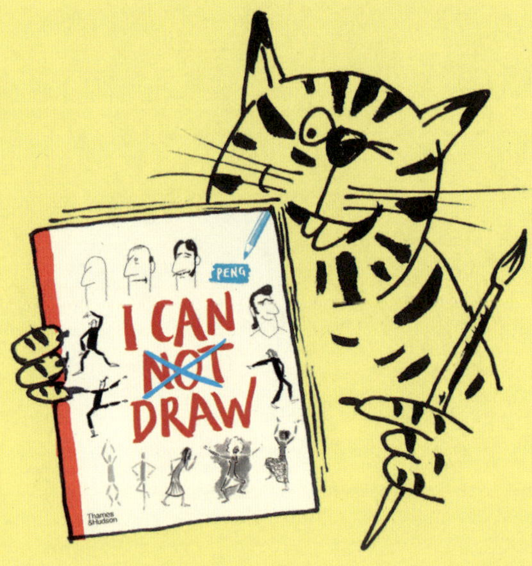

Translated from the German *Ich kann ~~keine~~ Katzen zeichnen* by Jill Phythian

First published in the United Kingdom in 2024 by
Thames & Hudson Ltd, 181A High Holborn, London WC1V 7QX

Original edition © 2023 Dumont Buchverlag, Cologne
This edition © 2024 Thames & Hudson Ltd, London

All Rights Reserved. No part of this publication may be reproduced or transmitted in any form or by any means, electronic or mechanical, including photocopy, recording, or any other information storage and retrieval system, without prior permission in writing from the publisher.

British Library Cataloguing-in-Publication Data.
A catalogue record for this book is available from the British Library

ISBN 978-0-500-29816-9

Printed in China by Shenzhen Reliance Printing Co. Ltd

Be the first to know about our new releases, exclusive content and author events by visiting
thamesandhudson.com
thamesandhudsonusa.com
thamesandhudson.com.au